# NOSTALGIA

# Nostalgia

## Going Home in a Homeless World

Anthony Esolen

REGNERY GATEWAY

Regnery Gateway™ is a trademark of Salem Communications Holding Corporation; Regnery® is a registered trademark of Salem Communications Holding
Corporation

Cataloging-in-Publication data on file with the Library of Congress

ISBN 978-1-62157-801-7
e-book ISBN 978-1-62157-848-2

Extracts from The Book of Common Prayer, the rights in which are vested in
the Crown, are reproduced by permission of the Crown's patentee, Cambridge
University Press

Scripture quotations from The Authorized (King James) Version. Rights in the
Authorized Version in the United Kingdom are vested in the Crown. Reproduced
by permission of the Crown's patentee, Cambridge University Press

Scripture quotations taken from the New American Standard Bible® (NASB),
Copyright © 1960, 1962, 1963, 1968, 1971, 1972, 1973, 1975, 1977, 1995 by The
Lockman Foundation. Used by permission. www.Lockman.org

Published in the United States by
Regnery Gateway, an imprint of
Regnery Publishing
A Division of Salem Media Group
300 New Jersey Ave NW
Washington, DC 20001
www.RegneryGateway.com

Manufactured in the United States of America

10 9 8 7 6 5 4 3 2 1

Books are available in quantity for promotional or premium use. For information
on discounts and terms, please visit our website: www.Regnery.com.

# CONTENTS

# Man, Far from Home

The man is sitting on the shore, looking out upon the sea, his arms about his knees. That's what he has done for a long time now, longer than he can remember. He sheds a tear.

All around him is beauty. The sea glints with the light and play of wine. The breeze is gentle, and the plane trees and the oaks dapple the hill behind him with shade. He hears the chatter of a bird above—a kingfisher, circling about and suddenly plunging into the shallows beak-first. Will he come out with his dinner? The man is distracted for a moment. Yes, there he is—but no dinner. Well, he will get his fish before long. All is well with the bird, and with the fish that swam away from his enemy.

In all the world, only the man is lost, only the man is not well.

It's a beautiful world, often a world of terror and pain, but always beautiful. So it seems to the man when he is not sighing and sitting on the shore. He has lived all his life in places where the weather was warm and mild and men and women spent most of their waking hours out of doors, by the sea, atop high and rocky hills, on windy plains beneath the endless sky, and in deep mysterious valleys where the winding river was so clearly a god that it seemed a holy thing to bathe your feet in his waters. He has an eye for beauty. It is the great heritage of his people.

She, the woman who is keeping him here on the island, she the goddess, who spends most of her day weaving and singing, is beautiful. There is no doubt of that. She loves him, as she might love a favorite pet. In days to come, he will meet a girl who will save his life, when he washes up on a foreign shore naked, half-dead, soiled with seaweed and brine. She will be taller than her girlfriends, and a goddess will fill her heart with courage, so that she will not run away from him as they do but stand her ground and listen to his tale of suffering. "I was on the island of Delos once," he said, "and I saw a palm tree, slender and perfect, and I thought I had never seen so beautiful a thing in my life. You remind me of that palm tree."

Then there was the beautiful and cunning and dangerous woman, the cause of the war that he and his armies were compelled to fight. He too had been a suitor for her hand in marriage, he and many others. She made her choice, whether out of cunning or caprice or both, he never quite could decide; she chose a good man, but not the best, strong in battle, but not the strongest, certainly no half-wit, but slow to make a decision, handsome enough with his red hair, but not such a form as to cast in bronze. That man was a fool to take her, but he'd have been a greater fool to refuse. Yet that marriage had undone the knees of thousands of good men, whose ashes were scattered by the winds in that faraway land, the land where he had spent ten long years, fighting.

All those women were lovelier than his wife. And when he thought of that, he shed another tear.

Is it a countryside he longs for? What is special about that place, what makes his heart yearn to see it again? You can't do much with thoroughbred horses there, because the terrain is too rocky. It isn't a center of commerce, where you might meet many strangers traveling to and fro. It's good for wheat and raising pigs. He had quite a few pigs, hundreds of them, and many head of cattle; who knows how many of them would be left now?

Is it a large family he left behind? No, the gods never blessed him that way. He was the only son of an only son, and he himself has one son, who was but a baby when he left home with his army, twenty years ago. He remembers one day in particular, and a small and mischievous smile comes to his lips, even with the tear in his eye. He didn't want to leave. To Hades with the vow he made, to support his red-headed friend if someone should ever try to steal the dangerous woman from him. He pretended to have lost his wits, and strapped himself to his plow like an ox, zigzagging across his fields and making chaos out of them. But a couple of his fellow generals saw through the ruse. They knew his ways. So they took the little baby—Fighter-from-Afar was his name—and placed him in his father's path. Every time they did that, he would swerve aside.

"Odysseus," they said, "master mariner, man of many turnings, come now, we see that you are not mad. You too made the vow. You must join us in the war."

He did, against his will. By now the son must have grown to manhood, and his wife's hair would be turning gray.

Would it not be easier to give up hope, to stay here on the island, and let things go as they must go, faraway? The goddess is kind. And she has promised him much more than her loyalty. He will not age, so long as he remains with her. Perpetual youth, utter security, on a beautiful island, with a goddess who loves him as you love a pet, and who takes him into her bed every night; plenty of good food, wine, and peace.

A flutter of wings and spray—the kingfisher, with a fish in his beak. All is well, except with the man. He suffers the pang of something bitter and sweet, and more bitter than sweet. Yet he does not wish that the feeling would go away. He cherishes it. It is in his language the *algea* for the *noston*: pain for the return, ache for the homecoming.

The Welsh call it *hiraeth*, "longing," and in one of their folk songs they say that nobody can tell what exactly *hiraeth* is, but it brings both great joy and intense pain. That song was written at a time when poor Welshmen were leaving the mines and quarries in the land they loved to go to America or Australia, or Argentina of all places, where there is still a small Welsh-speaking outpost in the pampas, called *yr Wladfa*, "the colony."

In German, it is *Heimweh*, "home-woe," or *Sehnsucht*, "seeking to see again"—in English, *homesickness*. In Italian, you feel *mancanza di casa*, that is, you are "missing the home," literally the "house"; it is like a hole in your heart. The Italians also express it by the Greek word that has entered English and is the subject of this book: *nostalgia*, the ache to turn back home.

### Hatred of the Present

Before I return to Odysseus on the shore, I want to spell out what this book is not. It is not a book of misty-eyed adulation of an imagined time that never existed, or of a past *that is not ours*, and that we half invent, less out of love for anything real than out of hatred of what is. It is not nostalgia as despair. I do not intend simply to be a *laudator temporis acti*. The poet Edwin Arlington Robinson captured the spirit of that kind of man who indulges fantasies of the past because he sees nothing around him worthy of his love. I will present it in full, because it bears upon our current situation in a most surprising way:

> Miniver Cheevy, child of scorn,
> Grew lean while he assailed the seasons;
> He wept that he was ever born,
> And he had reasons.
>
> Miniver loved the days of old
> When swords were bright and steeds were prancing;
> The vision of a warrior bold
> Would set him dancing.
>
> Miniver sighed for what was not,
> And dreamed, and rested from his labors;

He dreamed of Thebes and Camelot,
And Priam's neighbors.

Miniver mourned the ripe renown
That made so many a name so fragrant;
He mourned Romance, now on the town,
And Art, a vagrant.

Miniver loved the Medici,
Albeit he had never seen one;
He would have sinned incessantly
Could he have been one.

Miniver cursed the commonplace
And eyed a khaki suit with loathing;
He missed the medieval grace
Of iron clothing.

Miniver scorned the gold he sought
But sore annoyed was he without it;
Miniver thought, and thought, and thought,
And thought about it.

Miniver Cheevy, born too late,
Scratched his head and kept on thinking;
Miniver coughed, and called it fate,
And kept on drinking.

Miniver Cheevy rests from his labors as if he were almighty God beholding the world he has made and all that is in it. He has responsibilities, which it appears he is slack in fulfilling, because he sometimes is short of money, the gold he scorns, but it's not pleasant for him to be without it, either. No medieval monk, he. He "dreams" of Thebes, the seven-gated city. Do those dreams include the sagas of parricide and incest and civil war, of Laius and Jocasta, of Oedipus and Creon and Antigone, of Eteocles and Polynices, which in the ancient world made Thebes a byword for unnatural wickedness? He "dreams" of Camelot. Robinson did more than dream of Camelot; he wrote poems set in the Arthurian world. Do Miniver's dreams include the adultery of Lancelot and Guinevere, which brought destruction to the fellowship of the Round Table? He "dreams" of Priam's neighbors. Were they the ones who fought alongside the Trojans against the Greeks, or the ones who joined the Greeks out of vengeance or lust for gain?

He flits from the ancient world to the Middle Ages to the Renaissance, or rather what he imagines were these worlds; and they have nothing in common other than that they are *not* the time and the place where he was born. He calls it "fate," and gets drunk. John Henry Newman warned against wishing that you were born in another time or place, because the providence of God has willed us to be here, now; these are the neighbors we are to love as ourselves, this is the land which we honor as we honor our mother and father, these are the times that try our souls. That does not mean that we accept everything that happens about us. Newman certainly did not. Nor does it mean that we ignore the wisdom of the past. Newman did not do that, either.

If we think about it, we can see a strange family resemblance between Miniver Cheevy, dreaming of an airy past that never existed while hating the ordinary things in front of him, and the self-styled "progressive," dreaming of a future that never shall exist, if he has a visionary goal at all, while hating the ordinary things in front of him, too. The secular pessimist and the secular optimist are the same man, with differences not in the mind but in the digestive tract, and neither one is a man of hope. Miniver "views a khaki suit with loathing" because it is not armor. The progressive with an overheated digestive system views it with loathing because it is khaki and not red. The progressive with a pacifist digestive system views it with loathing because it is a military suit of any kind at all. Miniver dreams of ancient

Troy, which at least has the virtue of having existed on earth and having been the inspiration for three thousand years of poetry, drama, and art. By no means was all of it in praise: for Dante, that city, queen of Asia, was an exemplar of pride going before a fall:

> Mark Troy, in gutted palaces and ash.
> Alas, Ilion, the signs for all to see
> now show you for a thing of scorn, and trash![1]

The progressive dreams of a city that does not exist and can never exist. He ends up building what Edward Banfield called the "Unheavenly City." I am far from the first to make this observation. The progressive has turned original sin, which afflicts all mankind, into political error, which conveniently afflicts his opponents and not himself. To be saved, in his mind, is not to be transformed by God into newness of life. It is to vote for the right program. How gray, how small! It is to applaud the raising of New Babel, a city of what he imagines to be perfect justice, to be recognized and administered by man, man the foolish, vain, greedy, slothful, vindictive, violent, and lecherous. Miniver may look in the mirror and detest what he sees. The progressive does not own such a mirror. He does not repent of his sins. He turns to a new political candidate. The old and worn-out may then be disposed of, like Trotsky, in blood, or like the mild Hubert Humphrey, in dismissal and oblivion.

Miniver is no lover of tradition. He lives in the United States, but he seems to be moved by none of his people's songs, holidays, customs, or art. He "would have sinned incessantly," says Robinson with understated hilarity, "could he have been" a Medici, one of the brilliant and grasping and corrupt overlords of Florence, "albeit he had never seen one." He might as well long to be an Eskimo, or a Maori spearing the emu on the South Island of New Zealand.

The progressive shares Miniver's scorn but not his naive generosity. He looks with delight upon nothing that has been. The history of man is a long tale of misery from which we learn nothing except, perhaps, how to avoid doing what people used to do. Only the future, which no one can know, is real to him. For the sake of that idol, all manner of evil and folly can be justified and, in the terrible wars of the twentieth century, has been justified. C. S. Lewis's shrewd demon, Uncle Screwtape, reveals the general principle:

> The Future is, of all things, the thing *least like* eternity. It is the most completely temporal part of time—for the Past is frozen and no longer flows, and the Present is all lit up with its eternal rays. Hence the encouragement we have given to all those schemes of thought such as Creative Evolution, Scientific Humanism, or Communism, which fix men's attention on the Future, on the very core of temporality. Hence nearly all vices are rooted in the Future. Gratitude looks to the Past and love to the Present; fear, avarice, lust, and ambition look ahead.[2]

Hence also does the progressive pontificate about the "judgment of history," by which he does not mean that we learn from the ineluctable reality of the past about the unchanging features of human nature. He means instead that the *future*, like a god, or like the Minotaur lurking around the next corner of the maze—the "Minotaur that is history," said the philosopher and playwright Gabriel Marcel, with trenchant wit—will have its inexorable judgment, which will be in accord with what the progressive desires. That Minotaur is the deity to which he sacrifices mankind. A childless Seattle is his paradise.

I could say more. Robinson's Miniver has not given himself over to the perverse. He may be wary of trains and cars and modern improvements in the daily stuff of human life, but that is not because he dreams of a world in which computing devices are implanted into human brains. He may weave fantasies of Tristan and Isolde, adultery after the natural fashion. He does not weave fantasies of Tristan and

Mark. He sighs for a romance he has never known. He does not feel a frisson of delight in contemplating the surgical mutilation of an ordinary boy. His problems are scorn and ingratitude. He is foolish, but he is not insane. The progressive, assuming that he has signed his soul over to an endless and increasingly chaotic devolution of sexual being, is both foolish and insane. Liquefaction of ice is good. Liquefaction of the brain is not. Miniver loves some things that are beautiful: the prancing steeds. The educational progressive—the "Gaius" and "Titius" of C. S. Lewis's *The Abolition of Man*—has adopted as a tenet of his aesthetic faith that there are no such things as good and bad aesthetic judgments. These are all mere brute feelings, and do not touch the question of truth. He therefore no longer believes in beauty as such. But because he wishes to be *au courant* with the resultant artistic deterioration, he ends up having to pretend he enjoys what is hideous. Hence we have modern architecture, the continual assault upon a normal human being's perceptions and love; and in this regard, as in many others, the progressive and the culture-dissolving capitalist who finances the progressive's fun-houses are but ungrateful son and indulgent father.

### Beauty and the Home

Neither Robinson's unfashionable man of the hazy past nor the far more malignant man of the future properly possesses a *home*. I do not mean to say that no individual human being who calls himself progressive has a roof over his head and cherishes his tomato patch. Men are seldom as bad as the worst of their ideas. I mean that he has no home in principle. Witness the common and continual and changeless call for "change" for the sake of change and the contempt for people who dare to ask whether a particular change is actually for the good. What can "change" without a subject or an object possibly mean? Does a man who loves his wife want to change *her* from year to year? "Yes," says the *laudator mutationis*, "a river runs through our village, a beautiful river. Many are the days I walked along its banks when I was a lad, but it has been also a disappointing river, a river stuck in its mud, a bedridden river, running in the same course for a thousand years and giving nourishment to the birds and beasts and fish, always the same kinds. Why, the green swallows sang the same song when I was a child as they do now. Therefore," he says, with a sigh, as if making a great sacrifice for other people who may not understand the blessing he confers upon them, a painful decision—that is, painful for others—"therefore, I shall have it dammed a mile upstream, so that I will not have to endure any longer its endless whisper, which speaks of eternity."

What we love we want to endure.

No man ever said, "I used to play ball on a field that was here—I think it was here. There was a stream at its far end, and a ball hit into it on the fly was a home run. I can't imagine where any stream would be now. But I am glad, glad indeed, that it no longer exists. I am glad that there's a tangle of highways here. I am glad that the slender blade of grass is now a mile-broad clover leaf. That's progress." Even if he understands that the highway had to be built, he is not *glad* of the loss. I have never met a single person who was happy that the school he attended, the church where he worshiped, or the old house where he grew up is now dust. It is natural for man to long for home. It is not natural for him to knock out its posts and feed its beams to termites.

The kingdom of God, says Jesus, is the reward of children new-made. If so, then I trust they will feel as did Shakespeare's wistful King Polixenes in *The Winter's Tale*, remembering what it was like to be a child:

> We thought there was no more behind
> But such a day tomorrow as today,
> And to be boy eternal. (I.ii. 65–67)

We will take some time, in this book, to ponder the relationship between man's return to childhood and his going forth from time into eternity. It is what the modern progressive denies, having once been advised of it by a man named Jesus, and what the pagan can hardly imagine, having never heard of it before.

Why does Odysseus want to go home?

We must rule out all merely sentimental reasons. Calypso's island is more beautiful than Ithaca is. Calypso is more beautiful than is Odysseus' wife, Penelope. Odysseus has been told that when he reaches Ithaca, he will have to deal with more than a hundred suitors for Penelope, who have descended upon his estate like an invading army. They have devoured his goods and turned his home into a banquet hall and brothel. He has no idea what kind of young man his son, Telemachus, has become. He cannot depend upon the loyalty of any single person; even his wife, who he supposes will have been true to him, is not utterly beyond suspicion. He cannot depend upon the citizens of Ithaca. Many of them will wish that he had starved on an unknown shore or been cut down in battle. The goddess Athena has told him that he will return and will succeed, but she is a crafty liar, as he himself is, and in any case, if you trust the gods, you will deserve what you get.

Odysseus wants to go home because it is his home. It is as simple as that.

But we should not let that simplicity deceive us. We must not be reductive. We cannot say that Odysseus will be happy when he has come home. He may be happy, he may not, but happiness is not the point. Odysseus' name itself suggests suffering and strife, and the telltale upon his flesh that gives his identity away when his old nurse washes him is not a birthmark. It is a long scar across his knee. He got it when he was a boy, hunting the wild boar with his maternal grandfather and his uncles. Grandpa Autolycus was something of a renegade and thief, ever at odds with other men, as the more virtuous but by no means saintly Odysseus has been.

Pleasure is not the point. Pleasure is what he enjoys now, with Calypso. The hedonist does not go home, because it is too arduous a journey, and who knows what difficulties await? Had Odysseus given his heart to pleasure, he would have remained in the land of the Lotos-Eaters, who do nothing all day long but eat the flower that banishes care. Tennyson captured the quiet despair of pleasure-seekers, or, what is much the same, the resignation of those who shy away from heartache, in his remarkable poem "The Lotos-Eaters," inspired by the scene from Homer. Here the mariners guess what will await them should they go home, and Tennyson has them guess correctly, although Odysseus is the only man who will survive the voyage and experience it:

> Dear is the memory of our wedded lives,
> And dear the last embraces of our wives
> And their warm tears: but all hath suffered change:
> For surely now our household hearths are cold,
> Our sons inherit us: our looks are strange:
> And we should come like ghosts to trouble joy.
> Or else the island princes over-bold
> Have eat our substance, and the minstrel sings
> Before them of the ten years' war in Troy,
> And our great deeds, as half-forgotten things.
> Is there confusion in the little isle?
> Let what is broken so remain.
> The Gods are hard to reconcile:
> 'Tis hard to settle order once again.
> There is confusion worse than death,
> Trouble on trouble, pain on pain,
> Long labor unto aged breath,
> Sore task to hearts worn out by many wars
> And eyes grown dim with gazing on the pilot-stars.

"Let what is broken so remain," say the weary men. If it were not for Odysseus and his demands, leading them back to their ships against their will, they would be content to cherish the memories of what was, perhaps with a pleasing tang of salt spray and sorrow, but never move one limb to return to it. This is the false nostalgia, one that has reduced the past to a room in the curiosity shop of the mind. It is a kind of suicide, and in fact Tennyson's other inspiration for the poem was Spenser's portrayal of Despair in *The Faerie Queene*, who tries to persuade the Knight of the Red Cross to give up hope and rest in his failure and his sin:

> Sleep after toil, port after stormy seas,
> Ease after war, death after life doth greatly please.[3]

These men, I say, are patterns of those who in our time do sense that we have strayed far from home, but who do not choose the heartache of the battle. They are not deceived. They know that many things are wrong and that the vanguard of what we indolently call our culture is quite mad, but it seems too great a task to fight it. "Let what is broken so remain," they say, and shrug, and wish that things will work out somehow. "I am certain," says Mr. Micawber, hastily casting a glance down a side street lest the grocer be waiting there with a bill, "that something—something *will turn up.*"

The hashish smokers, they who steep their minds in television that bores them, they who sign their children over to an institution we still call a school and do not inquire too closely into what goes on there, know that there should be an *order* in their lives and in their homelands, but they say that restoring that order is hard, and that "there is confusion worse than death." There is the key: *order.* The word has unfortunate associations for Americans; we imagine Puritans such as never were, keeping their suits and their tables spotless in a life of interminable Sunday sermons. Not for the Greeks, as Tennyson knew. He is thinking of *cosmos, the world as an ordered whole, a beautiful world, wherein everything is in its proper place.* The converse is *chaos, confusion,* which can be, according to the mariners, "worse than death." The irony is that they are unwilling to endure the confusion of battle so as to establish again the cosmos of an ordered household and an ordered community. They would choose to die—not to die in pain, but to die in slow, degenerating, enervate ease—rather than to fight. There is a confusion worse than death, and it is the confusion of moral disorder, the man-made desert of passions that drag Reason from her throne and beat her senseless with her own scepter or stupefy her with drugs; perhaps the *nepenthe* that Helen, ever the sly woman, slips into the drink of Menelaus and Telemachus, to still their weeping for a real friend and a real father lost.

Odysseus longs to go home, because it is home. He belongs there, in the way that the figure of Apollo belongs in the sanctum of his temple, or in the way that a well-hewed beam stretches as the roof-tree of a good strong house. I do not mean to describe here the biological longing of salmon to return to the pool where they spawned. We are closer with dogs, who have been known to trek over many miles of unknown territory to return to the masters they love. But neither the salmon nor the dog knows the *beauty* of home, the fitness of it. It is this beauty that is everywhere in the *Odyssey,* when men do what is right: *to kalon,* in Greek, the right thing, the decorous thing, what fits well and is admirable. We might say that man both makes his home beautiful and finds his home *in beauty.* Again, I am not talking about the picturesque. If a fine beach and a comfortable bed and a lovely bedmate were all, Odysseus would stay with Calypso. The braggart suitors in Ithaca are good-looking. Helen of Troy was the most beautiful woman in the world, and see what happened on her account.

Perhaps I can illustrate what this homely beauty is by going to the first man in Ithaca who welcomes Odysseus, whose identity he does not yet know. He is Eumaeus, the swineherd. Living in his shack a mile or two from the manor house, he keeps the hogs on Odysseus' estate, penning them in, giving orders to the younger men who assist him in his work, and taking the night watch himself, armed with a good stout club in case of wolves or thieves. Everything he does is fit, is right: for there is a beauty even in keeping a fine herd of hogs.

When Odysseus, disguised as a beggar, shows up at the swineherd's hut, all is as it should be. Fierce dogs rush upon him, barking and baring their teeth, as is right and fit, and Eumaeus himself, who knows more than the dogs do, comes out running and hollering and driving the dogs away. He knows what kind of greeting is owed to beggars and strangers, who the Greeks believed come from Zeus, as a test to man. Eumaeus welcomes the stranger, gives him the most comfortable seat, sets about straightaway to preparing with his own skilled hands a hearty supper, and asks his guest to tell his story, to share his sorrows. The suitors, hedonists as they are, will find the telling of the stranger's story a bore; they would not want to sit to hear the very poem in which they play so great and so ignoble a part. They are the sort who would slip an old and dying man a drink so as to put him out of *their* misery. So it is with our euthanasia: good for me and death for thee.

But Eumaeus and the beggar freely share stories of where they come from and what pains they have endured, though Odysseus' story is woven with truth and falsehood, because he knows it is not yet time to reveal his identity. When Odysseus asks Eumaeus a leading question about how well he lives on the estate, the old swineherd replies in a way that the man of nostalgia—of heartache for the homecoming—can understand:

> My master? Well, no doubt the dogs and wheeling birds
> have ripped the skin from his ribs by now, his life is
>     through—
> or fish have picked him clean at sea, and the man's bones
> lie piled up on the mainland, buried deep in sand...
> he's dead and gone. Aye, leaving a broken heart
> for loved ones left behind, for me most of all.
> Never another master kind as he!
> I'll never find one—no matter where I go,
> not even if I went back to mother and father,
> the house where I was born and my parents reared me once.

Ah, but much as I grieve for them, much as I long
to lay my eyes on them, set foot on the old soil,
it's longing for him, him that wrings my heart—
Odysseus, lost and gone!
That man, old friend, far away as he is...
I can scarcely bear to say his name aloud,
so deeply he loved me, cared for me, so deeply.
Worlds away as he is, I call him Master, Brother![4]

We will learn that Eumaeus was kidnapped as a small boy and sold
as a slave far from his home across the seas. The *nostalgia* he feels here,
then, is not a superstition regarding his native land or his race. It is
bound up with the duties of gratitude and love. Because Odysseus has
been a kind master to him, because Eumaeus admires the wife Penelope and loves the boy Telemachus as if he were his own son, he remains
at his post, doing what is right for a swineherd to do. He is, without
exaggeration, a *beautiful* old man, though nothing much to look at. He
is rich enough, he says, to take a good part of the herd away and set up
on his own, with the blessing of the family, but he will not do so. That
is not because he has any hope that Odysseus will return. When the
beggar-king tells him that he saw Odysseus and that the man will soon
arrive, Eumaeus regards it as gossip or as a well-meant lie. He is sure
he will never see the king again. That makes his loyalty all the more
impressive. He is thus the antithesis of the mariners who want to lay
down their oars and sail no more, no more steer their ship by the silent
and certain pilot-star in the heavens, no more torment their hearts
with sorrow and longing. *Nepioi*, Homer calls them in the first few
lines of the poem: ninnies. They are babies, not fit to bear arms.

It is the duty of a man to fight for his home, even when the enemy
has overrun it like locusts. It is also his duty to love that home and to
want to protect it, and if it has been reduced to rubble, it is his duty to
build it up again. In doing so he does not pretend that it was perfect. It
was not. I will speak in its place about the heaven toward which we

turn our gaze. But the reason we love our home is because it simply is. It is more than a house and other than a house. "Other lords may build," writes Ben Jonson at the end of his tribute to the Sidneys' manor, Penshurst, "but thy lord dwells." In the home where man dwells, even such homes as wayfaring man may find and cherish in this life, we find things in happy order. The home is for man as natural as the grass.

## The Virtue of Piety

It is also natural for man to look to his elders for wisdom. They are the builders of his moral home. You will find this sense of reverence for the old in every culture in the world. The Roman Senate is literally a gathering of old men. Virgil turned that insight into perhaps the most important motif of the *Aeneid*. Aeneas turns to his crippled father, Anchises, for advice when they seek a homeland for their refugee people, and after Anchises, "the best of fathers," has passed away, he will be instructed to seek him out in the underworld, where the soul of the happy old man will reveal to him the glorious future of his people. The name that Virgil gives Aeneas is not Odysseus' *polytropon*, the man of shifts and dodges, but the Latin word *pius*. Aeneas embodies a virtue we hardly recognize in our time: *piety*, which meant for the Romans a willingness to do your duty by your father and mother, your elders, your household gods, the city and state, and the great gods above.

This piety is at once a deeply personal virtue and a powerful force to bring together the generations, allowing the young to take root in the soil of the old and the old to engraft their experiences onto the young, so that we sense that home is a place where the passing day partakes of long ages past and to come. If it is advisable in the young, it is a duty and a pleasure for their elders. Says Cicero's Cato: "I can think of nothing more agreeable than an old age surrounded by the activities of young people in their prime. For surely at the very least we must concede age the capacity to teach and train young men and fit them for jobs of every kind."[5]

That attitude was universal in the ancient world. Devotees of the Stoics, the Platonists, the Aristotelians, and the Epicureans might heave books at each other's heads, but not about that. The Epicureans, who had no use for temple sacrifices, still held as sacred the birthday of their founder. Every book of Lucretius' *On the Nature of Things* thus begins with praise for a man who had died hundreds of years before:

> Out of such darkness you who were first to raise
> So brilliant a light to show us the best of life,
> I follow you, glory of Greece, and in the deep
> Print of your traces I now fix my steps.

"Honor thy father and thy mother," says the commandment, the one that forms a bridge between our duty to God and our duty toward others. It is the only commandment with a promise: "Honor thy father and thy mother: that thy days may be long upon the land which the Lord, thy God, giveth thee" (Exodus 20:12). So also Jewish wisdom:

> Hear, ye children, the instruction of a father,
> and attend to know understanding.
> For I give you good doctrine,
> forsake ye not my law.
> For I was my father's son,
> tender and only beloved in the sight of my mother.
> He taught me also, and said unto me,
> Let thine heart retain my words; keep my commandments
> and live. (Proverbs 4:1–4)

Nothing here of the puerile dismissal of the father, characteristic of our time of spoiled, unhappy, and aimless children old in years and infantile in wisdom.

If anything, the ethos of the East, with its love for the changeless Order of Heaven, demands an even more faithful cherishing of the old and wise. "Since King Wen died," said Confucius, who was meeting opposition from the people of the kingdom, "is not the tradition of King Wen in my keeping or possession? If it be the will of Heaven that this moral tradition should be lost, posterity shall never again share in the knowledge of this tradition. But if it be the will of Heaven that this tradition should not be lost, what can the people of K'uang do to me?" That same reverence for what was old and true was to be accorded to Confucius himself in turn, in a measure never before known in China, and never known since. "There have been many kings, emperors and great men in history," said the Master Historian of the Han court, Szema Ch'ien, "who enjoyed fame and honor while they lived and came to nothing at their deaths, while Confucius, who was but a common scholar clad in a cotton gown, became the acknowledged Master of scholars for over ten generations. All people in China who discuss the six arts, from the emperors, kings and princes down, regard the Master as the final authority."[6]

When Mao Tse-tung embarked on his sanguinary "Cultural Revolution," he decreed that the "Four Olds" had to be destroyed: old ideas, old customs, old habits, and old culture. So much for the millennial wisdom of the world's oldest civilization. I recall an argument I had with a chubby and bespectacled young woman in the main plaza of my graduate school. She was selling Mao's Little Red Book. The bloodshed did not matter to her. It was a small price to pay for cultural destruction, and after all, what do the aged have to offer?

Central to a healthy attitude of reverence is an insight that the self-named progressive is ever in danger of missing, which is that man can no more discover a new moral truth than he can invent a new color of the spectrum. What we do instead is to develop a moral insight already grasped, or we allow a moral insight to lapse into forgetfulness or confusion, or we are fitful and foolish in our application of the insight; and here the conservative needs to be careful, lest he conserve the outward trappings and lose the soul. But the truths do not change. They make up what C. S. Lewis called the "Tao" and are not the results of moral inquiry but the premises upon which moral inquiry is based. We do not arrive by deduction at the conclusions that the elderly are to be honored and that the innocence of children is to be protected. An immediate grasp of the good allows us to see these things. Of course we can, after the fact, come up with fine reasons why it is sensible to honor the elderly even when they have entered their second childhood, or to protect the innocence of children even when they are precocious. But those reasons are supplemental, not primary.

Edmund Burke called such insights by the name of "prejudice," a word which has acquired in America an understandable opprobrium, given its legal significance and our sorry history of slavery and racism. But prejudice, as Burke uses the word, does not imply evil intent or foolishness. Here he flashes his rapier against a clerical supporter of the French Revolution just as it was slouching toward Paris to be born:

> You see, Sir, that in this enlightened age I am bold enough
> to confess that we are generally men of untaught feelings,
> that, instead of casting away all our old prejudices, we cher-
> ish them to a very considerable degree, and, to take more
> shame to ourselves, we cherish them because they are prej-
> udices; and the longer they have lasted and the more gener-
> ally they have prevailed, the more we cherish them.[7]

By "prejudices" here, Burke means accepted and time-honored sentiments regarding right and wrong. They are not the results of philosophical discourse; Burke fairly boasts that he is a man of "untaught feelings." He does not mean that he has received no instruction in those feelings. Perhaps we ought to say "unschooled feelings," because the sentiments of moral insight are in fact taught to us, though not much at all in schools. They are taught by our parents' precepts, but still more often by their quiet example, by the example of good and honorable people around us, and most mysteriously by the prompting of the human heart, made by God to thrive upon what is right, and to sicken and wither by what is wrong. Such feelings that have the approbation of the ages, that have lasted and prevailed a long time, are all the more to be cherished, says Burke. They build up the moral home.

The alternative is to cast aside the heritage and to build anew. A dangerous enterprise, given the insufficiency of the individual man:

> We are afraid to put men to live and trade each on his own private stock of reason, because we suspect that this stock in each man is small, and that the individuals would do better to avail themselves of the general bank and capital of nations and of ages. Many of our men of speculation, instead of exploding general prejudices, employ their sagacity to discover the latent wisdom which prevails in them. If they find what they seek, and they seldom fail, they think it more wise to continue the prejudice, with the reason involved, than to cast away the coat of prejudice and to leave nothing but the naked reason.... [8]

What applies to the individual applies all the more to the generation. A people that vainly thinks it has nothing to learn from its forebears, no wisdom to seek, is as foolish as a young man who scoffs at his father and grandfather. As foolish, but more devastating. As I write these words, the people of a once noble and now silly nation, Great Britain, are considering giving the vote to sixteen-year-old children. There was a time when a fourteen-year-old John Quincy Adams could act as the effective American ambassador to the Russian court in Saint Petersburg because he spoke fluent French and the official ambassador could not; even he was not so foolish and self-satisfied as to believe that he merited the franchise. But in our day, the typical sixteen-year-old in Great Britain, if he is like his American cousin, would find it hard going to read Quincy's letters back home—in English.

## Sed Contra

Here I should like to forestall objections. They are jejune, mere substitutes for thought. The first one is strangely "conservative" in the worst sense. It tricks itself out in a slogan and takes the slogan for wisdom. "You can't put the toothpaste back in the tube," they say, or, "You can't turn the clock back." If by those bromides we mean that we cannot take a time machine and return to the day before yesterday, so that we should not after all filch Lady Windermere's fan but leave it on the dresser where it belongs, who can disagree? What's done is done. But of course, I can put toothpaste back into its tube; I assume that it did not grow there from a tiny seed of dentifrice, or that the tube did not slowly envelop a lump of toothpaste patiently waiting for its abode. It is not easy, but I can do it. And I can turn the clock back. I get up, cross the room, take the clock, turn a dial, and there you go.

The adulterer cannot alter the past. He can certainly alter his behavior for the future. He can cease to commit adultery. The past may be a *fait accompli,* but the future certainly is not. The German people embraced the Nazi regime. They did not have to do that, and they did not have to continue doing it. We have embraced the sexual revolution. We did not have to do that, and we do not have to persist in it. Every bad thing in the world will seek to justify its continuance by conferring inevitability upon what is in man's choice. A stupid law may be revoked. A depraved custom may be repudiated. A forgotten virtue may be recalled. Otherwise we are bound as slaves to the most irresponsible and irrepressible among us, who wreak havoc and call it history.

It will appear that I have contradicted myself. Not so. I do not claim that a certain time in the past was a golden age. Ithaca was not Paradise. I claim, again, that human nature does not change, and that therefore we do well to look to our forebears for wisdom, because they have experienced far more than we in our individual lives ever can, and because their mistakes are rarely going to be the same as ours. Where they erred, we can see and forgive; where they were right, and where we err—*that is what is hard for modern man to see, and even harder for him to forgive.* Modern man enjoys his sense of superiority to those who came before. That is almost the essence of modernity itself: and underneath the pride of it all there lurks a persistent fear that the pride is empty. I am persuaded that there are men the modern feminist finds it even harder to forgive than her great-great-grandfather who beat his wife. They are her seven other great-great-grandfathers who loved their wives and would sooner have cut off their right hands than raise them in anger to the women they loved.

Others say that conservatives are nostalgic—and they mean that as an insult—because they want to return to a time when black people were treated miserably and all the women stayed home to bake, preserve vegetables and fruit, make and mend clothes, tend gardens, care for small children, make butter and cheese from raw milk, teach children their first lessons, see to the elderly and neighbors in need, organize social events with other women, and make a house into a home. Pro-life people, they say, oppose "choice" because they oppose "choices" for women generally speaking, as if the women I have described were not immersed in choices of moment all the time.

Such criticism is childish and not to the point. First, all that I say here applies, *mutatis mutandis,* to every people in the modern world struggling against the leveling force of a technocratic and culture-dissolving state. I write for the citizen of Lagos as for the citizen of Saint Louis. I speak to the farmer in Szechuan as to the farmer in Saskatchewan—and to those poor souls, the graduates of our expensively inept schools, who can no sooner locate either place on a map than they can label the mountains on the moon. As bad as the cultural destruction has been in the United States, it is still nowhere near as bad as what happened in China under Mao; as if all the topsoil of a civilization three thousand years old had been stripped away, leaving nothing but a moral dust bowl, a sad and dismal desert, swarming with people robbed of the treasure of their past—a billion people without a home. We in the United States still have the wherewithal to remember.

Second, we do not say that our forebears were saints. All we require is that they were not villains, and they were *our forebears.* Every great renewal of art, like every great renewal of the moral life, has come when people, seeing beyond their own time and sometimes beyond the recent past, have recovered forgotten virtues from the more distant past. We do not have to recover the vices. Wordsworth set Pope aside and returned to Spenser and Milton. That did not mean that he "writ no language," as Ben Jonson said of the archaizing Spenser, or that he believed that the Catholic Church was the whore of Babylon, as Milton did. A. W. N. Pugin set classicism to the side, not ignoring it altogether by any means, and returned to the Gothic. That did not mean that he hired illiterate masons, or that he reproduced the profound blue of the windows at Chartres—nobody has been able to do that. Dickens set aside the utilitarianism of his time to return to the Gospel, where he found wisdom far more useful than anything deduced in the boiler-maker mind of Jeremy Bentham. That does not mean that he took to wearing a tunic, or that he abandoned industrial England in disgust.

Mozart turned to Bach, as did Mendelssohn, but neither man was a church organist who wrote a cantata every week. Donatello dug up—with a shovel—copies of Greek statuary that had been buried in centuries of Italian rubble. But no sane person can view *Lo Zuccone,* his statue of the prophet Habakkuk, and miss the gulf that separates the Christian from the ancient Greek. Who are we to disdain to do what Wordsworth and Mozart and Donatello did?

Third, any particular person's motives are not relevant. A man may argue for a new road, knowing that it will cross land that he owns and can sell at a high price. But that does not touch the main point, whether the road ought to be built. His motives may be entirely mercenary or entirely selfless; it does not matter. Good people will sometimes promote a bad thing for a good reason. Perhaps they have not thought the matter through; perhaps they are deceived; perhaps their longing for a good end gets the better of their moral sense, and they elide the difficulties. Good people will sometimes promote a good thing but for a bad reason. Perhaps a baseball coach makes his boys work twice as hard as everyone else, partly because he really wants them to learn the game, but also partly because he hates the coach of the rival team. We may take his motives into account when judging him as a man or deciding what weight to give to his testimony, but ultimately they do not touch the main point. Bad people will sometimes promote a good thing, for a bad reason, as when Karl Marx, an energetic hater of mankind, defended the rights of miners in England, not because he loved miners, but because he hated capitalists. Bad people may promote a bad thing for an ostensibly good reason. All the tyrants of the world have done so. The best of men is a tangle of motives, often contradictory. Ultimately, we must base our decision for or against a law or a custom upon its merits.

But if ever we were justified in attributing a selfish reason to what someone promotes, we are justified in the case of someone whose philosophy admits in principle of none other than selfish reasons. We may take the materialist at his word. If he is correct, and all moral judgments are but camouflage for the powerful, then he invites us to apply his own reductive analysis to himself. Consider what the ancients tell us. What quicker way to debase a people and keep them subservient than to induce licentiousness in them? Who benefits from the evisceration of the working-class family? Whose bank account is fattened by feminism and its promotion of the double-professional household? Who have penned up for themselves a dependent clientele? Who is it who fairly reveals his own economic motives when he says, without blushing and with no sense of absurdity, that people who wish to protect the lives of unborn children—people like Mary Ann Glendon, the Learned Hand Professor of Law at Harvard, a devout Catholic and a champion of the unborn, or the redoubtable philosopher Elizabeth Anscombe, who in her old age was once dragged off to jail for protesting at an abortuary—want to rob women of their careers? Is that then to be the justification for killing the unborn child—that it is economically desirable for the mother? Was it not also economically desirable for the slaveholder to preserve *that* peculiar institution, propping it up with the lingo of the newest developments in biology? Was it not economically desirable for Hitler to unify the Germans by aiming their resentment at the Jews? If money is the arbiter, it is hard for me to see why we should look askance at robber barons or monopolists. People who see only money and power as the motives of their opponents unwittingly reveal a great deal about themselves.

I suspect, rather, that people who object to nostalgia are afraid that their achievements, such as they are, will not stand scrutiny. "No, you don't want to go home!" they cry. They must cry, they must make all the noise they can, because if they cease for a moment, we hear the calls of sanity and sweetness again, and we may just shake our heads as if awaking from a bad and feverish dream. Coming to ourselves, we may resolve, like the prodigal, to "arise and go to my father's house."

## Categorical Errors

But some will again say that although cultural customs can be adopted, rejected, or modified, the culture we possess is driven by technological advancements, and those, once in place, cannot be removed. We are not going back to the days of the horse and buggy. We are stuck where we are, like it or not.

We are dealing with three problems here. First, we have assumed that development in culture is like development in technology, whereby one machine replaces another, rather than like the growth of a living thing, whereby the natal and latent powers of the creature flourish and broaden in variety and scope. Second, we have assumed that technological developments must dictate terms to us, rather than our being in charge of the developments, always asking in what ways they serve us, if they serve us at all. The human purposes must come first. Third, we have failed to distinguish between instrumental goods and things that are ends in themselves, and technology is by its very nature instrumental. So we must ask, "Instrumental for what?" These three confusions are related to one another; where we find one, we usually find the other two as well.

Let us take trite old horse and buggy. Or rather, let us take those prior things called *legs*. They are for locomotion: they get us from one place to another. The legs do so, however, at some expense of energy and time. When we are small children, when we are sick or exhausted from work, or when we are old and our knees are giving way, we can hardly make ten miles in an afternoon, even in good weather. The horse-drawn carriage was an extension of the legs. It allowed us to do an ordinary thing with greater ease. It did not amputate or replace the legs or cause them to wither and die. One might still walk, and people did walk, all the time. The automobile, in turn, was an extension of the power of the horse-drawn carriage, making it possible for people to travel long distances. It has also, of course, made it *necessary* for people to do so, and without the slow pace that made a carriage ride more like walking from place to place than like speeding from one point not experienced as a place to another.

Now, since riding in a car is not an *integral human good* but instrumental to some other good things, we must ask how we are to procure or preserve those things, car or no, assuming that those other things are necessary for a truly human existence. We do not want to become the tools of our tools. We want our tools to help us secure and enhance things that are good in themselves, without compromising or destroying other things good in themselves that may be more important still.

For example, the hand-held telephone with internet connections allows us to speak easily with people far beyond the distance we can cross by shouting or waving flags or sending smoke signals. But when the use of such telephones shuts down communication with people three feet away from us, then we are talking about a tool whose use— if we do not learn to restrain ourselves—damages the very faculty that it is supposed to assist. It has become a suicide machine. Or if a student's laptop computer prevents him from acquiring the patience and the mental silence necessary to read a good book, then it is weakening the very faculty for which, presumably, it was adopted in the first place. It too becomes a suicide machine. It will not matter that the computer can place before the student's eyes many thousands of books he could otherwise never open. He will lack the mental habits to read them.

The local school *might* be an extension of the family and its role in educating young people; it might be like a library that extends the holdings in the private home, or an organized team that extends the reach and perfects the beauty of an informal gathering of young people playing ball. But if it attempts to supplant the family, or if it works against the common moral understanding of the parents, then it would be like a drug that at its best might enhance the function of one organ while causing the whole body to sicken. Families are more important than schools. Schools are for learning. Families are good in themselves. I dare say that the success of home-schoolers suggests, if anything, that the farther our schools remove themselves from the proximity of families, the oversight of families, and the time-transcending character of families, the more pathological they become and the less they serve either the function of schools or the good of families. We are left with something similar to the paradox of the over-organization of sport's leading to fewer and fewer players. Bloat as well as shrinkage can lead to atrophy.

And then there is the objection that all I want is for things to remain the same. Far from it! For the Christian, the return, in this life, is not the end of a journey, or the refusal to enter upon a journey. It is a return *to the journey,* the pilgrimage. Gabriel Marcel, in his preface to the perfectly named *Homo Viator,* expresses it better than I can: "Perhaps a stable order can only be established on earth if man always remains acutely conscious that his condition is that of a traveler."

To every repentant prodigal, to the fathers and mothers who await them, and to the home that we have not quite forgotten, I dedicate this book.

CHAPTER ONE

## Man in Time

*When I do count the clock that tells the time,*
*And see the brave day sunk in hideous night;*
*When I behold the violet past prime,*
*And sable curls all silvered o'er with white;*
*When lofty trees I see barren of leaves*
*Which erst from heat did canopy the herd,*
*And summer's green all girded up in sheaves*
*Borne on the bier with white and bristly beard,*
*Then of thy beauty do I question make,*
*That thou among the wastes of time must go,*
*Since sweets and beauties do themselves forsake*
*And die as fast as they see others grow;*
*And nothing 'gainst Time's scythe can make defense*
*Save breed, to brave him when he takes thee hence.*
—William Shakespeare, Sonnet 12

I once asked a college friend what he believed was the most important criterion for judging between good and evil. He gave me the Darwinian answer: survival. That got things backwards and was beside the point. What is good will allow man to thrive because it is good, and man has been made for good and not for evil; but not everything that gives a man an advantage in the struggle for existence is good. Robbing his neighbor is not good, though it would give him the

1

money to impress the vivacious Miss Lovegold, and that in turn might result in marriage—and then think how grasping he must learn to be.

If we make the Kantian move on the chessboard and say that if everybody robbed everybody else, there would no longer be any property to rob, I reply that such were the cultural habits of the pagan Germanic tribes, so long as it was other tribes they robbed. "That was a good king," says the Christian poet of *Beowulf,* speaking with a subtly ironical air of Scyld Sceafing, the deceased warlord of the Danes, whose claim to being good was that he smashed the mead-benches of his neighbors and made them pay tribute. If we combine Kant with Darwin and say that such habits do not conduce well to the survival of your people, I reply that they did not kill off the Germans who swarmed over the Roman empire, and besides, *mankind is no longer in any danger of disappearing from the earth.* We are going to be around as sure as the sky is blue.

If we are reductive materialists and say that our notions of good and evil have been bred in us by the pressures of survival back in the ages when that was by no means assured, I answer, besides that there is no evidence for that claim, that that turns things backwards again and evades the issue. What do we do *now*? It is not sufficient to say that Johnny *must* be honest with his employees merely because his parents taught him so, nor does it alter the question if you extend his parents backward into the days of stone knives and bearskins. We say instead that Johnny must be honest with his employees because honesty is good, and that because honesty is good, man does not merely survive by it, he thrives by it, as men have seen for as long as men have dwelt upon the earth, in every part of the world, in cultures at every stage of technological development. That is likely why his parents have taught him to be honest, and their parents before them, and we do well to heed the testimony of the ages.

But my friend was on to something after all. He didn't know it, because he had not read any philosophy or theology, and neither had I, at that time—keep in mind that we were American students at one of the most famous colleges in the world. We were not likely to have learned much from the past. He had intuited something about man's relation to time. But because of the pseudoscientific reductions he had uncritically accepted, he could express no difference in that regard between man and a flea. Those biters and burrowers also are driven to survive. We sense, though, that time for man is different from time for a flea, though the bodies of both should age and decay and turn to dust. What this difference means for man's home, and his homecoming, we shall see.

Consider the above sonnet by Shakespeare. In his day, a collection of sonnets was not a grab bag of love poems tossed in at random. It was a highly organized and intricate work of art, and each sonnet was a piece of the whole. Shakespeare has thus begun his sequence of sonnets with seventeen poems that all have to do with one way, the most obvious way, to defeat the fell purposes of Time. You have children.

So the narrator of the sonnets, whom we should not naively identify with the poet himself, begins by telling the young man whom he addresses that he had better get married soon and have children, because Time, that "delves the parallels in beauty's brow" (Sonnet 60, line 10), will be doing its inevitable work. As spring passes into summer and summer into fall, and as the sheaves are brought in on a bier, like the body of an old man with a white beard brought to the burial ground, so must we too pass away. The urgency is not for the human race but for the individual person. It seems but a few years ago when I was strong and not a single hair on my head was anything but glossy black. I have arthritis developing in my knees. If I eat as much as I used to, I will put on weight—and I have put on weight. The malady that will send me out of this world may now be working unseen and unknown in my body. And I see my fresh-faced children, and they, though not children anymore, cheer my heart.

Again, Shakespeare puts it most brilliantly, striking home to the point where childhood greets old age and makes a man feel young again. So says King Polixenes about his nine-year-old son:

If at home, sir,
He's all my exercise, my mirth, my matter;
Now my sworn friend, and now mine enemy;
My parasite, my soldier, statesman, all;
He makes a July's day short as December,
And with his varying childness cures in me
Thoughts that would thick my blood. (*The Winter's Tale*,
    I.ii. 199–205)

We are not talking merely about boosting the old man's metabolism. He has *thoughts* that would thicken his blood; these thoughts, in our quiet moods, in our old age, must be of the passing of time, the loss of loved ones, the things we have done that we cannot undo, the things we should have done that we left undone, and death. No other creature upon earth experiences anything remotely resembling these thoughts. We are immersed in time, as all things are, but we alone can grasp it as it passes, can stand above it or beside it. We alone are conscious of age and death. We alone can sin and know that we have sinned. We alone can mourn our lost innocence.

It is not then *survival* that we ask from our children, but hope. I am not yet speaking in specifically Christian terms. At the beginning of the same play I have cited above, two gentlemen are speaking about another young lad, the son of King Leontes. The counselor from Bohemia tells the counselor from Sicily that his people "have an unspeakable comfort of your young Prince Mamillius; it is a gentleman of the greatest promise that ever came into my note." The Sicilian agrees: "It is a gallant child, one that indeed physics the subject, makes old hearts fresh. They that walk on crutches ere he was born desire yet their life to see him a man" (I.i). The boy "physics," or gives healing medicine to, those who look upon him, and the lame man who is near the grave wants to live if for no other reason than to see how a boy of such intelligence and grace should grow to be a man worthy of his childhood.

Although the child is at the center of both the sonnet and these reflections in *The Winter's Tale,* there is a difference. The speaker of the sonnets has a narrow view of the child. The proposed son is to be a mirror in which the young man will see his beauty born again, an heir to that beauty, a bounty that comes from using your wealth wisely while you have it rather than to "make worms thine heir." The child is an instrument of egotism.

But Shakespeare—I am speaking of the author, not the voice in the sonnets—is the playwright of his age who most boldly shows his love of children and his sense of the peculiar evil in offenses against them, which he never leaves unpunished. The child, like every other living person, is a bearer of legal rights, though no more than that, and if we are to believe the philosopher Peter Singer, *much less* than that, particularly if he is newborn or if a defect of birth makes him more vulnerable to someone's desire to have him out of the way. The child is a vessel of hope—the foot soldier in the vanguard against time, which is also a battle against the ruins we have made in time. He is the bearer of a hope not in mere survival but in spiritual regeneration, not in life as *bios,* which vitality the sheep and cattle have, but in the life of life, the *zoe* that is divine. Yes, we know that the child will grow into a man, a sinner who will likely spoil some things in his turn, but when we see him uncorrupted, we can understand, even if not yet in any specifically theological sense, why Jesus said, "Let the little children be, and do not hinder them from coming to me, for of such is the kingdom of heaven" (Matthew 19:14).

Perhaps that explains why people in our time who have no faith tend also to have no children. You might think the reverse, that if you do not dwell in the precincts of heaven, looking to the horizon whence glory shall come, you will be thrown back with all the greater force upon the natural expedient and attempt to "live" forever through your healthy brood of progeny. But that is to think mechanistically, as if the human soul were an overheated boiler, so that the steam that would be released through a clogged valve must press the more urgently upon the valve that is still free. But we are not so. Hope will color the whole man—hope, not its impostor, optimism—or the whole man will be pallid and frail. Marcel again, considering the adventurousness of the large family, notes "the horror of this very risk which prevails in an ever-increasing fraction of a country on the way to progressive devitalisation." Such people think you can use life as an element "to obtain a few patent satisfactions, without which the world would be nothing but a prison." Life, for such, has all the glare, the noise, and the triviality of an amusement park.

But soon that speaker of Shakespeare's sonnets leaves off recommending a child as a stay against the onslaught of Time and turns to another expedient. He introduces it briefly in sonnets fifteen through seventeen, then makes it the center of number eighteen, one of the best known in the sequence:

> Shall I compare thee to a summer's day?
> Thou art more lovely and more temperate;
> Rough winds do shake the darling buds of May,
> And summer's lease hath all too short a date.
> Sometime too hot the eye of heaven shines,
> And often is his gold complexion dimmed;
> And every fair from fair sometime declines,
> By chance, or nature's changing course, untrimmed.
> But thy eternal summer shall not fade,
> Nor lose possession of that fair thou owest,
> Nor shall Death brag thou wanderest in his shade,
> When in eternal lines to time thou growest.
> So long as men can breathe, or eyes can see,
> So long lives this, and this gives life to thee.

The sun declines to westward, the summer fades, the flowers wither, but into you, you callow and inactive lump of humanity, I will breathe the breath of life, or inject the ink of life, and you shall live.

What kind of life that is is an open question and not one that critics have wanted to ask. That is because they assume that Shakespeare, confident in the staying power of his poetry, really believed that he was conferring upon the young man a kind of eternal existence. A strange existence it is, when the greatest creator of characters the world of letters has ever known describes not one of the man's features other than his fair skin, when we do not know the man's name, and when his behavior implied by the poems is at best dubious and at worst treacherous. So why do we take the speaker at his word? I think we are disarmed by something else we take for granted: that our *creations* can live on after us. We achieve an ersatz eternity by means of "children," that is, by works of art and culture. "Exegi monumentum aere perennius," boasted the poet Horace: "I have made for myself a monument more enduring than bronze" (Odes, 3.30.1).

No one would deny that "so long as men can breathe, or eyes can see," people will be reading Shakespeare. "Dante and Shakespeare divide the modern world between them," says T. S. Eliot; "there is no third."[2] This is hardly the opinion only of academics. After all, until a century ago, the works of Shakespeare were not even taught in colleges. They were written in the mother tongue, and there was no reason to engage famous scholars to help you read and understand *English*. But the judgment of Shakespeare's greatness was early indeed and was rendered by those who should know best and who would have had selfish reasons not to praise Shakespeare but to depreciate him. From the youthful John Milton, for example, writing "On Shakespeare" about fifteen years after the playwright's death:

> What needs my Shakespeare for his honored bones
> The labor of an age in piled stones,
> Or that his hallowed relics should be hid
> Under a star y-pointing pyramid?
> Dear son of Memory, great heir of Fame,
> What needst thou such weak witness of thy name?

Thou in our wonder and astonishment
Hast built thyself a livelong monument.
For whilst to the shame of slow-endeavoring art
Thy easy numbers flow, and that each heart
Hath, from the leaves of thy unvalued book,
Those Delphic lines with deep impression took,
Then thou, our fancy of itself bereaving,
Dost make us marble by too much conceiving,
And so sepulchred in such pomp dost lie,
That kings for such a tomb would wish to die.

Shakespeare, says Milton, needs no pile of slave-dredged bricks to build himself a pyramid pointing to the stars, such as the pharaohs of old Egypt had and such as Horace boasted to have erected for himself. He has a finer monument than that, a *livelong monument,* one that is alive and always shall be. Milton is not saying in a sentimental way that Shakespeare will live on in his work. The very spirit of Shakespeare, what he thought and felt, what he saw of the truth and what he imparted of that truth in power and beauty, seizes the souls of his readers just as the prophet god Apollo seized his human votaries whether they would or no and literally astonishes them—turns them to marble with the amazement of "too much conceiving," thoughts too great for them, a progeny of the mind. We who read Shakespeare and are stunned by his genius are the sepulchers, alive, in which not we but the poet speaks. Kings build grand tombs for themselves, but Shakespeare needs none. He has us, alive with gratitude and struck still with wonder.

Eliot would agree, with a stern proviso: Without tradition, it cannot be. When tradition is scorned, when the love of home has vanished, when man has neither the longing for home nor its brother-longing, the spirit of the pilgrim, Milton's words make no sense. We are the walking dead. We do not grow but shrink into obsolescence and oblivion.

This life that transcends the limits of death warrants some careful thought. It is not conferred upon great artists, thinkers, and statesmen alone. Nor is it sufficient that somebody or other, several hundred years hence, may open your book and muddle about in it. The plays of Shakespeare are a gift bestowed upon the receivers. We require both those who give and those who receive: we require the living, who take and cherish with gratitude what has been bequeathed to them. Otherwise the "life" of Shakespeare on this earth is a bumpy line on a statistical graph—meaningless. We are here in the realm of *culture*.

## Culture, against Decay

As always, I wish to fend off misunderstandings. By "culture" I do not mean what people with a lot of money do—going to La Scala to hear Rossini and then boasting about it at a luncheon the next day. I do not mean culture as commodity or as a sign of social prestige. I certainly do not imply what has happened to "high" culture in our time, in the so-called *Regietheater* of the opera, turning works of tremendous power into crass political statements laced with the profane and the obscene.

The word suggests the inner reality. It is *culture* because a farmer (Latin *agricola*) has tilled (Latin *cultivare*) the soil. Not with a machine for razing everything in sight; the true tiller of the soil has nothing in common with Mao. You must be careful of the soil, and the seeds you plant now may come to full fruit long after you have passed away. A man gathers the apples from a tree planted by his grandfather, and grafts into hardy stock a slip of a peach tree in the hope, not the optimism, that his children and his children's children will reap the rewards.

Charles Péguy, in his magnificent lyrical meditation *The Portal of the Mystery of Hope*, has captured the essence of culture in the plain work of a farmer with sons:

If they don't inherit his house and his land.
At least they will inherit his tools.
His good tools.
That served him so often.
That have grown to fit his hand.
That have so often dug the same earth.
His tools, from use, have made his hands callous and shiny.
But he also, from using them, he made the handles of his
  tools all polished and shiny.
At the handles of his tools his sons will gain, his sons will
  inherit, the hardness of his hands.
But also their skill, their great skill.[3]

With good work, it is not possible to distinguish between the man
and the instrument or between the man and the field, as the meter is
in Shakespeare and Shakespeare is in his meter, and as the hands of
Michelangelo are scarred by the hammer and chisel and stone, and in
the stone are his thought and his love and his wish to bestow upon
other men the gift he so cherished and cultivated. Péguy's good farmer
is in his small and local way like Shakespeare, like Michelangelo.
Working his land is already an act that transcends his own day, for
there is no shine on the hands and the tools without the long and quiet
past, and with every thrust of the hoe against the earth, he prepares a
world for his sons to be.

We know of no human society, except perhaps our own, without
culture so defined. Every people we know of, except perhaps ourselves,
has sung the songs its fathers and mothers sang and celebrated the holy
days and prayed the prayers and prepared the food and carved the
shillelaghs and done the thousand other things that are the more precious to a people because it knows, in its heart, its mind, and its very
fingers, that they *have been* done just so, and *will continue to be* done.

Without the acknowledgment of a gift, there is no culture, even if
scholars still compel sweating students to forget their debauched lives

for a moment, to gaze instead at the *corpus* of Shakespeare, like a piglet preserved in formaldehyde and lying on a laboratory table, to which poor thing they apply their galvanic shot of politically tendentious criticism to get the trotter to twitch and jerk.

We have heard tell of people in possession of some rare work of art or craftsmanship, some precious memento of an historic battle, a batch of unknown correspondence between Grant and Sherman bound with string and forgotten in an attic, who toss the things away and let the Landfill of Progress swallow them up—and only later realize what they have done. For the most part, our schools from kindergarten to the doctorate are a vast waste-management operation, hauling the past away to be buried while passing out the flyers of social and antisocial fads. A well-read and relatively unschooled woman of the nineteenth century, such as Sophia Hawthorne, could and did write letters and read books that would tax the minds of almost every college student today. Those letters and books would be filled with references as unintelligible to today's professors as the hieroglyphics on the tomb of Cheops. If Sophia and her husband, Nathaniel, are dead to them, it is because they, the professors and students, have never come to cultural life to begin with.

I do not exaggerate the incapacity. Students can find on the internet a variety of sites that will help explain to them what the letters of Abraham Lincoln mean. I would say that newspapers will soon be stocked with their own cheat-notes, but it is hard to imagine even now that anyone would need help reading "See the President run."

People who scoff at the past rob us of our soil. Better to have your pocket picked than to have your cultural field sown with salt or the works of your hands left to gather mold and spiders.

Culture shows us that, as I have suggested, man's relation to time is as far from that of a clump of matter as it is possible for a bodily creature to be. It is far also from the mere animal. Man does more than remember. He recalls. He does more than anticipate the near future, as my dog, Jasper, does when, hearing that I have stopped playing the piano, he knows it may be time for a walk. Man plans; he looks far into the future. He can contract long vistas of time into a single perception, as when he sums up his life and says, with Jacob, "few and evil have the days of the years of my life been" (Genesis 47:9), or with Job, "My days are swifter than a weaver's shuttle" (Job 7:6). He can do so not only for himself but for his forebears and his children, his neighbors and the men and women and children who fall to their knees beside him in prayer.

Consider how great a crime it would be to infect someone with a disease that would cut his life short by five or ten years. But to deprive him of *an entire dimension* of his temporal being, the dimension that allows him to transcend his three score and ten, or that steeps those years in long years past and years to come—to cut him off from the wellsprings of culture and set him adrift in the river of time like a dead thing among the flotsam of what used to be rich and human—that is a crime that would undo the word of the Creator who said, "Let us now make man in our image." Man without culture is an inert thing, acted upon by the psychological manipulators of mass education, mass politics, mass marketing, mass entertainment. It makes no difference that those in apparent control of these mass phenomena are themselves carried along by their swell and flow. If anything, it makes matters worse. George Orwell's linguist in *Nineteen Eighty-Four*, Syme, knew all about the ideological aim of Newspeak and explained it to Winston Smith with the chilling enthusiasm of a destroyer. A few weeks later, Syme was no more to be seen. Evil eats its own.

Hence in our time, the longing to go home must also be a longing for a heritage lost. Again, I note a paradox. If we adopted that hydraulic view of man, we might guess that people who do not have many children would be all the more committed to preserving the arts and letters and folkways of those who came before, intuiting that their own descendants might do the same for them in turn. Or they may conversely fear that if they treat their forebears with contempt, they will instruct those who follow them to do the same: to heave their works away along with their stiff and empty shells. But it is not so. They who have lost their faith in God generally have little good to say about the past and resent anybody who retains an attachment to the time-gathering and time-transcending power of culture. It has been those most committed to the Landfill of Progress who have rubbed out of our schools almost all the heritage of English literature, replacing diamonds and emeralds with costume jewelry, cheaply acquired and quickly discarded. But show me a young person who reads Milton, and I will show you someone looking over his shoulder, catching sight of a nearly overgrown path, and seeing in his mind, a thousand miles along its adventurous way, something that looks like a home.

### It Is Not Good for the Man to Be Alone

I have said that culture is one of the means by which man makes his dwelling in time and beyond time, and that it therefore requires generosity and gratitude; I must accept with thanks what I have been given and preserve all that is good in it, which will be great indeed, and seek to measure my works by its high standard and pass it on to my children with love. The iconoclast—the icon-smasher—is not generally a lover of mankind. Here let me add something that is hard to see when we are thinking *only* of selves and their survival. It is that the longing to go home, to a real culture, is also a longing *not to be alone anymore*. They who are cut adrift in time are like survivors of a shipwreck, each clinging to his own spar or beam. They who are at home in culture dwell in something that spans the generations and renews them, throwing bridges across the divides of class and sex and age. Think of a black man and a white man who both love the poetry of John Keats, and what a profoundly beautiful thing they share in the depths of their souls. At the best of times the rich man and the poor man do not share enough. In our time, the rich man and the other rich man share almost nothing. We are alone.

I return to Shakespeare to illustrate the point. Not this time to the often confused and exceedingly selfish narrator of the sonnets but to

the rustic comedy *As You Like It*. We are in the Forest of Arden with
Orlando, a young man whose elder brother has sought his life. With
the lad is his servant, Adam, a loyal man of more than four score years.
The forest is wild, it is winter, food is scarce, and the poor old man is
near to death. So Orlando tries to cheer him up, keeping him as warm
as he can, before he sets off to catch something to eat: "Yet thou liest
in the bleak air. Come, I will bear thee to some shelter, and thou shalt
not die for lack of a dinner if there live anything in this desert. Cheer-
ily, good Adam!" (II.vi)

The Forest of Arden happens also to be the wilderness where
the good Duke Senior, his own brother having usurped his throne
and driven him out, has retreated with his loyal retainers. They are
about to have some venison for dinner—they too feel the pinch of
the cold and of the empty belly. Orlando, frantic and half crazed
with fear for Adam's life, bursts upon them, sword drawn, demanding food—as if he were a savage and so were they. When the Duke
answers him in a gentle voice, Orlando begs pardon, and no longer
demands but asks:

> Speak you so gently? Pardon me, I pray you:
> I thought that all things had been savage here;
> And therefore put I on the countenance
> Of stern commandment. But whate'er you are
> That in this desert inaccessible,
> Under the shade of melancholy boughs,
> Lose and neglect the creeping hours of time;
> If ever you have looked on better days,
> If ever been where bells have knolled to church;
> If ever sat at any good man's feast,
> If ever from your eyelids wiped a tear,
> And know what 'tis to pity and be pitied,
> Let gentleness my strong enforcement be:
> In the which hope I blush, and hide my sword. (II.vii. 107–120)

To which the Duke responds in kind:

> True it is that we have seen better days,
> And have with holy bell been knolled to church,
> And sat at good men's feasts, and wiped our eyes
> Of drops that sacred pity hath engendered:
> And therefore sit you down in gentleness,
> And take upon command what help we have,
> That to your wanting may be ministered. (121–127)

Every man in this scene, including the desperately weak Adam offstage, is an exile, and yet we do not feel *homeless* here. That is not merely because the Duke is kind. I have sometimes stopped in my car to pass a ten or a twenty to a homeless man begging on the corner, but still the man is homeless, and there is little human connection between us. Let us look closely at the terms of Orlando's question and Duke Senior's response.

Orlando begs on condition that the Duke and his men have shared not only his trouble but a way of life—nothing less than a culture. What does it mean to have "known better days"? We learn immediately. It means to have been called by the church bell to join your fellow men in the service of God. It means to have sat at the table of a good man and enjoyed his generous gifts. It means to have shared intimately in the humanity of your fellows assailed by sickness or loss or death, and to have shed a tear of *sacred* pity: pity set apart from the necessities of the workaday world. It means to have been merciful to others and to have been shown mercy, as Orlando applies the words of Jesus to the situation at hand, an allusion that would not be lost on the Duke. They are in the middle of nowhere. If they returned to what should be their homes, it would cost them their lives, yet they are home with one another. They share nothing less than the world.

Man without religion walks the streets of an interminable film noir but without the talents of Orson Welles or Paul Muni to transform it into art. He cannot know what he is missing. Consider the words of the Eucharistic prayer in a Catholic mass, immediately after the elevation of the Host: *Unde et memores*: we declare ourselves to be *mindful, in remembrance*, and not only of some event long ago, but of the re-enacted sacrifice of Christ before us now. My Jewish readers should think of the Passover supper, meant not just to celebrate the dread night when the angel of death passed by the houses marked with the blood of the lamb, but to re-enact it ritually, with your loins girt as if for flight, eating the unleavened bread of haste: "And it shall be when thy son asketh thee in time to come, saying, What is this? that thou shalt say unto him, By strength of hand the LORD brought us out from Egypt, from the house of bondage" (Exodus 13:14).

Nor only once a year, this remembrance. Many of the psalms dwell upon the *magnalia Dei*, the great works of God for the Jewish people. The psalms were the treasured prayer book of the Jews, central to the worship of God in the Temple and still at the heart of Jewish piety and liturgy to this day, *three thousand years later*. The psalmists know very well they are composing acts of remembrance. They have it specifically in mind, because it was God who commanded the remembrance in the first place—God, the maker of time and of times himself:

> For he established a testimony in Jacob, and appointed a law
> in Israel,
> which he commanded our fathers, that they should make
>     them known to their children:
> That the generation to come might know them, even the
>     children which should be born;
> who should arise and declare them to their children:
> That they might set their hope in God, and not forget the
>     works of God,
> but keep his commandments. (Psalm 78:5–7)

When Jesus and his apostles ate the Passover supper on the night before he died, they said the prayers their forefathers had said and sang the songs, and so when Jesus himself commanded remembrance of that moment, he was doing far more than asking the apostles to think of him when they were in their cups. He was instituting a new rite of remembrance, a new re-enactment of the liberating *magnalia Dei*, those past and that which was soon to come, his sacrificial death upon the Cross, as "the Lamb of God, which taketh away the sin of the world" (John 1:29). That is why Saint Paul insists upon a faithful tradition, a handing on, from one believer to the next, from one generation to the next, of what Jesus did before his own blood would be spattered on the posts and lintels of a world in bondage to sin and death:

> For I have received of the Lord that which also I delivered unto you, That the Lord Jesus the same night in which he was betrayed took bread: And when he had given thanks, he brake it, and said, Take, eat: this is my body, which is broken for you: this do in remembrance of me. After the same manner also he took the cup, when he had supped, saying, This cup is the new testament in my blood: this do ye, as oft as ye drink it, in remembrance of me. For as often as ye eat this bread, and drink this cup, ye do shew the Lord's death till he come. (1 Corinthians 11:23–26)

This is more than habit or custom. Dogs have habits. People have plenty of customs which are little more than commonplace ways of greeting someone or saying goodbye. This is tradition in the strict sense: the bequeathing of a heritage. It is also *more* than that. It is a grasping of time past, time present, and the time to come, in communion with your fellow worshipers in the church where you are kneeling, and before all the altars of the world, at all times, so long as time shall be. It is exuberant in the literal sense, as of a womb overflowing with life. It is, as Josef Pieper puts it, "the spontaneous expression of an inner richness," far beyond mere utility, for such richness causes people to build "not merely a functional meeting hall but the basilica of Ronchamp or a cathedral."[4]

Nothing in the experience of secular man is like it. I state the obvious. When does secular man read and hear words spoken two thousand years ago, not as curiosities but as urgent revelations and warnings and commands and consolations, as still present, as if spoken to him and to his fellows face to face, words that interpret for him the whole journey of his life and the journey of the life of mankind from Adam to the men of the last day? And if it should happen to him once, what is that but an accident? It is not a tide-surpassing experience as regular as the tides. Secular man, having lost the dimension of the eternal, must be swept along the rapids and eddies of time; he has no stay against them. He is "lost in the cosmos," as Walker Percy says. He builds houses in time but no *home*, either in eternity or in the here and now.[5] For man is meant to rise above time or to step aside from it, even as he is immersed in it. A house that is no protection against the elements is not much of a house. A home that is no protection against oblivion is not much of a home. It is as if you were to "build" on a flat piece of paper a two-dimensional domicile for three-dimensional beings. For man, height and width and depth will not suffice.

## Tradition and Sex

And now I return to the child. Dogs breed, man pro-creates.

The sexual equivalent to the rejection of culture is a crass and mechanistic hedonism, seeking the pleasure of the day for its own sake. In our time of pills that fool the taker into thinking that youth can endure, the hedonist seeks his pleasure in the least human way. He fools himself into thinking that it can last. He is without that sad and salutary sense of self-defeat that shades Horace's poem whence we derive the saying *carpe diem*—seize the day, as a low-hanging fruit to be plucked and enjoyed, because no one knows what the morrow will bring. So said Lorenzo de' Medici, the Magnificent one whose faith was residual, and who wrote poems when he was not managing far-flung business interests and keeping the city of Florence under his iron rod:

> *Chi vuol esser lieto, sia!*
> *Di doman non c'e certezza.*

> Who would be happy, let him be!
> Tomorrow knows no certainty.

So one body preys upon another, and the last thing in the mind of either "partner"—note the business term—is that what they are doing should partake of time long past and time to come. The man is planting seed that contains within itself unnumbered generations, and the woman bears the egg, the haven for that seed, to be penetrated by it and fertilized, so that what begins from that moment is a new human life, a new instantiation of the divine image, a new dweller in time, oriented to eternity. That is in fact what is happening, but the hedonist denies it. He says that the child-making thing is not for making children. It is how he strips the topsoil or avoids the green fields, to live instead in an arid and hopeless plain. We might put it this way:

> They are not half in love with easeful death,
> They are not half in love with anything;
> No field in summer makes them catch their breath
> Where the corn ripens, and the sparrows sing;
> The man wishes he had no seed to cast
> In the warm spring upon the ready earth;
> The woman, that her womb were bolted fast.
> Death they may fear, but birth
> Is perfect terror, or the sad and slow

Contraction of the little life they play,
Without a germ or root or bloom to show,
Numb to the pulse of both the night and day.
Nor do they go where Moloch's flames appall,
Because they would not bear a child at all.[6]

Rape, assault, and even consensual fornication are still rightly *felt* as violations of a sacred act and of the sanctity of the womb, that fearful haven which is to be set apart and never reduced to a tool or a factory. But we have lost the language of the sacred, so we are left naked to the winds. We can speak only of *will*, a vague and shifting thing. We breed no children but disillusionment and antagonism between the sexes.

Shakespeare could have told us about that too. He began his sonnet sequence with a sometimes unpleasant and strangely mechanistic appeal to the young man to beget a son. He deliberately and fittingly ends that same sequence not with marriage and hope for fruitfulness, but with descriptions of sterile and treacherous sexual action, madness, and venereal disease:

Past cure am I, now reason is past care,
And frantic mad with evermore unrest:
My thoughts and my discourse as madmen's are,
At random from the truth vainly expressed,
For I have sworn thee fair, and thought thee bright,
Who art as black as hell, as dark as night. (Sonnet 147, lines
    9–14)

That is what you get when you do not understand what the child-making thing is.

To give yourself over in love to a little child, the most economically useless creature in the world, is to forget yourself and your immediate purposes, unless you imitate the aims of the sonnet-speaker, and have your child's career planned out, turning him into a protracted business proposition, a thing bound to time, like bonds with interest. There is in a healthy person's self-forgetfulness before the child something of the time-leaving and time-transcending character of culture and of sacred worship. And perhaps that is why those who would *use children* to further their political purposes have ever been those who despise what culture is all about.

Let me illustrate. Many a feminist critic of Shakespeare's *The Tempest*—note that it is not *The Storm* but *The Tempest*, with its suggestion of the action of time—has abhorred the idea that the young and pure Miranda should not be "in control" of her sexuality but must submit to the moral law as embodied in and propounded by her father, the mage Prospero. Shakespeare would have found such criticism to be callous to the beauty of woman and the profundity of sexual being. The desire to be "in control" of what you do down under is like a mechanistic and merely chemical view of agriculture. It is to marriage what agribusiness is to tilling the fields. Nor does it matter that you are the one in charge of your own denuding. Your commitment to technical control bespeaks, to cite Marcel again, "a spirit of suspicious vigilance, which is perhaps incompatible with the inward eagerness of a being who is irresistibly impelled to welcome life with gratitude."[7]

Hence such critics have little to say about the masque that Prospero directs for the benefit of the newly betrothed Miranda and Ferdinand. It is a celebration of chastity and *therefore* a celebration of fruitfulness. It is in harmony with the order of creation, and the seasons, and *therefore* it transcends the seasons; it is within the world of change and above it. So Juno, the goddess of marriage and childbirth, and Ceres, the goddess of the harvest, pour their blessings upon the young and happy couple:

*Juno*: Honor, riches, marriage-blessing,
Long continuance, and increasing,
Hourly joys be still upon you!

Juno sings her blessings on you.

*Ceres*: Earth's increase, and foison plenty,
Barns and garners never empty;
Vines, with clustering branches growing;
Plants, with goodly burden bowing;
Spring come to you, at the farthest,
In the very end of harvest!
Scarcity and want shall shun you.
Ceres' blessing so is on you. (IV.i. 106–117)

And to show that this is not just a piece of elaborate politeness, Juno then invites harvesters—youths and maidens—to leave their work in time and step beside it, in the joyful and truly culture-making spirit of the time set apart, the holy day:

You sunburned sicklemen, of August weary,
Come hither from the furrow, and be merry;
Make holiday; your rye-straw hats put on,
And these fresh nymphs encounter every one
In country footing. (124–128)

At which they all dance.
Prospero will momentarily disperse the spirits putting on this show when he suddenly remembers a plot against his life. We are still in a world of folly and sin. But the boy Ferdinand's reaction to the masque shows the power of goodness and holiness. He loses all sense of time, and all sense of Italy and Naples, whither he and his father and their retainers were bound before the storm cast them up on an unknown shore:

Let me live here ever;
So rare a wondered father and a wise
Makes this place paradise. (113–115)

Paradise is, literally, a special kind of garden, as Christian painters and poets had long known:

> A garden inclosed is my sister, my spouse; a spring shut up, a fountain sealed.
> They plants are an orchard of pomegranates, with pleasant fruits; camphire, with spikenard,
> Spikenard and saffron; calamus and cinnamon, with all trees of frankincense; myrrh and aloes, with all the chief spices:
> A fountain of gardens, a well of living waters, and streams from Lebanon. (Song of Solomon 4:12–15)

So is marriage, as they also knew. And here we return to time and eternity.

Nobody throws rice at the signing of a business contract. A couple will not wear a special suit or dress when they sign their first mortgage and then save the clothing for their children when they in turn will put themselves in hock. Again, dogs breed, but human beings marry. Theirs is a promise not for a long time, but forever. To include some kind of escape clause is to destroy the essence of the thing. It is like running a bank inside a church, and inviting the rebuke of Jesus: "Stop making My Father's house a place of business" (John 2:16 NASB).

If you are in the middle of what looks like an adventure, but you can clap your hands or wave a wand and, presto, you are sitting in your recliner with a beer at your elbow, you are not on an adventure at all. It is not real. If you say the word "forever" and do not mean it, it is as if you had merely pretended to launch away from the shore. You are playing at sailing the seas, like a child in a sandbox, with a pail of water, except that the child is innocent and you are not, and the child may be wholly in the spirit of the thing, and you are not. Your anchor is wedged in the mud. But you cannot go home unless you leave the safe shore. So it is that the longing for home is not a longing for safety. It is a too strong attachment to safety that keeps people from returning home. To save our lives, we must lose them.

That is why Shakespeare's speaker of the sonnets, at his most lucid, places not one reservation upon marriage. If it does not go beyond time, it is neither marriage nor love:

> Let me not to the marriage of true minds
> Admit impediments. Love is not love
> That alters when it alteration finds,
> Or bends with the remover to remove.
> O no! It is an ever fixèd mark
> That looks on tempests and is never shaken;
> It is the star to every wandering bark
> Whose worth's unknown, although his height be taken.
> Love's not Time's fool, though rosy lips and cheeks
> Within his bending sickle's compass come;
> Love alters not with his spare hours and weeks
> But bears it out even to the edge of doom.
> If this be error, and upon me proved,
> I never writ, nor no man ever loved. (Sonnet 116)

His language is that of the marriage service. Says the priest, in the words of the Book of Common Prayer (1552):

> I require and charge you (as you will answer at the dreadful day of judgment, when the secrets of all hearts shall be disclosed) that if either of you do know any impediment, why ye may not be lawfully joined together in Matrimony, that ye confess it. For be ye well assured, that so many as be coupled together otherwise than God's word doth allow, are not joined together by God, neither is their Matrimony lawful.

The impediment warned against here might be consanguinity or compulsion. But the impediment that Shakespeare thinks of is a willingness to change. If minds are *true*—faithful, with the carpenter's sense of being straight—they will not seek to "bend with the remover to remove," nor to "alter" even when they find alteration. Good looks will fade and youth depart, but the true mind will not change. The ship wanders on the high seas, but love is the cynosure, the pole-star, that guides it through tempests. Love is not the "fool" of Time but, says Shakespeare, echoing Saint Paul (cf. 1 Corinthians 13:7), "bears it out even to the edge of doom."

Sexual desire without the moral law is disoriented and gone astray. The tempests batter the ship to flotsam. Marriage is not marriage without the promise of eternity. Home is not home if it is only for a time. All these truths are one.

# CHAPTER TWO

## Man in Place

*Breathes there the man, with soul so dead,*
*Who never to himself hath said,*
  *This is my own, my native land!*
*Whose heart hath ne'er within him burned,*
*As home his footsteps he hath turned,*
  *From wandering on a foreign strand!*
    —Sir Walter Scott, *The Lay of the Last Minstrel*, Canto Sixth

When I was a boy, I used often to go for long walks in the woods—four or five square miles wedged in between two county roads and our neighborhood—which were graced with the stubborn works of nature and pocked with the abandoned works of man. The latter included lines of tall telephone poles crossing a ridge from one end of town to the other and a series of poles, rotting and sinking, without any wires on them at all. There were "strippings," gouges in the earth twenty or thirty feet deep where coal had been taken right off the surface, and "canyons," mining holes fifty feet deep, filled with bright green water from leached copper compounds, I suppose. There were a bus chassis and a couple of cars left to sink into the ground in the middle of nowhere, a paved mining road that had not been touched in many years, leading nowhere, and a hundred-foot-high escarpment built up out of a hillside and heaps of coal. Here I would pick my way among the slabs like a goat, searching for fossils and stuffing my jacket pockets with the best of them. When I cracked open a slab sideways at an obvious fissure, I found that there was almost always a fossil of some sort within, often colored, too, with the odd rainbow tints that you find when somebody's car leaks oil on blacktop.

If I were a geologist, I'd be able to tell why the ridge was as it was, with sudden heaps of stone such as granite, barely covered with enough topsoil to grow low-bush blueberries, wintergreen, lichens, and wild juniper; what made the sheer wall that in those days still had a name, Corey Cliff, now most likely forgotten; and what that strange red ash was that the miners left behind in one place the size of a football field, where nothing would grow but scrubby white birches. Possibly it was the residue of a fire, reducing the coal to cinders. One little stream drained a swampy area on its plateau and eventually found its way along the side of my next-door neighbor's property, to be channeled into the ditch on our street. There were a couple of what we called "ponds," shallow water atop poorly drained areas, with the little stumps of trees that had somehow managed to take root there but died and rotted after a couple of years. From the top of the ridge, you could see ten miles to the southwest and fifteen to the northeast, but to the southeast, the first streets and settlements of my town snuggled against a mountain side that rose up like a wall.

There was little that was picturesque about it—though we should keep in mind that to call something "picturesque" is to make light of it, to praise it faintly. The downtown was shabby, with more beer gardens than anything else, and a little half-rotting movie house that had been shut for many years, whose sign out front, "The Grand," I remember fondly, I don't know why. The parish church was grand and solemn, and to enter it was to wonder how it got to be there, what with the coal mines and their leavings all around. The field where I played many a baseball game didn't have a grass infield or a fence, so we traced a line in the outfield with chalk, and any ball that went over the line on the ground was a double.

If you take things slowly—if you walk, or ride a bicycle—you might actually see the beauties of your home. I walked all the time, as did everybody else; the bus was only for the handful of boys and girls in my class who lived more than a mile from the school. Behind that rather plain baseball field, there was an abandoned trestle perched high above the river. If you wanted to go to the west end of town, the trestle would save you half an hour, but you had to be careful, because there was nothing between each of the big train-ties and the river far below. My collie did not enjoy crossing it and took her footing slowly, but she would cross it nonetheless. The trestle had a stark beauty about it.

All kinds of things do, if you bother to look, if you bother to care. Think of old lithograph postcards. Yes, sometimes they depict the Grand Canyon or Old Faithful. But there are many thousands of postcards of a little town hall, a school, a factory, a bank, an ordinary riverside, a bridge, a farm, a quarry—all that is human and that people are fond of, because the things are theirs in ways that surpass the power of words.

I think of a lovely folk song, "My Little Welsh Home," whose singer longs for the small and unimposing homestead he looks upon, and the village, and the heart of the village that makes the past present again and beckons toward eternity:

> I can see the quiet churchyard down below,
> Where the mountain breezes wander to and fro;
> And when God my soul shall keep,
> It is there I want to sleep,
> With those dear old folks that loved me long ago.

The land of Sir Walter Scott may now be blowing the bagpipes for the tourist shillings, but when he wrote the poem with which I began this chapter, Scotland was near to his heart for a forbidding beauty that only a native could really cherish:

O Caledonia! stern and wild,
Meet nurse for a poetic child!
Land of brown heath and shaggy wood,
Land of the mountain and the flood,
Land of my sires! what mortal hand
Can e'er untie the filial band,
That knits me to thy rugged strand!
Still, as I view each well-known scene,
Think what is now, and what hath been,
Seems as, to me, of all bereft,
Sole friends thy woods and streams were left;
And thus I love them better still,
Even in extremity of ill.

So I believe the heart of an old Inuit fisherman, his friends and kin having passed away, must beat more warmly when his boat rounds the cape and enters the bleak and treeless and beloved cove where his fathers and his grandfathers caulked their canoes and set out among the waters and the ice.

### A Bitter Fountain

Let me not suggest, then, that man loves his place because it would make a nice postcard. He loves it because it is in him, and he is in it; it bears the impress of his fingers, and it touches the nerves of his soul. The place that has once been seen and worked and loved by man is no longer a mere intersection of longitude and latitude. The scrawl of my printing remains, forty-five years later, on the plywood walls of our old garage, as do my fingernail scratches in the trim around the bathroom door, where I measured, week after week, how tall I had grown. There are big rocks overgrown with weeds that still bear traces of my cousins' names, painted on them fifty years ago.

I cannot belong in any place in quite the same way as I belong there. The experience of place transcends ideology. The conservative who understands what it is to conserve feels it no more powerfully than does the liberal who defines his worth not by autonomy but by loyalty, and there are many such liberals, better men than their philosophy might warrant.

I think here of the Italian author Ignazio Silone. He helped to found the Italian Communist Party but broke with what he would call "the god that failed" when he saw that the Stalinist reds were just as fascist as the Fascists he loathed. Silone returned from exile in Switzerland to the forbidding lands of Abruzzo, dry and mountainous, with little good soil available for the poor peasants. That was his land. He wrote about it in a trilogy of novels: *Fontamara*, *Bread and Wine*, and *The Seed Beneath the Snow*. We gather how difficult the life was by this description of a small watercourse outside of the imaginary village of Fontamara, "Bitter Fountain":

> Right where the road comes in to Fontamara there used to be a little spring of water that trickled forth from under some dripping stones. It made a kind of small pool. After a few feet the water then worked itself into the stony soil, dug a hole for itself, disappeared and came out again at the foot of the hill more abundantly, in the form of a stream. Then before starting for [Lake] Fucino the stream-bed made several curves. The farmers of Fontamara used to take water from it to irrigate the few fields they had down on the level land, which were the sole resource of the village. Every summer when the stream water was divided among the farmers there would be stormy quarrels. In years of dearth the quarrels would end up with knives.[1]

That was the land to which Silone returned, to bring justice for the people among whom he had grown up. Lake Fucino had already been drained, and the exposed land, much of it very fine, had been parceled out among people from the nearby city of Avezzano and not given to Silone's brother peasants. But his love for them and their place was love, not devotion to an ideology.

We see that love in the defiant foreword he wrote to *Fontamara*, justifying his occasional use of the Abruzzese dialect instead of standard Italian, the latter of which he and his people learned in school "like Latin, French, or Esperanto." "Though we may borrow the Italian language," he says, "the manner of telling the story is our own. It is an art of Fontamara."[2] The words and the very form they take in the local jests and folk tales are "what we learned in boyhood, lying awake long nights beside the loom, following the rhythm of the loom."[3] It is emphatically not the same art that holds sway in the city. For Silone, it was an art like weaving, and it made for stories that were slow, deliberate accretions of small and beautiful details. "First one sees the stem of the rose," he says, "then the cup of the rose, then the corolla of the rose; but from first to last everyone knows that it is to be a rose. That is why the things we make seem naive and unfinished to city people. But when have we ever tried to sell them to the city?...And likewise, have we ever asked city people to tell about themselves in our manner? We have never asked it of them."[4]

Silone is not, let us note, fond of emigration from Italy to places that the peasants had never heard of before, though he opposed the Fascist policy of keeping the poor at home against their will. Several of his characters in Fontamara have emigrated and returned, among them the hero of the work, Berardo, who sold what little land he had to go abroad but did not succeed there. He works hard at odd jobs but without, in his mind, any warrant to marry the only woman he has ever loved. Another has found himself in New York City selling ice and soda water. The only word he learns—a word his boss hollers at him constantly—has become his new name: "Sciatap"—Shut Up. A third is called the Impresario, or in some translations, the Promoter. With his ethic of hard work and sharp dealing, he has the whole political apparatus of Avezzano in his pocket, along with most of the land of the former Lake Fucino. He will, with the approval of the government in Rome, divert the water from that lone straggling stream upon which the Fontamaresi have so long relied, to water his own lands, which of course are more productive. He is a money-maker, out of place where he has settled; he turns "place" into a profit-making concern.

The point is not whether people ought to emigrate or not. God commanded Abraham to leave forever his homeland in Ur of the Chaldees and travel with all his household to the land that God would show him, a land flowing with milk and honey. The Anglo-Saxon Seafarer in the poem to which we have appended that name feels strongly the yearning to set sail upon the sea alone, even though he knows it will bring him not milk and honey but heartache:

> He has no thought for the harp or the world's high bliss,
> for the ring-giving or the glad joys of women,
> or for anything else but the whelming ocean,
> setting out on that lake, his longing ever.
> The woods take on their blooms and the berries grow
>   lovely,
> the fields are adorned, and the world hastens onward;
> and they all urge the eager heart
> that it is time to go forth, time for the one who longs
> to leave and sail far on the floodways.[5]

This man, unlike Silone, cannot go home, because home no longer survives. The depredations of man, a wolf to man, have destroyed it. So says another sad speaker, the Wanderer of the Anglo-Saxon poem by that name:

> He who thus wisely considers this wall, the world,
> and into our dark life casts his mind deep,
> his heart old and keen, calls back from long ago

that wealth of slaughters, and utters these words:
"Where has the horse gone? Where has the hero? Where are
   the hall-joys?
Where the giver of gems? Where the gathering for feasts?
Alas, the bright goblet! Alas, the burnished mail!
Alas, the prince's power! How that time has passed,
   now dim under the night-helm, as if it never were!"[6]

What binds together the Wanderer, the Seafarer, Ignazio Silone returning to his poverty-stricken native land, and even Abraham, who has left behind the fields and the gods of Ur, is the persistent sense of place—the holiness of the place that human beings have made their own. Abraham the sojourner died and "was gathered to his people," and Isaac and Ishmael his sons buried him beside his wife Sarah "in the field of Ephron" he had purchased east of Mamre, the same place where God in the persons of the three visitors came to him to eat dinner and reveal that Sarah would bear him a son in his old age (Genesis 18 and 25:8–10). But for the Impresario, the lands around Avezzano do not make up a place—only resources to be put to use. He is home-less. And that brings us to one of the great questions of our time. Scripture puts the sad experience of human futility in these words: "neither shall his place know him any more" (Job 7:10). But what happens to man himself when he no longer knows a place that is and has been his own?

### The Unplaced Person

What happens is that he is a modern man, rootless, a tourist but not a pilgrim, apt to leap over fences to find that the grass on the other side is yellow too.

When one of the scribes said to Jesus that he would follow him wherever he went, Jesus warned him about what it would mean: the foxes have their dens and the birds their nests, but the Son of Man had nowhere to lay his head (Matthew 8:20). When the disciples went about

Jerusalem with him, happily showing him the magnificent walls and buildings, he warned them that "there shall not be left here one stone upon another, that shall not be thrown down" (Mark 13:2). When he looked out from the Mount of Olives upon the city below, he himself cried out, "O Jerusalem, Jerusalem, thou that killest the prophets, and stonest them which are sent unto thee, how often would I have gathered thy children together, even as a hen gathereth her chickens under her wings, and ye would not!" (Matthew 23:37) His sorrow was like that of Jeremiah, whose experience of persecution by the city he loved and whose witness of its destruction have long been used by the Church in its prayers on Good Friday: "How doth the city sit solitary, that was full of people! how is she become like a widow! she that was great among the nations" (Lamentations 1:1).

Jesus had nowhere to lay his head, but he did not recommend to us that same nowhere as the aim of our hearts. He goes before us, he says, to prepare a place (John 14:2). Jeremiah did not rejoice at the gutting of his enemy, his beloved Jerusalem. Abraham was by his own description a stranger in a strange land, and his grandson Jacob, who ended his days in Egypt, would say of his own life, his pilgrimage as he called it, "Few and evil have the days of the years of my life been" (Genesis 47:9). Yet the greatest son of Jacob, the same Joseph who was raised to an authority in Egypt only nominally less than that of the Pharaoh himself, begged his sons that when they should leave Egypt to return to Canaan, they should take his bones with them and bury them there, as he had himself traveled from Egypt to bury in Canaan the bones of his father (Genesis 50:25). We have no abiding place upon earth. But that does not mean that we are to love no place at all.

But just such indifference to place seems to characterize the modern man. The ancient Greek felt the numinous in every stream. It was as if a sacred being, a nymph, were glancing upon him from behind the tree whose branches hung low above the trickling water. So Socrates rested one afternoon with the young Phaedrus under the plane tree on the road from Athens, along the stream Ilisus, and spoke of the transports of love. And though Christians were to clear away the mists of error from this holy reverence of the natural, it was, at its wisest, an appreciation of the will and the wisdom of God in all of creation, so that every place, rather than no place at all, could be the threshold to the divine. For without the divine, man loses the human also, reduced to mere stuff, a usable resource like iron or tin. Nor does it matter if he himself is the user.

A natural and therefore supra-natural reverence for place is at the heart of Flannery O'Connor's story "A View of the Woods." The scene is a plot of land in rural Georgia. A dirt road leads up to it. There is a ramshackle house on it, with a long stretch of grassy flat in front, then a lake, and beyond the lake, the woods. An old man owns the land, some six hundred acres. He lives in the house with his daughter, his son-in-law, whom he despises, and his grandchildren. The only one of those children with whom he has anything to do is the youngest, a ten-year-old girl who he believes takes after him. She is chubby, as he is, and self-willed, as he is, and rapacious, as he is—although he would call it shrewd self-interest, not rapacity. He insisted that she be named after him: she is called Mary Fortune. He believes that he and she agree in all things.

To humiliate his son-in-law and to show him who is the real boss on the property, the old man has been selling off parcels to be "improved" because he is all for "progress," unlike the dirt-poor relations he has to live with. He takes a spectator's enjoyment in that progress taking place before his eyes in the form of a ravenous backhoe seeking land to devour. So, for a time, does his favored granddaughter: "He sat on the bumper and Mary Fortune straddled the hood and they watched, sometimes for hours, while the machine systematically ate a square red hole in what had once been a cow pasture." But why should a cow pasture matter? "Any fool," says old Mr. Fortune, aptly and sardonically named, "that would let a cow pasture interfere with progress is not on my books."[7] Progress here is not the destruction of beauty. There is no great beauty. It is the destruction of a place.

All goes well for Mr. Fortune, if we can call "well" his alienation from family, place, and the poor scrub-beauty of the land he owns, until he decides, as an act of ultimate vengeance, to obliterate the plot of land dearest to the family he hates. He tells Mary Fortune his plan, believing that she will be happy to hear it:

> "I'm going to sell the lot right in front of the house for a gas station," he said. "Then we won't have to go down the road to get the car filled up, just step out the front door." The Fortune house was set back about two hundred feet from the road and it was this two hundred feet that he intended to sell. It was the part that his daughter airily called "the lawn," thought it was nothing but a field of weeds.[8]

But the girl gets her back up. The place means something to her. She too calls it "the lawn." She says it is where she and the other children play. She says it is where her daddy—a sullen man who takes out his anger against his father-in-law by whipping the back of Mary Fortune's legs and ankles with his belt—grazes his calves. And if a gas station were built on it, she says, "we won't be able to see the woods from the porch." O'Connor lets us know what kind of gas station it will be. Old Mr. Fortune wants to sell it to a man named Tilman, who is looking to set up another establishment like the one he runs already, "a combination country store, filling station, scrap-metal dump, used-car lot and dance hall," a "one-room wooden structure onto which he had added, behind, a long tin hall equipped for dancing," which hall is "divided into two sections, Colored and White each with its private nickelodeon."[9] There's progress for you.

The story will not end well for Mr. Fortune. But he merely represents a tacky and grubby version of the same contempt of place that characterizes our time. What Mr. Fortune wants to do to a field full of weeds—"the lawn" that is the long vestibule to the sacred woods beyond—modern architects, city planners, consolidators of schools, and international businesses have done to other once human buildings and places. Brutalist architecture, boasting of its great flat boxes without decoration, looking as if machines had learned to copulate and engender other machines, numbs the very sense of place. The mode became "international," which meant that a building in Sydney, Australia, would look pretty much like another building in Chicago or Berlin or Novosibirsk, without relation to the history and the culture of the actual people who lived in its vicinity. It is as if a dead thing were to lodge itself in the midst of a breathing body, slowly spreading its death to everything contiguous.

I am looking at the modern city of Brasilia. It is a no-place. Its cathedral looks like a gigantic sea-anemone in stone, its great curving flanges and spikes quite naked of any relation to the human body or to human history or to Jesus Christ. It is a thing, not a place. It does not belong. I am looking at an aerial view of the city. I see one great hulking glass and steel rectangle after another, again without any relation to the nature roundabout, or to the people and their history. It is noise in stone, constant drumming noise.

We need not pick on Brazil. I am now looking at a photograph of the infamous Pruitt-Igoe housing complex in Saint Louis. Whole neighborhoods were razed to put the complex up. They were razed for reasons that Mr. Fortune would understand. The old neighborhoods were like "the lawn"—a big stretch of weeds, yet human beings loved that lawn. The old neighborhoods were unsanitary, the buildings in need of repair; yet instead of cleaning them and repairing them, the architects and planners in Saint Louis did the easy and "progressive" thing. They destroyed them and put in their place an enormous stretch of concrete prisms, indistinguishable from one another, faceless and characterless and ugly as only an ideology can be. Such architecture, like bad air, makes men sick. Some thirty or so years later, Pruitt-Igoe was razed in turn, unfit for human habitation.

The well-known author and raconteur Father George Rutler lives in the rectory of Saint Michael's Church on West Thirty-Fourth Street in Manhattan. It is the only human habitation remaining on that long thoroughfare, he says. All others have been torn down and replaced with gigantic glass-faced things. Saint Michael's is graced within and without by the works of human hands: paintings, stained glass, plaster moldings, finials, balusters, arches, newels, hand-hewn and finished pews, the marble altar, the beautiful and quiet side chapel where I have seen local Hispanic women, not making the great salaries conferred upon the ants under glass, praying in silence before going to work in the morning. Naturally the archdiocese wants to sell the property, so I am not sure it will still exist by the time you finish this sentence.

All these criticisms have been made before. I claim no originality here. Jane Jacobs wrote in *The Death and Life of Great American Cities* that modern planning does not reflect how people live their daily lives, and it is fascinating that a woman with no academic credentials in the field but with a great fund of reading and human observation could bravely and confidently stand alone against the massed "wisdom" of the architectural professionals and academics. She predicted what destructively modernizing plans would do to such cities as Detroit, but no one listened. Perhaps it took a woman to notice that it is children above all that bind a neighborhood together and turn a cartographical coordinate into a human place: children walking home from school, visiting the small grocer, the barber, the druggist, and the short-order cook at the diner, turning a vacant lot into a ball field and giving the grownups something to watch while providing them with a free security system. For children see everything.

In *The Golden City*, Henry Hope Read shows that modernist architects ruined place after place, motivated by their hatred of the classical style, which was sufficiently versatile to be adapted to a culture's needs and to the building materials available. He places side by side, for our instruction and dismay, pictures of what used to be and what now is. There is the old Penn Station in New York City, for example, destroyed in 1963, alongside the structure that took its place. In the old interior, great shafts of light stream in through semicircular windows high above the hall. It looks like a basilica in honor of transportation: its exterior echoes the Parthenon, with graceful Greek columns and pediments, and a grand but human approach. What we have now looks like a roll of steel wool perched atop a prism. If you are so unfortunate as to look upward from the interior, you see girders pitched at odd angles, like the wings of predatory birds in descent, or a flat and low ceiling, as you make your insect way from terminal to terminal. Big, not grand; flashy, not warm with light.

### Man on the Way

"Where are you going?" I ask our progressive fellows, and never hear an answer. You do not ask a whirlwind about its destination.

We might ask Hilaire Belloc the same question. Belloc was a bulldog of a man, built like a fighter, powerful in shoulders and jaw, possessed of immense stamina and determination and relish for the earthy, ordinary things of life. He was a man of the conservative left, a phrase that now means nothing; he wanted to lead England and Europe forward to the mirth and faith of the Middle Ages. (His female counterpart is that stout battle-ax of Norway, Sigrid Undset, who likewise saw Europe's only hope in what she called a Return to the Future.) Belloc once walked from Calais to Rome, jabbering in dialect with the natives, eating heartily what he could get at farms and public houses, sketching what he saw and writing down the conversations. He walked from New York to San Francisco to propose marriage to the woman who would be his wife. Note that he did not ride a train from one place to another, skipping all the places in between.

Such a man, an inveterate traveler, was also an ever-youthful lover of his home and the homes of others. He was not a tourist. "There is a valley in South England remote from ambition and from fear," he writes in "The Mowing of a Field," and to this valley he returned as a man to see again the fields and the downs of his youth. It did not disappoint:

The many things that I recovered as I came up the country-side were not less charming than when a distant memory has enshrined them, but much more. Whatever veil is thrown by a longing recollection had not intensified nor even made more mysterious the beauty of that happy ground; not in my very dreams of morning had I, in exile, seen it more beloved or more rare. Much also that I had forgotten now returned to me as I approached—a group of elms, a little turn of the parson's wall, a small paddock beyond the graveyard close, cherished by one man, with a low wall of very old stone guarding it all round. And all these things fulfilled and amplified my delight, till even the good vision of the place, which I had kept so many years, left me and was replaced by its better reality. "Here," I said to myself, "is a symbol of what some say is reserved for the soul: pleasure of a kind which cannot be imagined save in a moment when at last it is attained."[10]

Belloc did not come there to enjoy an aesthetic experience. He came to mow a field, so he launches into a discussion of when it's best to make hay and how best to sharpen and swing the scythe. He remembers what his father taught him, his arms and his legs recover the art of it, and he sweeps forward, "cutting lane after lane through the grass, and bringing out its most secret essences." He is not "the bad or young or untaught mower without tradition, the mower Promethean, the mower original and contemptuous of the past," who leaves heaps of grass uncut, gets his blade stuck in the ground, and twists the scythe and loosens the handle till the tool is dull or broken. It is with mowing, he says, as with "playing the fiddle," and "dozens of other things, but of nothing more than of believing."[11]

The progressive believes that things grow old and outworn, to be discarded. Hence the strangely tubercular wheeze of "youth movements" detached from the old. Pert seedlings without deep roots, they soon wither. "It's 2018," tweeted a female reporter in response to a college football player who expressed dismay that she was in the locker room while he was disrobing. She might as well have declared that it was Monday, or a minute before midnight. What difference? But if yesterday's news is yesterday's news, to line a bird cage or wrap fish withal, then my own youth is yesterday also, leaving me with nothing to bind my old self and my young self together. I am temporal detritus.

But when Belloc thinks from afar about the place where he grew up in his poem "The South Country," past and present and future are real to him still:

> I will gather and carefully make my friends
> Of the men of the Sussex Weald,
> They watch the stars from the silent folds,
> They stiffly plough the field.
> By them and the God of the South Country
> My poor soul shall be healed.
> If I ever become a rich man,
> Or if ever I grow to be old,
> I will build a house with a deep thatch
> To shelter me from the cold,
> And there shall the Sussex songs be sung
> And the story of Sussex told.
> I will hold my house in the high wood
> Within a walk of the sea,
> And the men that were boys when I was a boy
> Shall sit and drink with me.

Secular man may want a home because he is human, and he may do fine work in his local Historical Society preserving old homes for their beauty. People are rarely as bad as their worst ideas, and the rich can afford to insulate themselves from the effects of their bad ideas. But a mere belief in "the future" is a pallid and frail mimic of that longing for an eternal home. It does not lay the foundation. It does not build the spire. Looking upon an exhausted Europe, Belloc describes in "A Remaining Christmas" how the Christmas season is observed and celebrated in his own beloved house, where the faith has taken root. "Man has a body as well as a soul," he writes, thinking of the things we do and where we do them, "and the whole of man, soul and body, is nourished sanely by a multiplicity of observed traditional things," especially in the face of death and the lesser features of mortality, such as weariness, forgetfulness, sickness, and disappointment. In that house where the birth of the Lord was kept with festivity and a hundred beloved habits great and small, wayfaring man can find the home that prepares him for home:

> [I]ts Christmas binds it to its own past and promises its future, making the house an undying thing of which those subject to mortality within it are members, sharing in its continuous survival.

It is not wonderful that verses should be written of such a house. Many verses have been so written, commemorating and praising this house. The last verse written of it I may quote here by way of ending:

> Stand thou for ever among human Houses,
> House of the Resurrection, House of Birth;
> House of the rooted hearts and long carouses,
> Stand, and be famous over all the earth.

Belloc understood that man would lose his sense of place along with his cultural memory itself. We are not disembodied spirits. Those things seem to stand and fall together. To that dreadful oblivion, with closer attention, we now turn.

CHAPTER THREE

## Lost among the Ruins

"You can't go home again," wrote Thomas Wolfe, as if that were what he wanted to do.

Here is the protagonist of the ironically named novel *Look Homeward, Angel,* considering his young life with his drunken and histrionic father, his shrewd, land-grubbing mother, his frustrated sister, his three variously unhappy brothers, and the people of "Altamont" (Wolfe's fictional Asheville, North Carolina), part shabby old Southern town, part tacky new resort for the rich and weary:

> [H]e became passionately bored with them, plunged into a miasmic swamp of weariness and horror, after a time, because of the dullness and ugliness of their lives, their minds, their amusements. Dull people filled him with terror: he was never so much frightened by tedium in his own life as in the lives of others—his early distaste for Pett Pentland and her grim rusty aunts came from submerged memories of the old house on Central Avenue, the smell of mellow apples and medicine in the hot room, the swooping howl of the wind outside, and the endless monotone of their conversation on disease, death, and misery.[1]

It is a characteristic passage. Quite different from the feeling for home expressed by Dante, the political exile. In Purgatory, he and Virgil meet an apparently solitary spirit on the lower slopes of the mountain, and an ordinary question is the occasion for an outburst of love—love for the place of one's birth, the homeland:

> Virgil approached the spirit nonetheless
> and asked of him to point us the best way
> to climb the mount, and he made no response
> But to inquire about our native land
> and who we were in life; and the sweet guide
> began with "Mantua," when that desert shade
> Rose up from where he'd stood so firm in place—
> "We share one country, you of Mantua!
> I am Sordello!"—and the two embraced.[2]

Virgil does not get to the verb in his sentence, much less to his own name. When Sordello learns of that, he falls to his knees, addressing his fellow poet as the "glory of the Latin tongue" and the "everlasting honor of [his] land." (7.16–18)

No one ever cast Thomas Wolfe out of the Carolinas and confiscated the boarding house that his mother operated in Asheville. No one did to him the violence that the Florentines did to Dante. So what explains his protagonist's revulsion against the place, the womb that bore him? "O lost!" he writes in his novel, again and again. "We shall not come again. We never shall come back again." This is no mere elegy of sorrow before the chances and changes of time; that note has been sounded ever since man was banished from the garden. It is something more— something sadder, more sinister.

We sense what it is from the novel's climax, when the young protagonist Eugene has a dream-conversation with the spirit of his older brother Ben, who has died of pneumonia, without any of the consolations of faith or even of a stoic philosophy. The young man asks, urgently, "Where, Ben? Where is the world?"

"Nowhere," Ben says. "*You* are your world."

The emphasis is in the original. Wolfe has collapsed the universe into a solipsism. Eugene's words end the conversation: "No leaf hangs for me in the forest; I shall lift no stone upon the hills; I shall find no door in any city. But *in the city of myself, upon the continent of my soul,* I shall find the forgotten language, the lost world, a door where I may enter, and music strange as any ever sounded; I shall haunt you, ghost, along the labyrinthine ways until—until? O Ben, my ghost, an answer?"

Ben turns away with burning eyes, and does not reply.

The young unbeliever has seen "in the tortuous ways of a thousand alien places, his foiled quest of himself."[3] That quest has also been "the blind groping of a soul toward freedom and isolation."[4] A powerful phrase, that; a powerful error, and one that gnaws near to the heart valves of the American. The heart that does not beat warmly in the neighborhood of its original loves longs for a freedom *from*, a freedom that Dante would not have recognized as freedom at all. To him, as to nearly all Christian and classical thinkers, freedom is to the soul as health is to the body—it is a power. It is the unimpeded capacity to realize the perfection of the kind of being that you are. Legs are for walking; freedom is for virtue; and virtue, intellectual or practical, is a perfective power. But since man is a social animal by nature and not by mere accident or necessity, his freedom is incomprehensible apart from love and life in a community.

That is what man's spiritual powers are for, and they find their most exalted expression in a communion of divine worship. No human life without feasts, and no feasts without what the progressive man has labored to eliminate, replacing the sacred celebration with labor and vacation, toil and vacancy. Josef Pieper writes in *Leisure, the Basis of Culture*:

> [H]owever dim the recollection of the association may have become in men's minds, a feast "without gods," and unrelated

to worship, is quite simply unknown. It is true that ever since the French Revolution attempts have been repeatedly made to manufacture feast days and holidays that have no connection with divine worship, or are sometimes even opposed to it: "Brutus days," or even that hybrid, "Labor Day." In point of fact the stress and strain of giving them some kind of festal appearance is one of the very best proofs of the significance of divine worship for a feast; and nothing illustrates so clearly that festivity is only possible where divine worship is still a vital act—and nothing shows this so clearly as a comparison between a living and deeply traditional feast day, with its roots in divine worship, and one of those rootless celebrations, carefully and unspontaneously prepared beforehand, and as artificial as a maypole.[5]

But there is no God in Wolfe's sad and sagging world, and the only feast he mentions, without a trace of mystery or prayer and therefore without any real mirth, is Christmas, the residue of a culture he has no part in. Wolfe has never known the wassail bowl from which the heartier and saner Belloc has drunk. Man without God loses his grasp of the world around him; mud is no longer the shining "plough-down sillion" of Gerard Manley Hopkins's "The Windhover," but only mud, sludge, the obliterating slag of dust and rain, and mud-man himself is "a flash of fire—a brain, a heart, a spirit," as the cynical and drunken doctor at Ben's deathbed says, and "three-cents-worth of lime and iron—which we cannot get back."[6]

"I've had nothing out of life," says Ben, enumerating his failures, and crying, "What's it all about? Can you figure it out, 'Gene? Is it really so, or is someone playing a joke on us? Maybe we're dreaming all this. Do you think so?"

Eugene answers in the affirmative and wishes that somebody would wake them up. "To hell with it all!" says Ben. "I wish it were over."[7]

The moment of brotherly love is genuine and filled with pathos. Yet aside from these ineluctable moments of human feeling, here today and shucked on the morrow, no *brotherhood* can survive an un-culture, and the false freedom of the individual will. Eugene has "a horror of all bonds that tied him to the terrible family of the earth," the family he thinks of "with fear, almost with hatred." "Am I never to be free?" he thinks. "What have I done to deserve this slavery?" You might as well rise up in anger against being bound to arms and legs and not remember that your legs can take you places, and your arms can embrace someone you love.

Neither of Eugene's parents has ever raised a hand in anger against him. Eugene has never been abused. Indeed, he has been a bit spoiled, admired by his mother, envied by his eldest brother, and looked on with favor by women and girls for his tall stature and handsome face. He has not known poverty. But his attitude toward family, home, and what remains of a decadent postbellum culture is contempt. He cannot forget his home, but he very much wants to do so.

There is a strange resemblance between Eugene and the Margaret Mitchells of the American South, who bemoaned a lost civilization of courtly gentlemen and sweet slave-owning ladies while turning a blind eye to the human horror in their midst. The fickle and selfish Scarlett O'Hara, we are told in Mitchell's *Gone with the Wind*, loves one thing in the world with a fidelity she grants to no one and nothing else: the red earth of Tara, her Irish father's plantation. That love is in itself a good thing, as Eugene's refusal to love Altamont is in itself not a good thing, but in both cases the authors have missed the heart of the matter, which is not *cultural* so much as *culture itself*, the thing in its essence. And neither the false and dreamy lyricism of Ashley Wilkes, the sensitive Confederate officer and slaveholder with a conscience nor the nightmarish revulsion of Eugene can bring us closer to that thing—unless it is by the hard instruction of trial and failure.

## Bound to the Old Estate

What Eugene is missing may be suggested by the tentative steps homeward taken by Charles Ryder, the narrator of Evelyn Waugh's *Brideshead Revisited*. Ryder goes to Oxford and learns little enough from the dons there, but he does fall into a couple of romances. The first is with a young, charming, and dissipated Roman Catholic nobleman, Sebastian Flyte, the younger son of the Marquess of Marchmain. The second romance, long afterwards, is with the strange and appalling faith that some of Sebastian's family follow devotedly (even as a matter of course, not the worst way to pray) and that others of them flout and try hard to reject. Ryder is searching, as Eugene was and as Miss Scarlett was not. He becomes a commercially successful painter, with a certain charm and no originality. Appalled by the soulless philistinism of English cities, he turns with a poignant longing to the site of a once-living culture—to such homes as Brideshead had been for him:

> I published three splendid folios—*Ryder's Country Seats*, *Ryder's English Homes*, and *Ryder's Village and Provincial Architecture*, which each sold its thousand copies at five guineas apiece. I seldom failed to please, for there was no conflict between myself and my patrons; we both wanted the same thing.[8]

Ryder does in painting what Margaret Mitchell did in prose. Yet this antiquarianism, a skin of nostalgia and not its muscle and blood, does not satisfy him. He misses the heart-pounding life of Brideshead—its loves and antagonisms, its apparently atavistic faith and the equally atavistic betrayal of the faith—and the inspiration it had once provided him. Like Gauguin and others—Gauguin the vile, who went to Tahiti to experiment in painting and married two or three teenage girls—Ryder turns away from moribund Europe. He leaves his society wife behind and spends a couple of years in Mexico, trying to nurse from the breasts of a land he takes to be half savage. Of course, it is a cliché to put it in those terms, and Waugh is quite aware of it. Ryder returns to England with great fanfare, and the exhibition of his new paintings seems to be an unqualified success.

*Seems.* But it is another decadent Catholic, the flamboyantly homosexual Anthony Blanche, who takes Charles to a "pansy bar" to tell him otherwise. Eager to see "Charles's unhealthy pictures," he met with disappointment at the gallery. He found no inspiration, nothing fullbloodedly evil. "I found, my dear, a very naughty and very successful practical joke. It reminded me of dear Sebastian when he liked so much to dress in false whiskers. It was charm again, my dear, simple, creamy English charm, playing tigers."⁹

("Fiddle-dee-dee," says Scarlett, with a flounce of her shoulders and a toss of her hair. God save us from the charm of charm.)

Charles agrees. He knows he is a failure, a most successful failure.

What does he want? Perhaps what Lord Marchmain wants. The adulterous husband, accompanied by his mistress, comes home to Brideshead from Venice to die. Let us be careful to notice what is as big and clear as day. He might have stayed in Venice with his mistress and died there, fanned by the faintly sewerish air of the canals, while the gulls cried and the gondoliers swore cheerfully at one another in their incomprehensible dialect. He does not. Says the mistress: "He has come home to die."

Charles, an atheist, fascinated by the Catholic family despite himself, fights against what he knows they will try to do. "They'll come now," he says, "when his mind's wandering and he hasn't the strength to resist, and claim him as a death-bed penitent. I've had a certain respect for their Church up to now. If they do a thing like that I shall know that everything stupid people say about them is quite true—that it's all superstition and trickery." But when the moment comes, and the priest has anointed the dying man's head with the oil of salvation, Lord Marchmain raises his hand to his forehead in the only reply he can make, the sign of the cross. And Charles himself is kneeling there, longing with the rest of the family. "Then I knew," he says, "that the sign I had asked for was not a little thing, not a passing nod of recognition, and a phrase came back to me from my childhood of the veil of the temple being rent from top to bottom."[10]

Brideshead—the manor, a home no more—will be abandoned by the family and employed as a barracks by the British army during the Second World War. Charles, surprised to find himself stationed there, strolls through the house he knew so well, ending his visit at its heart: the chapel. "The art-nouveau lamp burned once more before the altar. I said a prayer, an ancient, newly learned form of words." For what is most ancient is always ever new. He considers the apparent futility of the builders over the generations, extending the house, wing by wing, stone upon stone, until, "in sudden frost, came the age of Hooper," a platoon commander in Charles's company and a comical philistine. "The place was desolate and the work all brought to nothing; *Quomodo sedet sola civitas.*" That was Jeremiah's lament over Jerusalem sacked, its people led into captivity. Yet that is not all. I cite Waugh's passage in full, because it reveals the life of something that the modern world has not been able to extinguish:

> Something quite remote from anything the builders intended has come out of their work, and out of the fierce little human tragedy in which I played; something none of us thought about at the time: a small red flame—a beaten-copper lamp of deplorable design, relit before the beaten-copper doors of a tabernacle; the flame which the old knights saw from their tombs, which they saw put out; that flame burns again for other soldiers, far from home, farther, in heart, than Acre and Jerusalem. It could not have been lit but for the builders and the tragedians, and there I found it this morning, burning anew among the old stones.[11]

Charles Ryder, the successful dilettante, the antiquarian, the Bohemian poseur, is finally woven into what is a true culture. Brideshead is his home, not because he grew up there (he did not), but because it has *placed him*, as if he were a stone, in an ancient edifice of meaning. He is in communion with the Crusaders who fought at Acre, now in ruins, and Jerusalem, also in ruins. He is in communion with the friend of his youth, the alcoholic Sebastian, now an exile, a pilgrim, and a man with a home, half in and half out of a community of monks in North Africa, where one morning, as his sister Cordelia foretells, "after one of his drinking bouts, he'll be picked up at the gate dying, and show by a mere flicker of the eyelid that he is conscious when they give him the last sacraments. It's not such a bad way of getting through one's life."[12] It beats secular exhaustion and a shot of morphine.

This being home is not a sentiment. It is a felt reality, and from this day on it gives form to Charles's life. "You're looking unusually cheerful today," a soldier tells him in the last line of the book.

### Common Memory

"If I forget thee, O Jerusalem," cries the psalmist from captivity in Babylon, "let my right hand forget her cunning. If I do not remember thee, let my tongue cleave to the roof of my mouth; if I prefer not Jerusalem above my chief joy" (Psalm 137:5–6). The modern man produces little to remember and much to forget—the stuff of his vast landfills, so unlike the honest droppings of horses and oxen as they pulled the plows over the farmlands of old. I do not mean to champion horse-drawn plows, underrated as they may be, but rather to note that our whole orientation is toward disposal, junk, burial, razing, obliteration. So it behooves me again to bring *culture* into clearer focus, lest we be led down a false alley—or boulevard, lined with posh restaurants, clothiers, and museums.

A "Lady in a Box" seat in Thornton Wilder's play *Our Town* uses the word in that common sense: "Mr. Webb, is there any culture or love of beauty in Grover's Corners?"

"Well, ma'am," he says, "there ain't much—not in the sense you mean." The townspeople of Grover's Corners, an imaginary village in New Hampshire, have the ordinary beauties of sun and mountain and birdsong to enjoy, and one of the ladies prevailed upon her husband after many years to take her to see the ocean, fifty miles away, "but those other things—you're right, ma'am,—there ain't much.—*Robinson Crusoe* and the Bible; and Handel's 'Largo,' we all know that; and Whistler's 'Mother'—those are just about as far as we go."

"So I thought," says the pleasant snob. "Thank you, Mr. Webb."

The irony is that *Our Town* is all about memory, of families extended in time, knowing all there is to know about one another, and the central events of the play are a marriage and a funeral, wherein all the people in town are somehow involved. We have seen already that culture is not a bit from Handel and Whistler or a tourist trip to Paris, which Mrs. Gibbs in little Grover's Corners dearly wants. We have seen that it is what Belloc knew when he went back to the Sussex downs and swung the scythe again, with cunning in his hand and a keen eye for cutting the grass while there was still some green in it, and breathing the salt breezes whispering from the sea, and singing the Sussex songs with men he knew when he was a boy.

The home may be a place of wild anarchy, blessedly beyond or beneath the statutory law and the hordes of beneficent mischief-makers who know everything, from how to change a diaper to what to do when your teenage son comes home late and unsteady on his feet. But calm or half wild, it has always been home, a haven. Imagine a culture that is *not* home because it is a place of aggression, suspicion, unrest, and threat. Imagine, from our own experience, that man's power over nature has become unmoored from human purposes and now proceeds by its inexorable logic, demanding, as Romano Guardini puts it in *The End of the Modern World,* "its own actualization," so that it becomes, in the strict sense, "demonic." Guardini writes in the aftermath of that upheaval of madness and wickedness, the Second World War, nor had the wickedness died with the suicide of Hitler and the surrender of the Japanese Empire. The world being built up before and during that war, and upon its ruins, was not a world of memory. "I know of no term with which to designate the culture of the future," says Guardini. "To speak of a 'non-cultural culture' would be correct in the intended sense," but hard to understand, unless we specify the characteristics of the world to come—our world. This Guardini does, with admirable clarity:

> The coming order by which man will be related to his own works differs radically from the older one. It lacks the precise elements which constituted a culture in the older sense; the feeling of a tranquil fertility, of a flowering, beneficent realm. The new culture will be incomparably more harsh and more intense.... The new culture does not promise that breath necessary for a secure life and free growth; on the contrary it presents a vision of factories and barracks to the eyes of the mind.
>     A single fact, we must emphasize, will stamp the new culture: danger.[13]

We are not speaking merely of direct threats to human existence, such as the atomic bomb that had been detonated in the soul of modern man. "Man today holds power over things," Guardini notes, "but we can assert confidently that he does not yet have power over his own power." Thus we now hear of scientists seeking to create beings that are "transhuman" because good old ordinary man is not sufficient for their pride, and that same ordinary man is powerless to resist it, even by political means, for the political machine also has been fruitful and has multiplied or has sprouted mechanical arms and legs and is in the control of no one singly and no one collectively: it moves on. Ordinary human institutions such as schools have been likewise mechanized; they are trans-schools—centaurs or chimeras, half human and half machine, or all machine, subsuming the human. And again, there is nothing that an ordinary human being can do about it, even if he works in the belly of the centaur. Try to sit in on a class and see how many barriers within barriers you have to breach before you are allowed to open the door. You are a wanderer in a bureaucracy out of Kafka, on trial before you know the charge.

No one is at home. Orwell's imaginary Oceania, in *Nineteen Eighty-Four*, is a vast sprawling anthill, both subhuman and transhuman, where no one is at home because everyone stands always under the glare of Big Brother and because the memory that builds up the home has been erased. The protagonist, Winston Smith, works at the Ministry of Truth, which Orwell conceived after his experiences working for the British Broadcasting Corporation. The Ministry of Truth, or "Minitruth" as it is called with shameless irony in Newspeak, is in the business of deceit and oblivion. Smith's job is to alter old newspaper articles to bring them into accord with whatever the official policy of Oceania is at the moment and to destroy all evidence that anything was ever otherwise. Such evidence is incinerated in the aptly named "memory hole." We need not travel to that imaginary horror. All we need to do is to visit our schools. What is remembered there? Name one story about George Washington that our young people will be taught to remember and honor.

Or we may think of the sole space where Smith believes he is free to think and to record his thoughts in a form that may triumph over time and oblivion. It is not a place at all, only an odd angle in the walls of his flat, where he believes he is just beyond the surveillance of the two-way television and camera, at once delivering propaganda and spying upon the state patients to see that they follow it. So also in schools, where everyone has a screen and submits to its glaring eye. What, here, is with free devotion brought forth into the future?

If I can call upon my experience as a college professor, not much. A few plays by Shakespeare and pretty much no literature written before our current political itching. In Canada, the same, bilingually: ignoring French literature as well as English. Not much history, and what there is, blackened or wrested to current political parades. Last year an Episcopal church in Virginia removed a plaque commemorating Washington, who sometimes worshiped there. What the church did with crowbars, the school does with textbooks—the ones they use, and the ones they have sent to the dumpster. Our craze of icon-smashing is like the spike of a fever the patient has been suffering for a long time. Good but flawed men like Robert E. Lee are tarred and feathered long after death and without any inclination to see them as fallible human beings who tried to do what they thought was right and who risked all they had for it. Thoroughly bad men like Che Guevara are fêted and made into modern-day saints, a canonization that requires effacing all memory of their murders. Out come the chisels, stage left, and the deceitful banners, stage right. Oceania has always been at war with Eastasia. No one is home.

## Moments Immemorial

I am looking at two paintings that illustrate what I take to be the heart of culture. About one of them I have written before:[14] it is *The Angelus* by Jean-François Millet. Two peasants—I use the word in the literal sense: they are of the *pays*, the countryside, and they work the land—stand in the foreground. A man and a woman, their day's labor ending, have paused to pray. The man has stuck his three-pronged pitchfork in the ground. They have been hoeing potatoes, as we can see from the ground and from the lumpy bags on a cart nearby. The man has the slender build and tanned complexion of someone who is outdoors all the time. The woman is full-bodied, with broad hips and an ample bosom, though she is by no means what you would call soft. Her form bespeaks fertility, and fertility is an earnest of the future. They wear the peasant's *sabots*, wooden shoes. He has his hat in hand. They are bowing slightly, in an attitude of prayer. In the background, we see a broad plain stretching to the horizon, the fields brown with stubble and rolls of hay, and behind those fields a distant village, marked by the spire of a church. Evidently from that church comes the tolling of a bell to call the people to prayer.

What really is going on? They are praying the Angelus. One of them, probably the husband, will say, in French but possibly in Latin—and keep in mind that they are peasants, these people who would be saying a prayer in a language not spoken in common conversation in over a thousand years—"The angel of the Lord declared unto Mary," and the other will respond, "And she conceived by the Holy Spirit." Then they pray the Ave Maria. The husband continues, "Behold the handmaid of the Lord," and the wife responds, "Be it done unto me according to thy word." Another Ave Maria. And finally, with a genuflection, the husband, "And the Word was made flesh," and the wife, "And dwelt among us." And the third Ave Maria.

Notice how their action is set in time and yet how it far transcends the moment. Whether they are conscious of it is beside the point. The things that are so habitual to us that we do not subject them to analysis are those most formative of our souls. They are *recollecting*. They place themselves at the moment, more than 1,800 years distant, when the angel appeared to a young maiden named Mary, who allowed her womb to become the haven of the incarnate Lord. Most paintings of the Annunciation show the calm holiness and grave beauty of Mary, portrayed as meditating upon the Scriptures, though Tintoretto portrays the violent irruption of the Word made flesh into a world once royal but now in ruins. However the Christian looks at it, the Annunciation is what Dante calls "the fulcrum of the everlasting plan," the hinge of time, the moment at which all changes. All of the previous history of salvation was a prologue and a foreshadowing of that moment, and all of the subsequent history of man will be the playing out of what that moment means: the Word was made flesh.

You do not have to be a Christian to see the import of this act of prayer. If I wander across the battlefield at Gettysburg, I may pause at a memorial to this or that army from the North or the South and say, "These men offered their lives here," or I may climb the rise upon which Pickett's men sacrificed themselves in their desperate charge. And such memorials, and such thoughts, are cultural, properly speaking. We ought to have more of them, not fewer, and everywhere, not only in places thick with the traffic of tourists. But I do not seek while I am walking there to see all of time as consummated in that moment, nor am I engaged in making that moment real and present to the world. I do not measure the time of day by Meade and Stuart and Lee.

Nor do I bring all of human action and all of the world's breadth into the place where I stand and the time when I collect my thoughts. The peasants in Millet's painting pause because it is time to do so, as they hear from the tolling of the bell, and they are aware that other people will be praying likewise: other peasants in fields far off, people in the village streets, master and students in a classroom, the priest in the chapel, and then, farther away, Catholics in Spain, in Italy, and wherever the evening sun shows that it is time for their daily labor to cease. They are at one with them. So also at the churchyard; mothers and fathers, grandmothers and grandfathers, whose bodies lie buried in the hallowed ground; they too prayed, as their children tagged along after them in the fields and learned the holy words.

The mysterious skies in Millet's painting, streaked with clouds and suffused with sunlight, ranging subtly across the palette of color, direct our eyes toward heaven, even while we glance toward the homely things—the cart, the potatoes, the shoes, the earth. The anti-Millet would give us a concrete floor, ceiling tiles, and a man and woman strangely sexless and sterile, at lunch or on the telephone or scribbling notes on a pad, without connection to heaven or earth, to time long ago or time present across the world, to things humble or holy. The peasants in Millet are at home. The functionaries in the anti-Millet have no home. If man has no roots in time and beyond time, he has no home. Life is only a long stay at a motel or flophouse, and when he leaves, he turns in his magnetic key card at the desk, and his room number knows him no more.

The second painting I am looking at is by the baroque Dutch painter, Jan Steen: *The Child Jesus in the Temple*. When Jesus was twelve, we read in Luke's gospel, he went up to Jerusalem along with his parents and his kin for the Passover and lingered to speak with the elders in the Temple, proposing and answering questions. The boy astonished them. When, on the road back to Galilee, Mary and Joseph realized that the boy was not with any of the cousins, they returned to the city in haste. Steen depicts the moment when, after three days, they have found him in the Temple, portraying Mary as a woman in full adulthood, leaning toward the boy in an act of appeal and protectiveness. "Son," she says to him, "why hast thou thus dealt with us? Behold, thy father and I have sought thee sorrowing." But he stands, his right hand on his heart and his left arm held out at his side, palm outward and fingers stretched forth, as he says, as if to explain something they should have known already, "How is it that ye sought me? Wist ye not that I must be about my Father's business?" (Luke 2:48–49)

The rest of the scene is crowded with men, most of them elderly: the high priest, seated beneath a baroque marble canopy flanked by winding pillars, a book opened before him; a turbaned elder seated in the center, one hand propping up his head, the other marking a place in an open book; an ancient scholar with a rugged beak for a nose, seated to the left, glaring down at a small book while a companion peers over his shoulder; others engaged in concentrated discussion, while one man in the background looks out from the scene directly to the viewer—Steen himself, in a self-portrait. We are beckoned to place ourselves in that Temple, amidst the love of the Holy Family and in the life of Jesus, whose first public act situates him within the long history of his people, even as he will bring that history, as Christians believe, to a new instauration. Mary and Joseph want to bring him home, but he is already at home and about his Father's business, and in a cultural sense, all of the other people in the scene are at home too.

## Advertisements for the Homeless

I once angered a number of students at the university where I taught by suggesting that "multiculturalism" is a sham. There is nothing "multi" about its uniform politics, I said, and it is too rootless and shallow to be a culture. When I met with some of them, I showed them Millet's *Angelus*. They grew uneasy. They did not want to concede that we were looking at what was essentially cultural. That was because they knew in their hearts that what I said about contemporary man is true: he has no home. One of them complained that I was imposing my view of culture upon them, but he had no reply when I said that my description fits every known culture until what, for want of a more accurate term, we call our own. Another said that "culture" means different things to different individuals, but such epistemological relativism implies that nothing is true, and so why should anyone be criticized for what he says? And what culture can be founded upon solipsism? Still another, a native speaker of English but of Hispanic ethnicity, grew petulant and said that if she had no culture, it was because others, Europeans, had robbed her and her people of it. None had any response to the point at hand, which was that the purported robbers or the descendants of the robbers, the descendants of Europeans on our campus, had no culture either, no home.

When I suggested that we meet again to talk these things over, recommending Romano Guardini's book as a starter, the robbery victim protested that I wanted them to read a book on "my" side, as if we were engaging in partisan politics, and not thinking about human realities that transcend the heat and mire of the controversy of the day. They were not interested. I let them go and did not go out of my way to meet them again.

Perhaps these students were not, strictly speaking, engaged in partisan politics, but this kind of activism is to genuine care for the *polis* as mass entertainment is to culture, or as the shudders induced by pornography are to married love. It is, we might say, sub-political or pseudo-political. It warms no heart, forges no friendship, admits no sin and forgives none in others, and hates the present almost as much as it hates the past.

I was not angry with the students. That would have been like being angry with a half-mad cripple waving a sign on a street corner while begging for alms. People who have no home are going to be insecure. They do not say, "I am a pilgrim on the road, like millions who have gone before me," because they have no destination. They do not say, "I am here under the canopy of grace, where my father and mother stood, and their ancestors also, back into time immemorial," because they have lost the faith, or it has been demoted to a hobby, a pass-the-time.

Thus do they perceive every criticism as a mortal threat, truth's sword-point aimed at what they take to be their very existence. The more tenuous their grasp of what they are in place and time, the more they shrink like sensitive plants from the merest touch, a hair's tickle. The more foreign to them the walls and the roof of a time-transcending and place-transcending Temple, the more jealous they are of their scrap of ideological plastic tarp propped up on sticks, which is all they know of shelter.

The phrase "identity politics" is a strange contradiction in terms. There is no identity, and there is no polity. For if I assign to myself my identity, I have none. I have donned a costume. What I don I may doff. If I take for my identity my skin color or the happenstance of my begetting, I am attempting to build a world upon a foundation that will not sustain it—a cathedral upon a sheet of paper stretched over emptiness. If I take for my identity a partisan movement that is political in the common sense of the word—having to do with elections, money, advertisements, and protests—I may as well have consigned myself to a mental ward.

"Who is it who can tell me who I am?" cries Lear, without a kingdom, spurned by his eldest daughter and about to be turned out on a foul night by his second daughter, like a mongrel kicked from the door.

"Lear's shadow," says the Fool.

No faith, no culture, no home. Matthew Arnold, that sad prophet of culture who had lost the liberal Christian faith of his father, saw it despite himself, and wrote about it in his conclusion to his poem "Dover Beach":

Ah, love, let us be true
To one another! for the world, which seems
To lie before us like a land of dreams,
So various, so beautiful, so new,
Hath really neither joy, nor love, nor light,
Nor certitude, nor peace, nor help for pain;
And we are here as on a darkling plain
Swept with confused alarms of struggle and fight,
Where ignorant armies clash by night.

Those students in my office had youth's natural desire to fight. But they had nothing clear for which to fight, no clear object of devotion. So their fight was endued with bitterness and madness. The hobbits of J. R. R. Tolkien's epic *The Lord of the Rings* could remain cheerful in dark times not because they had a natural predilection for fighting or for adventures. Hobbits were notorious for being stay-at-homes, except for the raffish Tooks. (The real name of Pippin, one of the four friends along for the sojourning and the fighting, is Peregrine Took, and "Peregrine," as the polyglot Tolkien expected his English-schooled readers to know, means "pilgrim.") They went forth to save their beloved Shire, which meant also to save Middle-Earth itself from the totalizing ambition of Sauron. My students had no Shire.

### Keeping to the Desert

It was, however, not likely that they would have agreed to have a Shire if I had managed to point them toward one. Their minds had been eaten up with political slogans, as with cancer. One among their number, a young man from Colombia, told me that he was not eager to read Calderón (1600–1681), the greatest playwright of his mother tongue, who flourished during the greatest period of Spanish drama. "European," he said, with disappointment. He might have made the same complaint about the architecture of the churches in his country and the language spoken there, although after four centuries the strands of European and native cultures have become so entwined as to form one fabric, a good and strong fabric, as the native stone and stucco of the New World was raised up into homes of worship, where speakers of Spanish uttered prayers in Latin to the Lord who hears all languages, even those that have no words.

I might have offended them worse had I suggested that there was a home for them, if they would rise up from the unsatisfying task of feeding husks to political swine. Let me present that home.

In the decades following the Civil War, Helen Hunt Jackson, a friend of Harriet Beecher Stowe and a liberal at a time when "liberal" did not imply a complete political program to banish all liberty from human life except for the sexual, went west to examine the plight of other peoples whom the United States government had treated badly. These were the Indians. She began with the California missions, writing a series of long articles for several consecutive issues of *The Century Magazine*, in which she described the death of the great and indefatigable missionary Father Junípero Serra. On the eve of his death, he walked from his bed to the church he had built to receive the viaticum—the inspiration for Tolkien's "waybread," because that is what the word means: food for the journey. As Father Junípero knelt before the altar, there "rose from choked and tremulous voices the strains of the grand hymn 'Tantum Ergo.'" Mrs. Jackson, who came from a Unitarian family in New England, gives the reader the verses in Latin, without feeling the need to translate them. Protestant English-speakers could enter into the profound spirit of a Catholic ritual spanning many centuries in a language that had passed from life and change to eternity, among people who were both Spanish and

Indian, in a land that had once belonged to Mexico and not the United States.

Suddenly, she writes, "a startled thrill ran through the church as Father Junipero's own voice, 'high and strong as ever,' says the record, joined in the hymn," to the sobs of his friends and fellow workers, and the members of his flock, both whites and Indians. When the bell tolled his death the next morning, the people thronged the church, weeping and lamenting, and "it was with great difficulty that the soldiers could keep them from tearing Father Junipero's habit piecemeal from his body, so ardent was their desire to possess some relic of him." Not without justification did the Indians want such memorials: "He loved them, and yearned over them as brands to be snatched from the burning. He had baptized over one thousand of them with his own hands; his whole life he spent for them, and was ready at any moment to lay it down for them if that would have benefited them more."[5]

Lest we think that Mrs. Jackson is indulging in prettiness, she is careful to present for us items from the friars' well-kept records regarding what was accomplished and produced at the missions in California, extending from San Diego to San Francisco. We must consider the wide variety of goods and trades the friars brought to the Indians, whose life in those dry lands had been ever marked by poverty, famine, and the threat of violence from stronger tribes. The Indians for the first time cultivated the vine and the olive. They planted orchards of apples, pomegranates, and oranges. They learned the arts of the foundry and the mill. They dug wells. They raised cattle and sheep. They grew corn and traded the surplus for goods from abroad. They built schools. They learned to play musical instruments:

> The picture of life in one of these missions during their period of prosperity is unique and attractive. The whole place was a hive of industry: trades plying indoors and outdoors; tillers, herders, vintagers by hundreds, going to and fro; children in schools; women spinning; bands of young

men playing on musical instruments; music, the scores of which, in many instances, they had themselves written out; at evening, all sorts of games of running, leaping, dancing, and ball-throwing, and the picturesque ceremonies of a religion which has always been wise in availing itself of beautiful agencies in color, form, and harmony.[16]

What happened to these *homes*? Governments happened to them, first the Mexican, ever levying goods and moneys from these successful enterprises, and then, after the Mexican War, the regional government of California, followed by the United States. The missions were sacked. Lands to which the Indians had a claim extending back two or three generations were sold to American speculators amid confusion as to the specifics of titles, sometimes justified confusion and sometimes bad faith. Jackson went there herself. There were still quite a few elderly Indians who remembered the days of the fathers. There were also still visible many of the ruins of what had been their homes, the homes that the fathers had made for them: a well filled with sand, a broken mill wheel, the side of a chapel, grapes gone wild, an orchard choked with brush.

Here was home, in a way hard for us to imagine. What the fathers did for the Indians united them with fellow worshipers across the world and across the centuries. The Indians did things they could not have conceived before, conducting international trade from California round the horn of South America and on to Europe and back. But what was all that, against the secular dreams of an ever-expanding progressive American state? Jackson sums it up so: "The combination of cruelty and unprincipled greed on the part of the American settlers, with culpable ignorance, indifference, and neglect on the part of the Government at Washington, has resulted in an aggregate of monstrous injustice which no one can fully realize without studying the facts on the ground." And this: "I have shown a few glimpses of the homes, of the industry, the patience, the long-suffering of the people who are in this immediate danger of being driven out from their last foot-holds of refuge, 'homeless wanderers in a desert.'"[17]

Abstract theories about what national progress meant, combined with not so abstract greed, destroyed a remarkable interaction between the people of two races. But what would those who ply insatiable grievances wish, since the past cannot be changed? To live on grasshoppers and small game and to pound corn in a mortar? That life is gone. I might as well desire to herd sheep on the Norwegian mountainsides with iron tools, no electricity, no gasoline, and no schooling, while pretending to worship an Odin I know is only a myth. That is not a homecoming. It is Miniver Cheevy again. The people of southern California never gave up the faith the fathers had taught them. The people of Peru have not done so either.

The question we face is not what people in the past, who were on the whole no better or worse by nature than we are now, should have done. The question is what we are to do now, and why. Where do we go?

People—there is such a thing as home. Time to rise up, and take a step in its direction.

# CHAPTER FOUR

# The Static Idol of Change

S hortly before he died—we do not know if he had any presentiment that he would die, as he was not an old man—Edmund
Spenser directed his mythmaking genius toward the central
sorrow of human life, the experience of loss:

> What man that sees the ever-whirling wheel
> Of Change, the which all mortal things doth sway,
> But that thereby doth find, and plainly feel,
> How MUTABILITY in them doth play
> Her cruel sports, to many men's decay?[1]

His "Mutability" is no abstract force but a goddess rising up against
the rule of the Olympian pantheon, a revolt that Spenser casts in terms
that remind us of the revolt of Lucifer and the fall of man from grace:

> For, she the face of earthly things so changed,
> That all which Nature had established first
> In good estate, and in meet order ranged,
> She did pervert, and all their statutes burst:
> And all this world's fair frame (which none yet durst

Of Gods or men to alter or misguide)
She altered quite, and made them all accursed
That God had blessed, and did at first provide
In that still happy state for ever to abide.[2]

Spenser will answer the challenge that Mutability poses, but for the moment let us recognize what the challenge is. In the last chapter I suggested that it was not quite honest of Thomas Wolfe to insist that we cannot go home again, since he seems to have been the last man in the world who really wanted to do so. At the least, his relationship with home was vexed and bitter. But let us set aside the emotional baggage, his and ours. The title of Wolfe's other well-known novel, *Of Time and the River*, alludes to the saying, attributed to Heraclitus, that you cannot step into the same river twice. It is why that philosopher suggested that *fire* was the fundamental element of the universe: fire, never stable, ever changing, flickering, leaping, burning, warming, destroying. His contemporary Parmenides posited instead the existence of a single eternal principle, so that all change in the world was superficial or illusory. We may say that meditation upon change and stability has ebbed and flowed, wave-like, between Heraclitus and Parmenides. But suppose we take Heraclitus' point. Then it does not matter whether we want to go home. There is no home. *Tempus edax rerum*: Time is the eater of things, cutting them down, as Spenser says, "with his consuming sickle."[3]

We cannot go home. The place where Ebbets Field once stood is now somewhere in or near an urban intersection. Miners in my home town, more than a hundred years ago, abandoned a village they had built atop the mountain, a village with a small school and a post office, and of that village nothing remains except for some foundation stones covered with the drift of soil and the growth of the woods reclaiming its territory. Things change. We do not ride in carriages. We do not tie our horses to hitching posts. We cannot sled down the hills in the middle of town because they are roads and cars go up and down them. Our grandparents have died, and with them have gone stories that only they could tell. Our teachers have died. Where are the snows of yesteryear?

So we must address the problem of change.

### *All Adrift*

First let us affirm that men in every culture have looked upon the fields and seen the wind sweep over them and known that, as the prophet says, "All flesh is grass, and all the goodliness thereof is as the flower of the field" (Isaiah 40:6). Something deep in us responds in sympathy to the honest words of the Preacher: "Vanity of vanities, all is vanity" (Ecclesiastes 1:1). "[A]t my back I always hear," says Andrew Marvell's lover to his coy mistress, "Time's wingèd chariot hurrying near." The time to love is now, or never: "Gather ye rosebuds while ye may," says the genial epicurean pastor Robert Herrick. Or we hear, in his sadder pagan vein, Lorenzo the Magnificent praising wine and love, not so much for their joy as for their distracting us from the terrible alternative.

Happy talk about how all change is good and change that wipes things we have known clean off the face of the earth is extremely good—nobody in human history has thought so or spoken so heartlessly. Nobody until our time. So we have presidential candidates floating downriver on a platform of "change" and accusing their opponents of being "afraid of change," and yet no healthy person longs to see a fundamental change in his constitution, and no one working for a firm on the edge of collapse looks forward to the day when his name is no longer on the roster. People write love letters and often save them; no one says, at the end of a love letter, "shred after reading," or "valid for ninety days." Let Robert Frost instruct us in his laconic and powerfully suggestive way—or let his "Oven Bird" do it:

> There is a singer everyone has heard,
> Loud, a mid-summer and a mid-wood bird,

Who makes the solid tree trunks sound again.
He says that leaves are old and that for flowers
Mid-summer is to spring as one to ten.
He says the early petal-fall is past
When pear and cherry bloom went down in showers
On sunny days a moment overcast;
And comes that other fall we name the fall.
He says the highway dust is over all.
The bird would cease and be as other birds
But that he knows in singing not to sing.
The question that he frames in all but words
Is what to make of a diminished thing.

It won't do to say that just as summer gives way to fall and fall to winter, there will come another spring, with light green leaves and the pear and cherry flowers all over again. We know that. Whether that matters, and how much it matters, I will discuss later. But what we note here is the universal experience of loss, of decay, dwindling down toward death: what to make of a diminished thing.

The Oven Bird is a realist, not a dreamer. In this sonnet, whose rhymes and whose structure seem prosaic, he does not sing to us so much as speak, and speak the truth. Youth passes like a dream. The flowers are few. The woods are mostly silent. The highway dust is over all. There is, it seems, nothing much to sing about, and so the oven bird would cease too, except that his song is to tell us the simple and unmusical truth.

We may put the truth more dramatically. The just man Job is sitting on the dung-heap, covered with boils which he scrapes with the shard of a pot. He has lost his children and all his wealth. When his three friends come to comfort him by "solving" the mystery of change and decay and the suffering they bring, saying that God must have willed it because Job must have deserved it, Job cries out in defense not only of himself but of poor mankind generally. This is what we are:

> [Man], as a rotten thing, consumeth, as a garment that is
>     moth-eaten.
> Man that is born of a woman is of few days, and full of
>     trouble.
> He cometh forth like a flower, and is cut down:
> he fleeth also as a shadow, and continueth not. (Job 13:28–
>     14:2)

That is true whether or not we can expect to live out our three score years and ten. Job, in his heart-tearing pleas to be heard by God, cannot be comforted because the bygone years cannot be recovered; the fading flower will not bloom again; the moth-eaten garment cannot be mended. He has nowhere to go. God, in whom he trusted, in whose eyes he was upright and just, has, he believes, crushed him to the dust. Where to turn? He has been cut adrift.

Frost hears the Oven Bird and asks a question with no answer, except perhaps a stoic resignation: we must make what we can of the "diminished thing" that life is. Job cries out for an answer, and stoic resignation is unthinkable. Frost was at least bound to the health-giving earth and worked at a hard and punishing but fruitful task. The poet of Job had more: he had the faith of his forefathers, a faith he is putting to its most severe test. Job may feel as if the earth beneath his feet had fallen into the abyss, but the poet has the old man express one certainty about God after another, for God "stretcheth out the north upon the empty place, and hangeth the earth upon nothing" (26:7) and surely punishes the wicked, for the permanence the rich sinner counts on is vanity: "The house which he builds is like a spider's web, or as a hut which the watchman has made," that is, a makeshift tent of sticks and skins (27:18). Job's trouble is how to reconcile truths about God with the waves of suffering that have crashed upon him and apparently wrecked his life.

Suppose you have no connection with the land or the sea—no regular experience of their terror or their brute resistance to human will—but also, to filch a fine phrase from Chesterton, cited by my favorite Dominican theologian, Aidan Nichols, no regular experience of "the warmth and wonder of created things." Suppose further that you cannot cry out with Job because in your world God has been banished to an attic or out-building. You have no hymns in your heart, no psalms in your memory. You have no strong attachment to the locality of your birth or to your family extended far back into time. For you, "tradition" is a word like "antique" if you are fond of it, or "antiquated" if you are not. You have no culture. Suppose, in short, you are in the situation I have been describing in my previous chapters. You may then embrace "change," without any clear object in mind, not because you love something that you do not possess, but because you do not love at all what little you do possess. You are a sick person tossing and turning on a bed. No position will satisfy. If you indulge yourself in change for change's sake, surrendering yourself to the undirected verb, you may end up like Milton's Satan: "For only in destroying I find ease / To my relentless thoughts" (*Paradise Lost*, 9:129–130).

## Homo Errator

Such undirected change goes in our time by the question-begging name of progress. Here we must make two distinctions.

The first is between organic change, a development—an unwrapping—of potentialities that a creature, by virtue of the kind of thing it is, possesses within, and change that cripples, dismantles, denies, or obliterates its subject or origin. Feminists have been fond of saying that the fetus in the womb is no more a human being than an acorn is an oak tree. Thus have they advertised their unwillingness or inability to think analogically or to appreciate the rich and wondrous reality they want to deny. The embryo or fetus is human in act: it is in the midst of constant change that is a real development, an unwrapping, of its potentialities. It is not like the inert acorn. It is instead like a seedling or sapling, which we would indeed call an oak tree, a young and tender oak tree, without bark perhaps, and with the tree's other "organs" in early and inchoate condition, yet a tree for all that. Its future, if it is given sufficient water and light and nutrients, will unfold from its present, and you might then hang an old tire from a limb and swing on it to your childlike heart's content. All that the oak tree is, is present *in potentia* in that slender shaft with the leaf or two.

Cardinal Newman applied this notion to Christian doctrine. It is not that Christians declare a thing to be good and holy at noon and five hours later declare it to be wicked. It is rather that "re-velation" is a verb, an unveiling or unwrapping, so that we see more and more clearly what was already there to be seen, or that the implications of our faith are worked out in more intricate ways, as a bud blossoms and breaks into full flower, *without however denying or destroying the bud.* The faith as it was and the faith as it has come to be are one: Christ yesterday, today, and tomorrow. "I am the first and the last: I am he that liveth, and was dead; and, behold, I am alive for evermore" (Revelation 1:17–18), says Christ to the apostle John, in the book called *apocalypse*—the uncovering, the un-hiding. So Christians believe that the first people to whom it was said, "I am the LORD thy God, which have brought thee out of the land of Egypt, out of the house of bondage. Thou shalt have no other gods before me" (Exodus 20:2–3), were thus admonished not to worship the idols of the peoples among whom they would live, even though perhaps they did not yet fully understand that the Lord was *the only God.* Man cannot stand too much truth at once. So also the Passover: it is not eradicated in the sacrifice of Christ, the Lamb of God who takes away the sins of the world, but brought to full flower and re-enacted, as Catholics and Eastern Orthodox believe, on all the altars in the world. Nor is this notion of development, of patient and subject-preserving unwrapping, foreign to Jewish thinking. The prophets both spring from the Law and bring the Law to greater clarity, or sometimes a fuller sense of the utter mystery and majesty of God, "For my thoughts are not your thoughts, neither are your ways my ways, saith the LORD" (Isaiah 55:8).

We will ask, later, in what way we may rightly look forward to a complete transformation of being, an ultimate change.

Organic change, not in its ultimate form, is unlike the modern rage to uproot and level, a rage predicated upon scorn for the past. Woodrow Wilson said that the object of higher education was to raise men who were *unlike* their fathers, even while it was those fathers who were paying Wilson's salary at Princeton. The "new math" did not build upon the algorithms and intuitions of many decades of American education but swept them aside in favor of teaching children set-theory, with all its jargon and abstraction. Modern sculptors did not build upon the classical and innovative work of such men as Rodin but gave us lumps and coat-hangers and blocks instead. Modern poets of free verse did not build upon the wildly various metrical innovations of such Victorians as Tennyson and Browning. They largely rejected them, and that is why the metrical craft has fallen into desuetude. The consolidated school did not develop from neighborhood schools; it devoured them. It goes by the name of "school," but the gigantic and impersonal and anonymous institution is a different thing in kind. Feminism did not build upon the father-headed household. It repudiated it.

The second distinction we must make is between change that leads to a clear and ultimate goal and change that has no such goal because people have rejected the it or forgotten that there ever was one. If we use the word "progress," we imply, like it or not, that we *have a reasonably clear destination in mind*. The men of the Middle Ages were inveterate pilgrims—they had a destination. A man who goes to the Holy Land not as a tourist but to perform an act of penitence, to tread the roads that Jesus trod and walk the Way of Sorrow up the mount of Calvary understands that he himself is a man on the way: *homo viator*. Every moment in his life is oriented toward one of two destinations. One is the presence of God Himself, or as the psalmist put it long before the full revelation of the promise of eternal life, to "dwell in the house of the LORD all the days of my life, to behold the beauty of the LORD, and to enquire in his temple" (Psalm 27:4). The other is the outer darkness, where "there shall be wailing and gnashing of teeth" (Matthew 13:50). That is the place of ultimate futility, motion that does not move, change that is like the suck of quicksand. I think of the ceaseless flapping of Satan's wings at the bottom of Dante's hell; the motion serves only to chill the River Cocytus and reduce it to the very ice that locks Satan in place.

Where are we going? "Progress" implies that there is a goal, because otherwise we would be walking for the sake of walking, as in an immense and trackless forest. What goal? Since the Christian has or should have a goal, change as progress is essential for him, for there is no standing still in the spiritual life. He who is not progressing, say the experts, is falling and retreating. But what happens when we substitute for that heavenly goal an earthly one, as if some merely human structure, with all the human failings that we cannot heal in ourselves, let alone in human race, could satisfy our longings? We long for democratic capitalism or the dictatorship of the proletariat or toothpaste with a cleaner, brighter taste, and then all shall be well and all manner of thing shall be well! We are bound for a fearful reckoning.

So allow me to suggest an aim for the progressive who never troubles to tell us where we are supposed to be going. The heaven on earth is this: endless technological progress, giving us more and more sophisticated machines for the elimination of labor and the procurement of pleasures; more and more autonomy for the individual in sexual matters, paid for by more and more state surveillance over and management of ordinary human affairs; and the gradual elimination of borders, skins, membranes, institutions that claim our fidelity and separate town from town, clan from clan, congregation from congregation. The magic word that is to accomplish all of this is *equality*—meaning, in practice, a staggering *inequality* of power between those who are to enforce the equality in certain preferred respects and those who are to suffer it.

If that is so, then progress is the progressive dissolution of what it means to be human. A man is not defined but un-defined by autonomy:

he loses his skin. If you are a law unto yourself, obeying the promptings of your pleasure within a state-sanctioned playground, you are no citizen but a subject, or a slave, both to your passions and to the dictates of a state which men no longer govern, either individually or collectively, but which has taken on a pseudo-life of its own, with all the trappings and the electoral apparatus of democracy and none of the soul. Unless, perhaps, democracy has an undemocratic soul and must lead inevitably to a terrible trade of actual for notional liberty. You are a paramecium swallowed up in an amoeba. Wherever you go, you go nowhere. You are not *homo viator* but *homo errator,* man without aim. "For he that once hath misséd the right way," says Spenser's Despair, "The further he doth go, the further he doth stray."[4]

There is a name for a creature that has lost its skin. It is called a bloody mess, or a corpse. We have progressed so far as to have persuaded ourselves that "male" and "female" are mere words, shape-shifters, dissolving into one another and into who knows what else. Some scientists want us to dissolve ourselves into computerized androids. That must end us, that must be our cure.

## *Change and the Journey*

I have often heard from progressives that a certain kind of change is impossible, meaning any kind of change of heart that would bring us back to *the way.* This is a denial of the purpose of change. It is to stick in the mud of events as they happen, like a dead thing washed up in the eddies of a sluggish river. Here we may say that *nostalgia* is an ache for the journey, that which leads not to the home we have known, but from that home and through that home to the home for which we have been made. It is the sweet heartache of a pilgrim spirit. Its steadfastness is not the desire to remain fixed in one place but to hold to a journey from and through one beloved place to the true and only beloved. "Being," says Gabriel Marcel, "necessarily means 'being on the way.'"[5]

Tennyson captured *that* heartache too in his poem "Ulysses," which seems to affirm the lust for wandering that must finally reject all homes. It does not, I believe, actually do so, but let us take the situation with its most obvious features. The old king Ulysses—the Roman name for Odysseus, and thus the name he bears in Virgil's *Aeneid* and in Tennyson's inspiration here, Dante's *Inferno*—has returned to Ithaca. Penelope and Telemachus are very much alive. But Ulysses feels that he is wasting his last precious years, doing no one any good:

> It little profits that an idle king,
> By this still hearth, among these barren crags,
> Matched with an aged wife, I mete and dole
> Unequal laws unto a savage race,
> That hoard, and sleep, and feed, and know not me.

Tennyson allows Dante to school him on two matters here. One is the idea that some of Ulysses' mariners survived with him the twenty years of wandering from Troy. The other is the idea that he abandoned Ithaca to sail forth—disastrously—into the western ocean. Dante implicitly condemns the man for his impiety. Unlike Aeneas, the refugee who had no home to return to, and who for the sake of his son and his descendants endured great suffering to settle his people in Italy, Dante's Ulysses leaves his home, his son, and his wife for the sake of knowledge, "for you were never made to live like brutes," says he to his mariners, "but to pursue the good in mind and deed!"[6] And that seems to motivate Tennyson's Victorian fellow. Every man and woman of means in America or England simply had to wander about Europe, especially that fascinating and filthy and fantastic matrix of culture called Italy. We too, if we are uncharitable, may say that Ulysses, as Tennyson imagines him, is an inveterate tourist. "I cannot rest from travel," he says.

But that is not quite fair. Ulysses is restless in large part because his *memory* cannot be still. He is not like the Lotos-Eaters, who want to forget their home. But he is also not like a self-satisfied man who is too stolid to move. He is not simply a hedonist. He is thirsty for life, and his thirst makes him a kind of pilgrim of the mind and heart, a pilgrim as yet without a clear aim for the pilgrimage:

> I will drink
> Life to the lees: all times I have enjoyed
> Greatly, have suffered greatly, both with those
> That loved me, and alone; on shore, and when
> Through scudding drifts the rainy Hyades
> Vexed the dim sea. I am become a name;
> For always roaming with a hungry heart
> Much have I seen and known; cities of men
> And manners, climates, councils, governments,
> Myself not least, but honored of them all;
> And drunk delight of battle with my peers,
> Far on the ringing plains of windy Troy.

Here Ulysses appeals to what will be his future by recalling his past. He cannot forget what he has been, or the "name" among men that he has become. He remembers that he is remembered; he will say to his men, to whet their desire to accompany him on the voyage, that they may perhaps "reach the Happy Isles, / And see the great Achilles, whom [they] knew." They are not any men, but the same who have always been with him, "Souls that have toiled, and wrought, and thought with me," says he,

> That ever with a frolic welcome took
> The thunder and the sunshine, and opposed
> Free hearts, free foreheads—you and I are old;
> Old age hath yet his honor and his toil.

Tennyson knew well that Ulysses' men in the *Odyssey* were mainly grumblers who opposed his will and were never cheerful in the face of thunder. What we see in his own poem is the fellowship of old men who have seen much and done much together and who are now called to remain true to what they have become for one another.

While Dante's Ulysses is a pattern of impiety, leaving the home where God has ordained him to be, Tennyson has him say, with something of an uneasy conscience, that the home is good, and being a king even over the sleepy beasts of Ithaca is also good and necessary:

> This is my son, mine own Telemachus,
> To whom I leave the sceptre and the isle—
> Well-loved of me, discerning to fulfill
> This labor, by slow prudence to make mild
> A rugged people, and through soft degrees
> Subdue them to the useful and the good.

The old man does not treat his son with disdain. He assumes that Telemachus is engaged in work that is related to his, in this sense: Ithaca will not remain as it is. Ithaca will change. Telemachus is to be a part of his people's lives but also the captain of the vessel as they make their slow way toward a better and more human life. "He works his work, I mine," says Ulysses, and I take it there is some affinity between them, Telemachus with his "offices of tenderness," paying "meet adoration to my household gods," Ulysses joining his men again, doing "some work of noble note.... Not unbecoming men that strove with Gods," those of Olympus, with their beauty, intelligence, power, and treachery.

Something has happened between Homer's poem and Tennyson's. There is no pilgrimage in Homer. Where would the pilgrim long to go? The life of man was a wheel. Aristocracy, says Plato, and his diagnosis met with broad agreement, degenerates into oligarchy, democracy, and tyranny, until we start the cycle all over again. But the revelation of God to the Jews had an aim: all nations would someday worship the Lord on Mount Sion. The Messiah would be a light to all peoples, and the kingdoms of the world would be consummated in his reign:

> Arise, shine, for thy light is come,
> and the glory of the LORD is risen upon thee.
> For, behold, the darkness shall cover the earth, and gross
>     darkness the people:
> but the LORD shall arise upon thee, and his glory shall be
>     seen upon thee.
> And the Gentiles shall come to thy light,
> and kings to the brightness of thy rising. (Isaiah 60:1–3)

Much of this forward force has shaped the Western mind and character. Sometimes for the worse: the biological trope of evolution, misapplied to human affairs, reduces man to a thing acted upon by historical "laws" and, as Jacques Maritain says, "disregards or ignores in practice the reality of free will in man,"[7] and so we are no more wondrous, really, than an aggregate of minerals or a crustacean. In perhaps a more pernicious form, it raises men to angels and fuels the naive progressive drive toward a city never seen before, the perfection of justice. But the progressive forgets that a human city is built with human stones, and so long as men and women are what they are, there will never be peace on earth, let alone bliss for all. *Homo homini lupus*, says the Latin proverb: man is a wolf to man. "We flee ourselves, whom we can never flee," says the materialist poet Lucretius,[8] who was honest enough to see that the problem of human life lies within man, not outside and around him. But we will not learn even from the materialists of the past, let alone from the saints. In our time of heretofore unimagined plenty, we still fight, slander, betray. Men are still aggressive and women are sly. Men still use their brute strength to get what they want and to intimidate and bully, and women plead their weakness to avenge themselves on their enemies or to dominate from the shadows. We did not need the evangelists to tell us so; Lucretius would have sufficed. Man is a sinner. That has not changed.

Tennyson was, in part, a believer in this forward thrust, a Christian faith transforming itself through human culture into a glory to be manifest upon earth. But when the faith that is the heart of this confidence in change is lost, we lose the pilgrimage and give ourselves over to change almost for its own sake. So says the spurned young lover in Tennyson's poem "Locksley Hall":

> Yet I doubt not through the ages one increasing purpose
>     runs,
> And the thoughts of men are widened with the process of
>     the suns.

God, we note here, is now a "purpose," and we do not have a clear sense of a *being* with a purpose, an all-comprehending providence. As the suns go on, men grow broader and freer in their thinking. So he says. But the speaker's confidence is not to be taken merely as Tennyson's. In context, he is compromised by seething resentment against his "shallow-hearted" cousin who obeyed her father rather than remain true to their love. She married an old man instead because of social convention, as the boy interprets it. So he will go forth and never see again the scenes of his disappointed passion:

> Not in vain the distance beacons. Forward, forward let us
>     range,
> Let the great world spin forever down the ringing grooves
>     of change.
> Through the shadow of the globe we sweep into the younger
>     day:
> Better fifty years of Europe than a cycle of Cathay.

In part this is an escape, with the grand gestures of a young man who wants to shake the dust from his feet and leave an old world behind. Yet notice in that reference to China how quickly and definitively he dismisses a way of life that goes nowhere. The "cycle of Cathay," a slow periodic turning of centuries, is not worth as much to him as fifty years of Europe. That is not because Europeans are more intelligent than Chinamen. It is because impatient Europeans, as the boy thinks, *are going somewhere*. Where that may be, other than toward some vaguely wondrous future, he does not specify. Perhaps it is toward "the Christ that is to be," if I may steal a line from Tennyson's "In Memoriam," his most mature meditation upon death and the changing fortunes of men. I do not know what Christ-to-be that is, as I believe in Christ who does not change, but far be it from me to heap gloom upon a man when he is steeped in sorrow.

### Escape from Change

When the promises of a world gone mad for change prove delusive, when the frenzy of ambition disappoints, when friends are fickle and allies are treacherous and the only thing that is constant is man's wickedness and folly, we may be moved to leave it all behind and retreat to the haven of a simple and private life. That is what the Epicurean poet Lucretius recommends. It is the best this life has to offer,

> when friends in the soft grass lie at ease,
> In the shade of a tall tree by the riverside,
> Their bodies refreshed and gladdened, at no great cost,
> Most pleasantly when the weather smiles and the season
> Sprinkles the grassy meadows with new flowers.[9]

Note here that the noblest of the hedonists of old, Lucretius and the master Epicurus, whose teachings he endowed with his tremendous poetic grace, did not recommend the heady madness of sex, moneymaking, political scrambling, fighting for glory, and all the other plagues of frenzy that daze the soul of man. Shall we say that their tastes were too aristocratic for that? They believed that an unwarranted fear of death drove men to these measures. They might well say, with the Christian poet, "Change and decay in all around I see," and their response was neither to accept the change nor to see any larger purpose in it but to retreat from its most powerful currents. "One thing gives rise to another, incessantly," says the poet flatly.[10] So also his personification of Nature, delivering a crushing rebuke to a man who clings to life and won't leave the table, even though he has feasted full of all that life has to offer:

> Give it up, old man, it doesn't become your years.
> Come, be content! Give way to your heirs! You must.[11]

The Epicurean proposes a modest life, making the best of it, pruning your desires down to what is merely necessary and to a few other things that make life becoming, such as having a friend or two to talk philosophy with, an agreeable wife, children if you are so blessed, a faithful dog—Lucretius seems to have been fond of animals generally—and bodily health, so long as it lasts. The world is not going anywhere. It presents us with change upon change. But it is a static change, for in the infinite expanse of time before us and behind us, says Lucretius, what is now has already been and shall be again. No purpose means just that—no purpose. He proposes for us the slow evolution of human society from the cave dwellers who ate wild strawberries to Roman senators at their elegant dinners, but he is temperamentally conservative and knows that material wealth does not go along with any sure improvement in goodness. "Poison they often drank unwittingly," says Lucretius about primitive men; "We are more skillful now—we give it to others."[12]

It is hard to deny the appeal of the Epicurean retreat. Its most sublime form may be what the Buddha gives us: the world is a wheel of change, and men torment themselves with desire; therefore we should no longer desire but should escape from that wheel. A calm and enlightened benevolence, yes; passion, longing, searching, pilgrimage, perhaps not. The West too has heard the call to leave the field of battle. I am thinking now of a scene in Tasso's *Jerusalem Delivered*, an epic romance in Italian, from the time of the Catholic Counter-Reformation, set in Palestine during the First Crusade. The princess Erminia, raised a Saracen, has fallen in love with Tancred, one of the leaders of the Christian army. She has, however, never revealed to him her love and has attempted, in vain, to remove herself from its occasion. But when, in exile in Jerusalem, she sees the Christian tents pitched on the plain below the city and sees the handsome young man from afar, the love in her heart surges again, and she cannot help it.

Trying to make her way by night to the Christian camp, she is ambushed, and her panicked horse carries her to a place she does not know. When she awakes, there is a pleasant stillness all around her. The birds are twittering; a brook mutters nearby; someone is playing on a reed. She looks round and sees an old man weaving a wicker basket while his two sons are singing. When she approaches him, she is amazed that he has found a haven of peace when everything roundabout has been roiled by war. How has he managed to live in this way, now of all times, and in this land of all places?

The old man replies with true Epicurean resignation. He does not fear because his wants are few, his lowliness attracts no seeker of glory, and his poverty no seeker of riches. Lightning strikes the mountaintops, not those who dwell in the low dales. But it was not always so with him. When he was young, he too had ambition. He too sought to climb, so he left his home to go to the court of the sultan at Memphis. And there he saw "the sins in which the court abounds," a life that brought no satisfaction. So he longed instead for "lost simplicity" and returned to this place, which he will never leave again.[13]

Erminia decides to stay with him and his family to see if her fortunes may change, to play the simple shepherdess, and to try—she does not try very hard—to forget her love. She sighs, she composes sad songs, she carves verses in the bark of trees, but she does not forget. The escape, Tasso gives us to see, is not for her. That is not because of her personality or her choice. It is because the escape *is not for man.* We would think less of Erminia if she could forget her love. Man is made for the war, Tasso suggests, and must fight on one side or the other. He is made for love, and what the old man holds forth, with all the sweetness and kindness in the world, is a slow spiritual death. It is the devil of the noonday sun, *acedia*, carelessness: and we are thus back to the Lotos-Eaters again.

The other way to try to escape from change is to *escape into change*: to yield to it as if you had been fighting against a stream and then lost heart. Spenser, following Tasso, gives us as an example the infuriated Pyrocles, who cannot control his rage and does not seek to avoid the occasion for it:

"I burn, I burn, I burn," then loud he cried,
"O how I burn with implacable fire,
Yet nought can quench my inly flaming side,
Nor sea of liquor cold, nor lake of mire;
Nothing but death can do me to respire."[14]

Spenser's epitome of female lust, a monster named Argante (who coupled with her twin brother, Olliphant, in utero, as had been said of the Egyptian deities Isis and Osiris), cannot slake her desires by means of her brother's flesh or by the ministrations of beasts but must, *horribile dictu*, roam about Faery Land seeking whom to deflower, attempting to satisfy herself by the delight of *change*:

But over all the country she did range,
To seek young men, to quench her flaming thirst,
And feed her fancy with delightful change.[15]

Indeed, it seems that for Spenser, the greatest sin against love is not hardness of heart or sexual congress before marriage—which are both bad things—but failure to be steadfast. So the sea-god Proteus attempts not to rape the virgin Florimell, whom he has saved *from* a rape, but to do something more sinister, as Spenser sees it. Proteus the shape-shifting god assumes a series of attractive guises to gain her consent, but

> Eternal thralldom was to her more life
> Than loss of chastity, or change of love.[16]

Instead, those who are apt to change their objects of love, as Spenser shows us, are more frequently motivated not by burning lust but by idleness and boredom.

### The Wandering Damozell

"I have often said," says Pascal, "that man's unhappiness springs from one thing alone, his incapacity to stay quietly in one room." Hence come wars, the drive of lust, the frenetic habits of hedonism, busyness of all sorts, moneymaking, ruining rivals, because if we were alone with ourselves for more than a few moments, we would have to come to terms with our wretchedness. We would have to take stock of the journey we are on, how far we have wandered from the path, how vain have been our best efforts at virtue, how empty our optimism, how trivial our pleasures. Such busy motion is not development but stasis.

Let a great poet illustrate the point. At the beginning of *The Faerie Queene*, Spenser gives us a young and callow and foolishly self-confident Knight of the Red Cross, on a journey to slay a dragon that has terrorized a land far away. He has been called for by the maiden Una, who loves him deeply and is accompanying him. But when the illusionist Archimago tricks him into believing that Una has played the part of a whore with a young page, Red Cross leaves her behind and goes off on his own. Immediately he lapses into what Spenser calls, with both physical and spiritual significance, *error*. The boy wanders from the path. From then until his baptism and confirmation near the end of his saga, we see him move about a lot, but to no purpose. He wins a fight that he had done better to refuse; he makes cold love to the witch Duessa, losing both passion and the possibility of joy; he lies in bed in the ominous House of Pride, bleeding from wounds that the leeches there do not actually stanch; he sneaks out of there but falls back into the company of that same witch anyway. Then, "poured out in looseness on the grassy ground, / Both careless of his health, and of his fame,"[17] quite literally diffuse and dissipated, having drunk from a fountain that saps the drinker of strength—Diana had cursed one of her nymphs for having "sat down to rest in middest of the race"[18] (cf. 2 Timothy 4:7)—he is taken captive by the giant Orgoglio and sent to fast and pine away in the bowels of a dungeon.

That is *homo errator*, moving from one mistake to another. He goes but never arrives. He exhausts himself and is never refreshed. He is weary with what is but finds no happiness in what comes to be. We see in Dante's Satan the futility of such motion for the sake of motion: he flaps his six vast wings eternally, changelessly, as if to say, "I shall arise by my power," and the flapping of those wings does nothing at all to raise him. They raise the gale that sweeps across the sinkhole of hell, reducing the river Cocytus to the ice that is his prison. Red Cross Knight, apart from Una, does a lot of moving and does not move at all. The scenes change, but they do not change. He is, as it were, stuck in the mud, the mud of a mudslide, or he flails about in quicksand. His being busy, his sweating a lot may hide from his mind any tickle of remorse, any awakening fear that he has not progressed one inch along the true way. He has changed, but has not grown, has not developed.

We have a name for corporeal change that has no organizing and directing purpose, that is not rooted in what a creature is and has been and is not aimed at the creature's perfection. We call it cancer. What is true of the flesh is true of the polity, including the polity of marriage. Una, the knight's bride-to-be, *does not change*: she is unitary, not double. She does not abandon her love, even when the knight has not been faithful to her. While he is playing his empty game of knight errantry, she has been searching for him hither and yon, at great danger to herself, all over Faery Land. Her steadfastness will bring him round in the end, and he will slay that dragon, and they will marry: and *for her steadfastness* she will earn the honorific name *The Errant Damozell*.

## No Stability, No Unveiling

How shall we characterize the contemporary itch for change, which aims not for the kingdom of God, which must ever be sought as a *gift*, a *grace*, and is not the production of man? It is easy to be steadfast to what has no place, to be loyal to no man and no God, and to keep a vow whose terms must change with the political winds. For, as Thomas Molnar puts it in *The Counter-Revolution*:

> The promise of the revolutionary doctrine is, then predicated on the denial of stable forms, whether of art, institutions, or the meaning of words, and on the denial of time, of the necessary and beneficent interval between conceiving and executing projects. The doctrine promises everything for "tomorrow," whether the classless society, the end of all wars, riches for all men, or a more human mankind. Hence, the destruction of the old becomes an urgent matter, an historic duty. Shirking this duty, let alone obstructing the avenue of progress, is a major crime, in fact the only sin the revolutionary recognizes.

*Plus ça change*, say the French, *plus c'est la même chose*. In our time, the identity of man and woman as such has been declared nonexistent, *unless* a man proclaims that he is "really" a woman or a woman that

she is "really" a man. It is easy to show the incoherence of simultaneously denying that there are any stable and conspicuous differences
between being a man and being a woman *and* asserting that these
differences are so decisive and penetrate so far down into a person's
conscious and subconscious being that we can imagine, as in a bad
piece of science fiction, that someone has been trapped by Nature in
the body of the wrong sex.

Easy, and beside the point. And this is what the ordinary human
being, with ordinary affections and attachments to reality, finds hard
to understand. The point is not to be consistent. The point is to destroy.
"The revolutionary," says Molnar, "lives in a permanent state of meta-
physical dissatisfaction." What Molnar calls the "totalitarian temptation" abides in revolutionary man like a soul-sickness. Because he is
restless, literally without rest—for it is not the Son of Man alone who
has nowhere to lay his head—he can play in his mind the part of a
pioneer. But in actuality, because he acknowledges no *telos*, because he
is radical only in having no roots, he is a pushover for the clichés he
and his fellows push by means of the mass media. If he had his way,
assuming that he has a way at all, *he would obliterate the meaning of
change itself* by locking mankind into an irresistible machine of continual political alteration. But where there is no stable subject, there
can be no meaningful change.

This point bears a closer look. The spatial analogue to change over
time is variety from place to place, or, to use the word that the revolu-
tionists now adore, *diversity*. A true appreciation for the diversity of
man would move us to let things be as they are, here and there, because
in each school, parish, neighborhood, workshop, and town, a precious
way of life has come to flower, assuming that the people there have been
left to grow slowly, preserving their traditions. And yet they who escape
from life *into change* fear that diversity. One precisely defined circle is
not merely similar to another; except for their size, they are indistinguishable. So too with the man to come, and I will quote Molnar again:
"The search for the ideal individual coming out of nature's hands fills

the pages of the impassioned Rousseau as well as those of the cold psychologist Condillac." We must not have that lively thing, that living thing, a real community, like Chesterton's Notting Hill. We must not wait upon Wimbledon. We must not bow to the folkways of those alien people in Cheapside. All must be the same. I call to witness the buildings that can be placed anywhere, because their purpose is to pulverize any remaining sense that there is a *where* at all.

A commitment to "change," then, is a longing for an anti-heaven, the reputed "end of history," and the more the revolutionary spirit is frustrated by reality—the more clearly and emphatically its dreams are shown to be dreams at best and nightmares at worst—the angrier and more intractable the spirit grows.

Consider two manifest failures of our time: the promised renewal of the Catholic Church after the Second Vatican Council and the promised flourishing of love and harmony and justice after the sexual and feminist revolutions. I used to wonder why such colossal destruction of parishes, schools, religious orders, and cultural influence has never caused the revolutionaries to reassess their ends and means. But I was reckoning on normal human beings with ordinary passions and ordinary views of the human good, let alone the divine. I assumed that if you invented a new kind of bridge, and it collapsed under the weight of cars and trains, sending people to an easily preventable death, you would hang your head, acknowledge your error, and leave bridge-building to wiser and more experienced heads. I had not reckoned on the rage to destroy, a deep-seated hatred of what is, and an inverted "religious" passion for a never-to-be-realized ideal, usually described in terms of absolute equality and requiring absolute and central control over every feature of human behavior and thought, a vast and secular anti-church or pseudo-church.

I had assumed that if, after your innovations in the realms of sex, marriage, and family, you saw marriage in free-fall, birth rates sinking into the suicidal, and relations between men and women, by the testimony of the revolutionaries themselves, characterized by suspicion, resentment, and bitterness—after all of that, you might say, "Maybe we were wrong, and there *is* a perduring reality to male and female." I had not reckoned that people would want to see such enmity. But then, as Molnar says, "the revolution has hardly any preoccupation with reality," for

> ... it goes its own way, paying hardly any attention to real needs, real abuses, real problems of justice. In fact, it subjects the little and defenseless people to new torments: it terrorizes peaceful populations, instigates troubles in orderly societies, inflicts stagnation on economies, prevent[s] masses of young from studying, scandalizes the faithful in their forms of devotion. In other words, as a consequence of the revolution, it is again, as always in history, the *poor* among us who suffer most.

So I assert that the conservative alone is capable of coming to terms with change and accepting it for what it is, neither making a god of it nor fearing its ravages. He grasps that change, if it is to be itself and not something else, must preserve its subject, and if it is to be good for man, it must be directed by God. Otherwise, man falls in idolatry of scientists, the state, the eructations of mass entertainment—something, anything—and the prone man goes nowhere. He makes an idol of change and stands in a stupor before it, impotent to resist. Such a person has no longing for home because he has cast into a dungeon his longing for anything at all. He has shut himself up in the prison of what he calls his liberty.

CHAPTER FIVE

# Lost Innocence

Not all the psychology textbooks in the world can teach us about the mind of man; neither can they teach us about the few chapters that begin the book of Genesis, or about why, wherever you go in the world, you will find stories of a lost Arcadia, a golden age, an Eden from which man has been banished. It will not do to suppose that such stories are natural to man because of his experience of the blessedness of childhood. It is not clear to me why that supposed experience should be the *cause* of the stories rather than one of their family features, or rather the *result* of the sense of a moral fall. Nor is it clear why we should look on childhood as a blessed time in the first place. After all, children are weak, of little economic use, under the law of their parents, largely ignorant of the world, and, until recently, vulnerable to communicable diseases and early death. It seems plausible that instead of projecting our lost childhood upon a legendary past, we project our shared sense of lost innocence upon childhood. That sense is not dependent upon any particular thing that has happened to us since we were children. We grow into an awareness of it as we learn about ourselves and the world. We carry it with us as surely as we breathe.

We know the story—or we all used to, before the great cultural amnesia. Adam, "the man," "the human being," and his woman Eve are placed by God in Eden, whose extent, for two people, is vast; think of an area the size of Pennsylvania. In the midst of Eden, God places a garden, a fruitful haven in the center of greenery and growth. He has not made the human beings, as in the Babylonian *Enuma Elish*, to get some unpleasant work done that the lesser gods do not want to do anymore. Nor have they sprung up, as in the Greek myths, by the spontaneous fertility of Earth. They are neither despised by Ishtar nor envied by Zeus. God has made them, the sacred author says, in his own image and likeness, to "have dominion over the fish of the sea, and over the fowl of the air, and over the cattle, and over all the earth, and over every creeping thing that creepeth upon the earth" (Genesis 1:26). That would be the entire physical universe and every creature in it. Just as God is not reducible to some animal totem or to any living thing that *man* can imagine, so no mere creature in the world is to be preferred to man or held sacred: "Thou hast put all things in subjection under his feet," says the psalmist (8:6), using a locution typical of kingship. And man exercises this dominion first in the work of his mind, for the Lord brings every beast to Adam "to see what he would call them; and whatsoever Adam called every living creature, that was the name thereof" (Genesis 2:19). When none proves to be a fit companion for man, God casts Adam into a deep sleep, and from one of his ribs he fashions a woman and brings her to him. Adam exclaims, in the first human words that Scripture records, "This is now bone of my bones, and flesh of my flesh: she shall be called Woman [Hebrew *ishah*], because she was taken out of Man [*ish*]" (2:23).

That is an expression of joy and complete satisfaction. The next words are crucial and not to be taken for granted: "And they were both naked, the man and his wife, and were not ashamed" (2:25). Milton made their nakedness one of the central motifs of *Paradise Lost*. Because they were sinless, Adam and Eve did not need "these troublesome disguises which we wear" (4.740). They were clothed not with fig leaves or the skins of beasts but with the virtues and a godlike majesty. So do they appear when Satan sees them for the first time:

> Two of far nobler shape erect and tall,
> Godlike erect, with native honor clad
> In naked majesty seemed lords of all,
> And worthy seemed, for in their looks divine
> The image of their glorious Maker shone,
> Truth, wisdom, sanctitude severe and pure,
> Severe, yet in true filial freedom placed. (4.288–294)

When Adam walks forth to welcome to the garden the angel Raphael, a visitor from heaven who has come to warn them of the approach of their mortal foe, he needs no extravagant clothing or any crowd of flatterers to accentuate his power. He meets the angel

> without more train
> Accompanied than with his own complete
> Perfections; in himself was all his state,
> More solemn than the tedious pomp that waits
> On Princes, when with rich Retinue long
> Of horses led, and Grooms besmeared with Gold
> Dazzles the crowd. (5.351–357)

He is clothed: we the guilty are naked. Says Milton, at the moment when Adam and Eve, now fallen, awake from unquiet slumber after sealing their sin with an act of unbridled lust: "He covered, but his robe / Uncovered more" (9.1058–1059).

Adam and Eve are naked—Hebrew *'arom*—and the serpent is not. The serpent is subtle, smooth—Hebrew *'arum*, pretty much the same word, from the same root. To be naked is to be smooth in one sense: the skin is smooth, not ruffled with woven cloth or animal hides. But to be subtle is to be smooth in another sense: to hide your intent under the cover of simplicity. We may add that the garden itself is not "smooth," not "bare" or barren as a desert would be. So on one side, we have the rich fertility of Eden, the joyous love of Adam and Eve for one another, the easy converse between the human couple and God, the nakedness without shame, and a God-like dominion over the physical world, expressed most powerfully by the grooves and corrugations of language. On the other side, we have the smooth, oily suggestions of the serpent.

For the essential feature of the serpent is that he hides. He pretends not to know that Adam and Eve have been commanded not to eat of the fruit of but a single tree in all the garden, in the midst of Eden, in the midst of the wide earth and the worlds roundabout. The name of that tree, of "the knowledge of good and evil" (2:17), does not suggest ignorance in man, since Adam immediately after the command names the animals, and God submits to the naming. The name of the tree suggests that man might know good and evil by his own power or by experiencing good and evil, good by losing it and evil by suffering it, as Milton will suggest. The serpent insinuates that God himself hides because he "doth know that in the day ye eat thereof, then your eyes shall be opened, and ye shall be as gods, knowing good and evil" (3:5). It is as if God were fearful of his own creation.

It is the first act of idolatry, because when Eve evaluates the tree as "to be desired to make one wise" (3.6), she attributes to a mere creature the life and gift-giving of God, while assuming the prerogatives of God's own judgment. Says the psalmist:

> The idols of the heathen are silver and gold,
> the work of men's hands.
> They have mouths, but they speak not;
> eyes have they, but they see not:
> They have ears, but they hear not;
> neither is there any breath in their mouths.
> They that make them are like unto them:
> so is every one that trusteth in them. (Psalm 135:15–18)

It takes a bestial heart to worship a beast and a wooden head to worship a wooden god. So what is the first thing that the "wise" Adam and Eve do after their fall? They hide. First they hide their nakedness from one another, using the broad leaves of the fig tree, and then they hide from God, as if they were rabbits in a warren. Genesis will continue to tell stories of people hiding. These run from the despicable envy of Cain, taking his brother Abel aside to slay him and then pretending to God that he knows nothing about it, to the just man Joseph, hiding his identity from the brothers who sold him into slavery not to avenge himself upon them—liars though they were—but to test their love for their father and their repentance.

We are not innocent. We hide. "Am I my brother's keeper?" we say with Cain, while the blood of our brother is still warm on the ground (Genesis 4:9). We have dark intents we would not acknowledge even to ourselves, so we are wise to repeat the prayer: "Cleanse thou me from secret faults" (Psalm 19:12). What man knows his own heart?

So man wishes to go back behind the Fall, which is not possible. He spins stories about Arcadia, where the worst thing that can happen to you is that you fall in love with a pretty shepherdess who does not return your love, so you play the oaten reed and sing sad songs on the hillside. The pagan poets, says Dante, may have dreamed about Eden in their stories of the Golden Age. Matelda, walking on the far side of the stream in earthly paradise, declares, "This was the nectar which the poets meant."[1] The nineteenth-century progressives who founded socialistic communities to bring about a paradise here on earth took it for granted that sin could be bleached out of the human soul as easily as you can smile and utter words of beneficence. The results were not good.

### Not Progress, but Detours

Nathaniel Hawthorne spent some time at such a community, Brook Farm, which was supposed to be, morally, the next "Great

Leap Forward" in the progress of mankind. He left disillusioned and made his experience the heart of his sad and satirical novel *The Blithedale Romance*.

Hawthorne was, essentially, always writing about evil and the vanity of believing that you can overcome it by ideological means—which included scientific or mechanical means. In his short story "The Birth-Mark," for instance, the chemist and ideologue Aylmer has conceived an irrational detestation of a small birthmark on his wife Georgiana's cheek. The birthmark resembles a tiny hand (cf. 1 Kings 18:44). It is a "character," an indelible sign, an imperfection, though others besides Aylmer find it beautiful, and indeed when Georgiana blushes with laughter the sign disappears, merging into the rose of her cheeks. Aylmer embarks on a dangerous and poison-laced "cure" for the imperfection, reaching deep into the heart of what makes Georgiana a living thing. The birthmark disappears at the same moment as Georgiana, fully approving of her husband's evil experiment, dies.

There was no sacrament of forgiveness in the Puritan system that Hawthorne inherited. Indeed, there were no sacraments at all, no physical means whereby God condescends to confer grace upon his flock. Such a system must turn inward upon itself with a soul-dissecting vengeance or turn outward against the world, as if some mechanical rearrangement of social conditions could manufacture the paradise for which men long. So there is a visible path from Hawthorne's great-great-grandfather John Hathorne, a judge in the notorious Salem witch trials, to the gentle George Ripley and his fellow transcendentalists at Brook Farm. If the fire-hearted old judge was narrow in his bigotry and blinded by his zeal to find evil everywhere—see the pathetic dupe in Hawthorne's "Young Goodman Brown"—the optimists at Brook Farm were narrow in their refusal to find evil where it was nearest, in their own hearts.

So too with the progenitors of Hawthorne's semi-fictional Blithedale. The very name is satirical in its bland self-advertisement, for little enough is blithe about the place, despite Hawthorne's generous attempt to concede all he can to the good intentions of the founders. The central male character is Hollingsworth, whom the narrator Coverdale calls a "philanthropist," which he distinguishes sharply from a "philanthropic man." The latter is a man who is benevolent towards others. The former, the philanthropist proper, is consumed by *an idea of philanthropy*, which he intends to impose upon the world: he is a tremendous egotist. You are either for Hollingsworth or against him. When he pushes Coverdale to commit to his single project, prison reform, Coverdale demurs, and their friendship ends. Hollingsworth will have no more to do with him. A century and a half before the term "politically correct" was coined, we see the same phenomenon: human goods, including friendship, are subordinated to an ideology and a political aim. It is Eden *or else*.

In his description of Hollingsworth, Coverdale lays the finger on what is wrong with all attempts to "cure" our birthmark of sin with extrinsic reforms:

> His heart, I imagine, was never really interested in our socialist scheme, but was forever busy with his strange, and, as most people thought it, impracticable plan, for the reformation of criminals through an appeal to their higher instincts. Much as I liked Hollingsworth, it cost me many a groan to tolerate him on this point. He ought to have commenced his investigation of the subject by perpetrating some huge sin in his proper person, and examining the condition of his higher instincts afterwards.

Nor is the delusion of a sociopolitical return to Eden a male temptation alone. The devout sex is prone to fall for it too, and the more, I believe, as people indulge the romantic delusion that women are especially virtuous. The principal female character in Hawthorne's novel goes under the pseudonym Zenobia, a queenly figure who is in love with Hollingsworth. The historical Zenobia was a queen of

Palmyra who declared her eastern empire to be independent of Rome. Her brief reign was apparently tolerant of religious differences and propitious for culture. Aurelian defeated her armies in A.D. 272, but her legend continued to inspire authors and historians, particularly in the nineteenth century, when Zenobia became an icon of intelligent and chaste feminism.

Hawthorne's Zenobia cuts that portrait on a slant. She is imperious, beautiful, intelligent, a staunch feminist, and a *woman*—from the hot-house flower she wears each day on her head to the shoes on her feet. Her presence at Blithedale makes what the denizens are doing seem to be an idyll, a May-day, an Arcadia. Yet she is compromised. Her trouble is not the *idée fixe* that concentrates the masculine and quasi-autistic mind. It is lack of discipline:

> I recognized no severe culture in Zenobia; her mind was full of weeds. It startled me, sometimes, in my state of moral and bodily faint-heartedness, to observe the hardihood of her philosophy. She made no scruple of oversetting all human institutions, and scattering them as with a breeze from her fan. A female reformer, in her attacks upon society, has an instinctive sense of where the life lies, and is inclined to aim directly at that spot. Especially the relation between the sexes is naturally among the earliest to attract her notice.

Hollingsworth wants to plant one tree and one tree alone. Zenobia wants, "with a breeze from her fan," to uproot everything, which means, particularly, to overturn the *modus vivendi* of men and women with one another. Not for her the patient and humbling work of clearing, harrowing, sowing, weeding, tending, and reaping, wresting a tolerable life from soil and rain and sun. She would have perfection, or her vision of it, and all with a gesture. Therefore, Zenobia is the one character in the novel who is quickest to wound other people, with a deliberate touch. And the work of Blithedale does not extend to the poor in the neighborhood. Most of the spare time is taken up with personal intrigues.

The novel ends for Zenobia in unrequited love and suicide. So much for Blithedale.

So much for every Blithedale that man can dream up. For the progressive's dream of Blithedale is not a march into the blissful future but an atavistic detour, a sour adult's longing to have childhood again without actually becoming a child. So we should not be surprised to find the progressive bound to a lie about the distant past. Friedrich Engels, the rich adulterer who financed the bad dreams of his friend Karl Marx, posited an idyllic past for mankind, the pre-agrarian matriarchies whereof feminists dream. Though we know that these never existed, feminists still hold fast to that version of the Fall, when men first sowed great fields and produced surplus food that could be stored indefinitely, and property was invented: property, the original sin. Alas, the reason that many aboriginal tribes were matrilineal was that women were the sexual playthings of men, so nobody could be entirely sure of paternity. As the historian Francis Parkman wrote about the American Indians more than a century ago, "By the rhapsodies of poets, the cant of sentimentalists, and the extravagance of some who should have known better, a counterfeit image has been tricked out, which might seek in vain for its likeness through every corner of the habitable earth." The Indian, says he, was a bundle of savage contradictions: "At one moment, he is wary and cautious to the verge of cowardice; at the next, he abandons himself to a very insanity of recklessness; and the habitual self-restraint which throws an impenetrable veil over emotion is joined to the unbridled passions of a madman or a beast."[2]

Perhaps Engels never got out of his European salons, but ethnologists have directly observed hundreds of human cultures with hardly any technological development and no settled ownership of land or goods. Contrary to feminist dreams, not one of those cultures has been anything but patriarchal—from the mild and peace-loving Navajos to the warlike Sioux. In the article "The Sun-Dance of the Sioux," for example, a late nineteenth-century witness describes how the medicine man cuts two holes in what little fatty flesh there is between a young man's nipples and collarbone, and inserts into them "a skewer of bone, about the size of a carpenter's pencil." This bone is attached to a rope fastened to the "sun-pole" around which the young men are arranged. Then, to the throb of drums and the wails of the people urging them on, they are to free themselves by straining against the rope, ripping the bone out of their flesh:

> The wonderful strength and extensibility of the human skin is most forcibly and fearfully displayed in the strong struggles of the quivering victims. I have seen these bloody pieces of bone stretched to such a length from the devotee that his outstretched arms in front of him would barely allow his fingers to touch them.
>
> I know it is not pleasant to dwell long upon this cruel spectacle. Generally in two or three hours the victim is free, but there are many cases where double and even triple that time is required.[3]

I will give the Sioux credit for something important: they understood that the boy must make that passage through the fierce rapids of puberty into manhood. We have forgotten it. We are simultaneously more domesticated than the Sioux and more negligent and foolish.

The progressive is strangely attracted to the primitive because he sees it as a secular way to go back, by one's own power, before the Fall. The Adamites of Bohemia, during the Enlightenment, worshiped in the nude as a sign of their having been blessed by God, by virtue of their faith, with a spanking-new innocence; the authorities were not amused. A childlike sweetness was attributed to the Pacific Islanders, which the amiable temperament of the native Hawaiians, depicted by the young sailor Richard Henry Dana in *Two Years Before the Mast*, seemed to confirm, but which was contradicted by the cannibalism of their cousins on the other islands and other habits that the Hawaiians, Dana noted with friendly skepticism, wanted to deny they ever indulged. Margaret Mead, the author of *Coming of Age in Samoa*, was duped into believing that she had discovered a sexual Eden, where adolescent lads and lasses naturally explored their emerging erotic interests through casual fornication followed by a smooth path into marriage. But then, Americans were willing to be duped, and so they bought into the evil primitivism of Alfred Kinsey, who hired pedophiles to masturbate baby boys to show that the serpent had always ruled in Eden, and that it was a good thing too.

In our time, the progressive young people who, ignoring the tragedies of Cuba and Venezuela, proudly reject "capitalism," which they cannot define, in favor of "socialism," which they also cannot define, are regressing to a land that never was and never can be. They have less in common with Emma Goldman, a hard-bitten socialist who opposed women's suffrage because she had no confidence in their voting the correct way, than with Peter Pan and Tinkerbell.

### Racism, Baby Style

The Golden Age is an allegory of Eden, and Eden recounts the fall of man, to which we are all subject. Jesus says that unless we become as little children, we shall not enter the kingdom of heaven. But we would have this transformation on the cheap. These days, one of the most vicious ways of pretending you can have it is to suppose that there were ever races that were pure and gentle until they were overwhelmed by the rapacity of people coming from Europe.

I am not saying that all cultures are the same. That is patent nonsense. I am not saying that the history of man has not been a saga of triumph and shame, of rare heroism and the more common venality, avarice, vindictiveness, and folly. I have been at pains to illustrate that saga and to insist that it continues in the same vein because *human nature has not changed*. Man is born a sinner and dies a sinner unless the grace of God transforms him into a saint, the very saint which the progressive denies or traduces or flees. I am not saying that Europeans treated the natives of the Western Hemisphere with any greater gentleness and justice than the natives would have treated them, had they been in their place. I am not denying that the study of other cultures is a good thing. I have spent my entire adult life studying other cultures.

I am denying the Enlightenment myths of the unspoiled savage and of secular moral advancement. We do not fall from Arcadia into Athens and Rome and London and Washington. We do not, in our essential humanity, rise from Arcadia into Washington. We make slow cultural progress in certain respects, and in the past century we have made quick progress in technology, but man is the same. If he advances in one virtue he lapses in another. There is *one stunning exception to this historical fact*—but I will reserve that to a later chapter.

Meanwhile, I cite here an author, friendly to the Indian tribes of North America, who cast a disapproving eye on the sorry treatment of the red man by the white. The Indian, wrote Edward Eggleston, cherished his freedom, yet lived under the yoke of "traditional custom and tyrannical public sentiment." Only rarely could the individual of strong will break loose from it. Freed by his hunting-and-gathering way of life, from tilling the soil and tending to large domesticated animals, the Indian enjoyed considerable free time. How did he dispose of it? Some excitement, wrote Eggleston, was necessary:

> The intervals between hunting and war-parties were filled up by an inconceivable number of ungraceful dances of various kinds, all regulated by a rather complicated etiquette, many mixed with superstition, and some ending in debauch. There were feasts of many sorts, at which those not invited might crowd the door-ways as spectators, or strip off the bark sides of the cabins to see the ceremonies; and there were athletic games, and games of hazard, with dice of bones or cherry-stones, in which the excited players would often

lose all their possessions, not sparing to wager their wives; the reckless gamester sometimes even staked his own liberty, and became a slave to the winner until his friends could redeem him. Sometimes the lucky arrival of prisoners in transit, who could be beaten as they ran the gauntlet, furnished diversion, and on grand occasions the savage could repair to the council-house as to a theater, to see the long-drawn torture of a captive—a sight as well suited to his taste as bull-fighting to a Spaniard's, or bear-baiting and cock-fighting to that of our English ancestors.[4]

Or, we might add, as brain-scrambling football and hormone-hopped martial artists of both sexes are suited to ours.

No doubt some reader will leap to accuse Eggleston of "racism," a cheap and cowardly charge in our time, associating the accused with centuries of chattel slavery in the Americas and the horrors perpetrated by the Nazi regime. American slavery was atavistic, not traditional, because Englishmen were not holding Scotsmen or even poor Irishmen for slaves, and so Southern theologians were led to posit for themselves a continuity reaching back behind the New Testament and its clear message of liberation all the way to the nomadic Abraham and his servants. And then the most startling and unapologetic defenders of slavery came to justify it by appealing to modern theories of evolution and the *biological* superiority of one race over another, theories unknown to the ancient pagans, the Jews, and Christians until that time. The Nazi regime was a grotesque mélange of progressivism and primitivism, with Jews cast as the great serpent in the garden.

We see now the same recipe, though not with the same pure wickedness, in the notion that "whiteness" is responsible for the evil in the world. If only we could get behind that whatever-it-is—sometimes it appears to be a race, sometimes a civilization, sometimes a culture, sometimes a set of social habits peculiar to people of our time—all would be well. It is the reverse of Booker T. Washington's rousing and courageous *Up from Slavery.* It is to chafe forever the still raw scars on *your grandfather's* wrists and ankles. It is likewise to toss away the pearl of great price, the faith that animated Washington and civil rights leaders such as Martin Luther King Jr., Ralph Abernathy, and Jackie Robinson, who achieved so much in such little time by rousing people out of the stupor of racism, pulling them out of its spiritual and political mud.

But Eggleston was no racist. He wrote of what was on record and what he had witnessed. What now brands you as a racist is a refusal to go along with "racism, baby-style." You decline to bow to the infantile dogma that you can find a race somewhere that shone forth in pristine innocence and splendor until it was soiled or destroyed by contact with whatever race you have decided to blame for all things wicked. In other words, you will be called a racist if you decline to participate in a racial revision of the Fall of Man. You will be called a racist if you believe that the most dreadful and deadly virus was not the smallpox that the Europeans unwittingly carried with them to the New World but the evil in the heart of man. That virus is everywhere.

I find that men who had most experience with cultures foreign to the West were least likely to fall for the notion that they held the secret we seek—the garden of delight, before civilization came to curdle everything. I think of men like Joseph Conrad and Herman Melville. Conrad's *Heart of Darkness* tells of the gradual moral corruption of a progressive, the enlightened Belgian Kurtz, who was going to bring bourgeois Christian morals and Western trade, not necessarily in that order, into the jungles of central Africa. Kurtz ends up as a kind of witch-doctor adored by the natives whom he has terrified and who have brought out the savage in him; and the narrator who returns to Europe can serve him only by preserving the illusion of his betrothed, that Kurtz died as a heroic man of faith and progress, whatever that latter word may mean. Melville, like Richard Henry Dana, sailed the high seas. The whale ship, he said, was his Harvard. He sweated and strained alongside men like his immortal Queequeg, tall and Herculean, sporting his incongruous top hat as he walked the alleys of New Bedford yet keeping close at hand his "kewpie," the wooden totem he worshiped.

Queequeg was a noble-hearted savage. Not so Melville's equally immortal Babo, the mastermind of the negro revolt in "Benito Cereno." Melville exercised as much patience with sentimentalists as he could muster, but the portrayal of that story's blandly good and progressively racist Captain Amasa Delano strained him to the utmost. Delano has boarded a Spanish ship clearly in distress on the western round of Cape Horn. To his sunny disposition, it appears that the blacks on board are orderly, though with a strange order. The captain, Cereno, assures him that all is well, but his faithful negro servant Babo sometimes answers for him, always keeping upon him a steady and affectionate eye. Particularly interesting is the moment when Babo calls Cereno for his throat's daily encounter with the razor. The American captain, a dupe of optimism, looks on the scene with the calm pleasure of a man who does not think carefully about good and evil:

> There is something in the Negro which, in a peculiar way, fits him for avocations about one's person. Most Negroes are natural valets and hairdressers, taking to the comb and brush congenially as to the castanets, and flourishing them with almost equal satisfaction. There is, too, a smooth tact about them in this employment, with a marvelous, noiseless, gliding briskness, not ungraceful in its way, singularly pleasing to behold, and still more so to be the manipulated subject of. And above all there is the great gift of good humor. Not the mere grin or laugh is here meant. Those were unsuitable. But a certain easy cheerfulness, harmonious in every glance and gesture, as God had set the whole Negro to some pleasant tune.

In actuality, evil is everywhere on the Spanish ship, a slave trader. The blacks, some of them not slaves for sale but "free" servants of the

Spanish, have risen in mutiny, led by the subtle and malevolent Babo.
The slightest word or sign on the part of the Spanish captain will be
his instant death. The figurehead of the ship is its original captain,
Cereno's friend, his skeleton nailed there by Babo. Nor were the black
women behindhand in taking pleasure from doing evil. So Cereno will
testify after being saved by the Americans: "Had the Negroes not
restrained them, they would have tortured to death, instead of simply
killing, the Spaniards slain by the Negro Babo; that the Negresses used
their utmost influence to have the deponent made away with; that, in
the various acts of murder, they sang songs and danced."

We should give people of other cultures this much credit at least:
they can be every bit as vicious as we are: "And God saw that the wickedness of man was great on the earth, and that every imagination of
the thoughts of his heart was only evil continually" (Genesis 6:5). To
pretend otherwise, again, is to engage in racism, baby-style.

### Shangri-La Syndrome

If we cannot recapture our lost innocence by moving to Samoa,
what shall we do? Where do we go?

Some people in our time say that the thing to do is to *be small*,
turning to "tiny houses," dwellings fitted out with a stove, a toilet, a
bunk for sleeping, and not much else; a home the size of a tree house.
Far be it from me to cast a cold eye upon living in a tree. I may live to
be eighty and still be a boy for whom that prospect still has its charm.
I think of Italo Calvino's young baron who, fed up with the brittle
habits of his aristocratic mother and father, decides one day to climb
up into the miles-long woods on the ancestral estate, where he spends
the rest of his life building shelters, scrambling from place to place,
reading literature and philosophy, falling in love, capturing bandits,
taking part in a revolution, and other such good things. Or the boy in
*My Side of the Mountain*, who spends a winter in the hills of upstate
New York living in the hollow of a tree, training a falcon to hunt for

him, catching and gathering his food, and getting called "Thoreau" by a professor who happens upon him there.

"Simplify, simplify," wrote the real Thoreau. "Our life is frittered away by detail.... Simplicity, simplicity, simplicity! I say, let your affairs be as two or three, and not a hundred or a thousand; instead of a million count half a dozen, and keep your accounts on your thumb-nail," wrote the man who lived on the lakeside and sent his laundry out to be done in town.[5] The advice is well taken, though. We "progress" into a mass of confusions, and then we may well find ourselves living more human lives if we can strip away the extraneous. Consider the madness of working to give a bad college education to your children so that they may acquire high-paying jobs to cancel out the debt for tuition and room and board and then send their own children to acquire an even sillier education, until bankruptcy or the end of the world, whichever shall come first.

Yet it is not improper, I think, to note that Thoreau was unmarried, the boy on the mountain was a boy, Calvino's *The Baron in the Trees* is a boyish satire, and if you live in a tree house or something smaller, there are many essentially human things you will never be able to do. Having a large family, for one, or welcoming many people to your home for a big celebration, or finding room for a library, or setting up a workshop, a pantry, a root cellar, or a sewing room for making things for you and your children. If we think about it, the tiny house is not so tiny, as its inhabitants depend upon all kinds of high-technology benefits for their existence and for their thriving, but they will have cut themselves off from the opportunity of *making*. It is, though an amiable and somewhat ambiguous relief to the environment, a sentimental retreat into childhood, or a refusal to leave childhood. It is as if you were returning to playing house. Some people now, I hear, make that retreat an olfactory matter also, curling up in cribs and relieving themselves into diapers. Hard to imagine them crossing a continent on foot or building a cathedral.

Or we may imagine a place of peace and plenty, far away—an escape.

That is what James Hilton did in his interbellum novel *Lost Horizon*. It tells of a climatically fortunate valley in the Tibetan plateau, almost inaccessible to the world, where mangoes and pomegranates grow alongside one another while ice-fed streams trickle from the walls of the enfolding cliffs, rising nearly to the height of Everest itself. In Shangri-La, the air is so pure and the way of life so simple and healthy that people live to an extreme old age, and since all that the body needs is easily procured, and there is neither the opportunity to acquire wealth nor anything to do with it if you did acquire it, people live in harmony with one another. A disillusioned English diplomat named Conway—a man with the heart and soul of an Oxford don, who ought to be construing Sanskrit verbs under the sweet colored light of a stained-glass library window—is hijacked along with three companions from the midst of war and rebellion in India to this unknown place for a purpose they do not know.

Their host, an elderly monk named Chang, reveals to them the secret of happiness in the valley below the lamasery:

> If I were to put it into a very few words, my dear sir, I would say that our prevalent belief is in moderation. We inculcate the virtue of avoiding excess of all kinds—even including, if you will pardon the paradox, excess of virtue itself. In the valley which you have seen, and in which there are several thousand inhabitants living under the control of our order, we have found that the principle makes for a considerable degree of happiness. We rule with moderate strictness, and in return we are satisfied with moderate obedience. And I think that I can claim that our people are moderately sober, moderately chaste, and moderately honest.[6]

Charming, and delivered in a kindly and witty understatement. We can almost believe that such a place might be possible, and that moderation, like the silken thread that Newman spoke of, might be able to restrain "those giants, the passion and the pride of man."

Children in Shangri-La come into the world in the ordinary way of nature, but they aren't present in Hilton's book. When Frank Capra made a film out of *Lost Horizon*, he added a strong love-interest for Conway, and in one scene we see the woman, played by Jane Wyatt—"Margaret Anderson" in the pleasant comedy of middle-class American family life, *Father Knows Best*—dismiss a big group of little boys and girls from their lessons and send them to the pond to play. They promptly take off all their clothes and happily waddle and plunge in. Capra thus gives us a breath of Eden, and we suspect that if his Conway were to stay in Shangri-La, he would certainly marry and have children of his own.

Marriage is not high on the list of James Hilton's concerns. Conway asks Chang about it, thinking that surely the sexual passion would give the inhabitants of Shangri-La the motive and the opportunity for strife, envy, treachery, and revenge. But it isn't so. The modestly chaste people are also modestly passionate—very modestly. If another man wants the woman you want, it's considered good form to let him have her. Good form—how English, how cultivated, how disinterestedly correct. Perhaps there's a little saltpeter in the water.

Conway, a bachelor with few close friends but a great success in his line of work, finds the pace of Shangri-La agreeable. A more "modern" fellow does not. One of the company, a brash and rather stupid young man named Mallinson wants to get back to the world of war and politics and real things like that. Mallinson complains that the lamas are "typically Oriental, you can't get them to do anything quickly and efficiently." Conway agrees, and yet thinks that the advantage is all to the Oriental: "It did not appear that the Eastern races were abnormally dilatory, but rather that Englishmen and Americans charged about the world in a state of continual and rather preposterous fever-heat." Conway dislikes the gigantism of record breaking, "progress," and doing a thing for the sake of doing it: "He was inclined to see vulgarity in the

Western ideal of superlatives." When he walks in silence among the
fantastic treasures of art that the lamas have managed to collect, he is
attracted most to the "world of incomparable refinements" that Chinese ceramics open quietly to the grateful observer. "His liking for
Chinese art," we hear, "was an affair of the mind; in a world of increasing noise and hugeness, he turned in private to gentle, precise, and
miniature things."

The lamas have an extensive library, hitherto unknown composi-
tions by Chopin, and such modern conveniences as porcelain bathtubs
from Akron, of all places. Hilton manages to explain it by means of a
*deus in machina*: the clefts in the mountains around the valley are thick
with gold. The lamas use the gold, which has no purpose in Shangri-La,
to trade with the outside world for books, old newspapers and magazines, works of art from both the West and the East, and such mechanical devices as would make life more comfortable in their lamasery
perched on the mountainside and down in the village below. Hilton
has taken a tip from Thomas More's *Utopia*, whose citizens use gold
for bedpans and toilets, instilling in their children and themselves a
contempt for it. Since the weather in Shangri-La is blessedly temperate,
and the people are governed by kindly masters, we have a kind of near-
Eden, and it is no small blessing to be in Shangri-La and *not to be in
London, New York, Peshawar, Chungking, Berlin*, or anywhere.

Conway eventually learns that he has specifically been chosen for
Shangri-La. The High Lama has been seeking a successor. Back in 1734,
a fifty-year-old Jesuit missionary named Perrault found himself in the
valley and began to preach the word of God. But he was impossibly far
from any contact with his superiors, and over the years he fell into an
easy way of living with the local Buddhism and Taoism, mingling with
it his own faith. The people revered him so much, and he governed
them in such a fatherly way, that he won their unshakable trust. He
was energetic at first, "a very earnest, busy, learned, simple, and enthu-
siastic person who, along with his priestly functions, did not disdain

to put on a mason's overall and help in the actual building" of the miraculous house itself. But he grew old, and calm, and he did not die, though he was ready for it. Instead he "had been granted a vision of some significance to take back with him into the world." For the sake of that vision he preserved his life with the help of a spare diet, the clean air, hours of peaceful contemplation, and "drug-taking and deep-breathing exercises," for he had become a proficient in yoga, too.

At the end of his first long interview with the High Lama, Conway suddenly perceives the truth: "*That you are still alive, Father Perrault.*"

Now, mere length of days is not the highest blessing that Shangri-La has to confer, but it is also not incidental. People in our world live longer than ever, yet their days are filled with jitters and noise, and they complain that they have no time. Time—that is what Conway will have, he sees, if he remains in Shangri-La: "He had Time, Time for everything that he wished to happen, such Time that desire itself was quenched in the certainty of fulfillment. A year, a decade hence, there would still be Time. The vision grew on him, and he was happy with it." We might call it leisure, the leisure of a life without worry about where your next meal will come from, or what you must do to satisfy your employer, or how your children will provide for themselves. Nor will you need to pump yourself up with energy for the next debauch, lest you experience in the very act the futility of it all. In a way it is just what Hilton says it is, the life of an ideal English don, translated to a hidden valley far removed from the miseries of the world. Or Thoreau on his pond: "Why should we live with such hurry and waste of life? We are determined to be starved before we are hungry. Men say that a stitch in time saves nine, and so they take a thousand stitches today to save nine tomorrow."[7]

Father Perrault has, without hurry, preserved his life for one aim, which he reveals to Conway. The world as it was when Hilton wrote, and the world that it would bring to birth in turn, was one of vulgarity and destruction:

There will be no safety by arms, no help from authority, no answer in science. It will rage till every flower of culture is trampled, and all human things are leveled in a vast chaos. Such was my vision when Napoleon was still a name unknown; and I see it now, more clearly with each hour.[8]

When Conway replies that the world seems to be lapsing into another Dark Age—he is thinking of the five hundred years between the fall of Rome in the West and the first flowering of the High Middle Ages—Perrault says that the darkness now will be worse, more complete. That is why he has been gathering great works of art and culture from East and West. He is preserving them for a better time. That will be Conway's intellectual and cultural calling:

I believe that you will live through the storm. And after, through the long age of desolation, you may still live, growing older and wiser and more patient. You will conserve the fragrance of our history and add to it the touch of your own mind. You will welcome the stranger, and teach him the rule of age and wisdom; and one of these strangers, it may be, will succeed you when you are yourself very old. Beyond that, my vision weakens, but I see, at a great distance, a new world stirring in the ruins, stirring clumsily but in hopefulness, seeking its lost and legendary treasures. And they will all be here, my son, hidden behind the mountains in the valley of the Blue Moon, preserved as by miracle for a new Renaissance.... [9]

I sympathize with Hilton, assuredly. My own teaching of literature, art, theology, philosophy, and history is in the Perrault line. I wish to preserve for a better day the love of the true and the good and the beautiful, and especially the knowledge of the great poets of our heritage. I am reminded of Ray Bradbury's *Fahrenheit 451*, a novel of a dystopian future, or of the very real dystopian *present*, wherein the great books and the good books of our heritage are unread because people have given their brains over to mass entertainment. In that novel, "firemen"—that is, men who set fires—burn whatever books they find smuggled away. They are called librarians and school super-intendents now. In Bradbury's imagination, a company of men and women known only to one another, otherwise outcast and despised by society, share books by committing them to memory, as much as each one can. They are modern monks without a monastery, living an ascetic life on the railway lines. They suffer for ungrateful mankind. Anyone in our time who reveres the works of Shakespeare, Homer, Dante, Milton, and Goethe will feel that sweet pang of brotherhood with those who remember and suffer.

What James Hilton wants is a monastery without monks, the good of prayer without prayer, contemplation without a God to contemplate, and, as Flannery O'Connor will put it in her uncompromising way, the Church of Christ Without Christ. It cannot be. A blandly warm affection for the good things of the past is no match for the modern progressive's ferocious drive to obliterate them or for the "evolutionary" social theories that prey upon man like monsters of the deep. The fawn is helpless against the tiger. When I enrolled as a freshman at Princeton in 1977, a sweet-tempered man named Fred Fox, an ordained minister with an office in Nassau Hall, was the official Keeper of Princetoniana. I do not think there was a more beloved man in the university, and yet his actual influence upon its life was nugatory. In a few short decades, after all, a school founded for the instruction of Presbyterian pastors, with a test in Latin as its entrance examination, had gone thoroughly secular and had abandoned its classical curriculum entirely. What was left of Princeton tradition? Many good little things indeed, but the soul—the soul was smothered.

So also at almost every college and university in the world. There is no soul. A few secular places remain committed to the learning that moved Hilton and his alter ego, Conway. That is like saying that a few

portions of a levee are still standing. The flood is victorious nonetheless. Half a dike is not better than none. Or half a pound of arsenic is
as bad as one pound; choose your analogy.

What the world needs is not a dream land like Shangri-La, lost in
a declivity of the most forbidding land on earth. The world needs *the
way*. Conway is without a home, and he never will have one unless he
takes up the cross and goes in the way that he does somehow sense is
the right way. Otherwise, Hilton never would have made his High
Lama a Jesuit priest.

Meanwhile, where are the children?

### Precocity in Evil

If you cannot recapture your lost innocence, and you have no
desire to take to heart the words of Jesus that you should become as
little children, then you can do the next best thing. You can infect
children with your confusion and evil. You can make them precocious
and hug yourself for being a "progressive" educator.

My readers can doubtless come up with plenty of examples: using
the pubic schools—I mean *public*—to instruct children in the glories
of septic erotic activity, confusing them about their sex, and encourag-
ing them to take detours in the swamps of the unnatural. The mental-
ity is like that of a vile old man who stashes dirty magazines in his
shack and entices boys to come inside and learn things, except that
schools can corrupt hundreds of children at once. If you find out about
the old man, the cops will be at his door in a heartbeat. Likewise, if you
find out about the school and show up to complain, the cops will be
there in a heartbeat—to escort you out. What could be fairer than that?

Those who wish to protect the innocence of childhood and those
who wish to make children owlishly precocious about sex have in mind
different destinations for the child. The ordinary parent wants the child
to grow up clean and sane, marry well, and have children in turn. The
ordinary Christian parent sees the future marriage as a vocation along

the way to the final calling, the beatitude of seeing God face to face. That is an expansive vision of the child's life, and it places him in a line of families reaching back in history and extending far into the future. For the Christian, the story extends from the first moment of creation to the consummation of all things at the end of time. When you have *that* view of the road, you are more likely to be patient and to wait for the slow maturation of the child. Puberty, legal majority, adulthood, and the acquiring of a good job are all stages on the way; they are neither the way itself nor the destination. If you are traveling from earth to heaven, Newark does not seem that impressive.

But they who instill precocity have no such patience. They insist they want the children to be mature, but that is not really so. They want them to be forced, like hothouse plants. Early precocity does not put a child farther along the way than his fellows. It is a *detour.* The child who is "like" an adult in ways that are unpleasant and not natural will grow up perpetually childish, clinging to the childhood he never experienced in the ordinary fashion. It is a grotesque sight: eight-year-old children who know more about sexual deviants than did my mother when she was twenty, and thirty-year-old children who lounge about in onesie pajamas, call their dogs their "children," turn the workplace into a slumber party, and copulate with fleshy robots.

*These progressives go nowhere.*

I will hear that childhood is an invention of the Victorians—Dickens is usually fingered as the perpetrator—and that in teaching children about sex, we are returning to the norm for the human race. Again, that strange conjunction between "progress" and a supposedly pure primitive state—think of Rousseau and his antisocial "sentimental" education in *Emile*—and at the same time the conjunction between "progress" and a frank acknowledgment that nothing was ever very good at all. We might as well cast aside any real progress we have made in ensuring that childhood is protected from the vices and interests of adults.

Let us look at the matter more carefully. Charles Dickens was no orthodox Christian in his theology, which was muddled, as we might expect from someone who wrote to keep food on his table and never had anything like a classical education. Yet he never took two steps without the gospels in mind, and the climactic scene of *A Christmas Carol*, when Ebenezer Scrooge is most powerfully convicted of his evil life, is wholly staged by children. Tiny Tim's crutch and braces are preserved lovingly in a corner. Peter Cratchit is reading to his younger siblings: "And he took a small child and set him in their midst."

That was no sentimentality on the part of Jesus, and to understand it aright involves us in no sentimentality, either. Not all of Dickens's children are saintly and self-sacrificing, like Nelly Trent in *The Old Curiosity Shop*. Some have the innocence of ignorance, like Pip in *Great Expectations*, or have already bred the serpents of selfishness in their hearts, like Charlie Hexam in *Our Mutual Friend* and young Tom Gradgrind in *Hard Times*. Dickens is rather hard on impecunious young men, like the eponymous Martin Chuzzlewit and *Bleak House*'s Richard Carstone, and it is a good woman who redeems them, if they can be redeemed at all, from their blindness or madness. Nelly's brother, Fred, is not redeemed. It was not nostalgia that led Dickens to look upon boyhood with delight, as the elder David Copperfield looks upon his time with his mother, Clara, and the matronly Peggotty, before the stepfather Murdstone came into the picture. Young David's childhood is not idyllic, as Dickens's own was not. It is fatherless and shadowed by the threat of poverty. Clara is called a mere child and treated as such by both the evil Murdstone and the blustery Aunt Betsy Trotwood, and her failure to grow out of childhood into the full measure of responsible womanhood is partly responsible for David's miseries after she dies.

Dickens is hard on adults who will not let children be children, creating a regular rogue's gallery of men and women, respectable and disreputable, ranging from those who are pleasant to speak with and those who are perfectly nasty. We have Fagin the viper, who picks boys off the streets and trains them in thievery, till it behooves him to betray one of them to the police to be hanged. We have the scatterbrained feminist do-gooder Mrs. Jellyby, who spends her days raising subscriptions to evangelize the natives of Borioboola-Gha (with shares in a coffee trade tossed in for sweetener), while leaving her household in appalling neglect. We have Gaffer Hexam, a naturally decent man in an indecent profession, who has his daughter Lizzie row his skiff as he trawls the Thames for salvage and dead bodies. And we have maybe his worst villain of all, Harold Skimpole, a man who calls himself "a child," who laughs at his financial ignorance and saves nothing, works at nothing, sponges off his friend, consigns his daughters to the edge of penury, and for a small bribe betrays a dangerously ill street-sweeper boy into the hands of the police. The boy dies. Nor will Skimpole learn from his sin.

## The Strength of the Child

The last thing Dickens wanted was to retreat into the idyll of childhood, for his own was troubled; he saw instead that we must progress *into the blessedness of spiritual childhood*, and in this progress, it helps to enjoy the love and examples of good and innocent children. If that is to be condemned as sentimental, then plenty of other authors must fall under the same ban, and one of those is named Shakespeare.

Shakespeare's plays, unlike those of most of his contemporaries, are filled with children. Their welfare is sometimes a sign of the spiritual health or malaise of their elders. Other times they become the *means* of spiritual regeneration. "O a cherubim / Thou wast that did preserve me!" cries Prospero in *The Tempest* when his daughter, Miranda, but a toddler when she and her father were treacherously placed upon a leaky boat to founder at sea, says she must have been a trouble to him:

> Thou didst smile,
> Infused with a fortitude from heaven,
> When I have decked the sea with drops full salt,
> Under my burden groaned; which raised in me

An undergoing stomach, to bear up
Against what should ensue. (I.ii. 153–58)

When Miranda asks how they managed to come ashore, Prospero replies, "By providence divine." It is the same providence that gave him help whence he least expected it, the help of his own child. Feminists rant about the unfairness of Prospero's tender care for Miranda's chastity, but that chastity is inseparable from her spiritual power. She is wondrous because she is innocent, and in her innocence, she possesses a fervor of love that lust-raddled men and women cannot know. The entire play moves toward a moment of consummate dramatic irony and theological wonder, when the guilty king Alonso—guilty, morally and by intent, of murdering Prospero and the girl—falls to his knees before her and begs forgiveness.

Again, we are not talking about sentimentality. We are not even talking about the natural affection that people have for small children who bring the breath of morning again to people whose childhood is long past. It is something stranger and more powerful than that. King Alonso, in his guilty mind, had come near to committing the unforgivable sin, the sin at the heart of all materialism, the denial of hope:

O it is monstrous, monstrous!
Methought the billows spoke and told me of it;
The winds did sing it to me; and the thunder,
That deep and dreadful organ pipe, pronounced
The name of Prosper; it did bass my trespass.
Therefore my son in th'ooze is bedded; and
I'll seek him deeper than e'er plummet sounded
And with him there lie mudded. (III.iii. 95–102)

Optimism is a slick, young, confident man. Shrewd planning is older and more crabbed. Alonso needs neither. He needs hope: he needs the child. Let us turn again to Charles Péguy:

Because my three virtues, says God.
The three virtues, my creatures.
My daughters, my children.
Are themselves like my other creatures.
Of the race of men.
Faith is a loyal Wife.
Charity is a Mother.
An ardent mother, noble-hearted.
Or an older sister who is like a mother.
Hope is a little girl, nothing at all.
Who came into the world on Christmas day just this past
   year.
Who is still playing with her snowman.
With her German fir trees painted with frost.
And with her ox and her ass made of German wood.
   Painted.
And with her manger stuffed with straw that the animals
   don't eat.
Because they're made of wood.
And yet it's this little girl who will endure worlds.
This little girl, nothing at all.
She alone, carrying the others, who will cross worlds past.[10]

Miranda cannot be the salvation of the sinner King Alonso and the one who reconciles Alonso's Naples with Prospero's Milan by pretending to know all about Italian politics and mingling sexual precocity with ambition. The world has enough of that and to spare. The child-virtue of Hope that Péguy describes is so not by calculation but by innocence and an orientation toward the world that is simple and receptive: "Happy, happy is he who puts off till tomorrow," he has God say in his poem. Rather than put our children to work, attempting to achieve something *by means of children*, Péguy says that it is only for children that man works at all. This is not just to feed them but to educate them. The children enjoy a priority. In them the father sees himself and his purpose most truly: "He thinks tenderly of the time when people will scarcely ever think of him except because of his children." The best of the pagans had some glimpse of this hope. So in the *Iliad*, Hector dandles his baby son in his arms and says with a glow of hope and happiness that someday people will say that Hector was a good man, but the son of Hector was better. The baby is fated to die, thrown from the ramparts by the Greeks when they finally put the city of Troy to the torch. But Hector's feeling is just.

### Child to Queen's Bishop Four

I conclude with a consideration of the *use of children* to bring about the Promised Land.

Saint Paul said, "When I was a child, I spake as a child, I understood as a child, I thought as a child: but when I became a man, I put away childish things" (1 Corinthians 13:11). I have discussed what Jesus said about becoming as little children, and the beloved disciple John echoes the Lord when he addresses his flock: "And now, little children, abide in him; that, when he shall appear, we may have confidence, and not be ashamed before him at his coming" (1 John 2:28). The Christian saints have always understood these adjurations to be in harmony with one another, just as Jesus, who "increased in wisdom and stature, and in favor with God and man" (Luke 2:52), did not remain a mere child, but grew into the fullness of manhood, meaning that he was ever more and more about the business of his Father. Thus we see in the greatest saints also, by the grace of God, a frolic childlikeness, the opposite of its evil secular parodies, old people who cannot give up their costly toys and young people who thumb the pages of a wickedness they cannot yet perform.

Now suppose you are moved, again, not by nostalgia, the ache to return home, but by a secular vision of a home such as never was and, on this side of the grave, never shall be. Dickens could shame the

Englishmen of his day to look at what their public policies were doing to children and families, but that was so that children should be free to grow naturally as children, and not so that there should be a new Children's Crusade. That sort of thing he abominated. It shows up in his novels in various forms, always associated with compulsion.

Its masculine form is embodied in Thomas Gradgrind, the schoolmaster at Coketown in *Hard Times*. "Facts, facts, facts!" he cries, as the principle of his educational manifesto. The children are to learn facts and nothing but facts; no works of the imagination allowed. The form of this reductive education is still with us, in political drag. We have not shaken off the utilitarian bigotry embodied in Mr. Gradgrind. We still believe that there is no point in reading good books for the sake of reading good books; we prostrate ourselves before the solely serious disciplines of Science, Technology, Engineering, and Mathematics, even though we're actually not very good at teaching the STEM subjects to our children. We don't have square-headed schoolmasters rapping out threats against Girl Number Twenty, who, although she has lived among horses all her life, cannot give a zoological *definition* of the horse as a graminivorous quadruped. We have what is in some ways worse. Employing the engine of compulsory and universal education, we have turned the school into a factory for the production and propagation of political opinion, uniform and relentless. If you cannot persuade the parents, you can stamp the children, as you would stamp molten wax with the same seal, hundreds at a time.

That is the "genius" of Aldous Huxley's *Brave New World*. The children are exposed to jingles and doggerel all their lives, from the incubator to the toddler-barracks to the school. These jingles break down their innocence, make them sexually precocious, and have them "think" according to the directives of the masters of the herd. The children are thus trained to make predictable responses and to be content with material well-being and mindless hedonism. Great books, books that have stood the test of time and that rise above any particular politics, books that tease the sluggish soul into thought, are forbidden. (It would be interesting to compare, for quality and provenance, the holdings of your local public library today with those of 1930, when Huxley was writing.) The genuine sexual nature of male and female, coming together to beget children, is treated as filthy and disgusting, while sex-play for kiddies is more than encouraged. If you shy away from it, if your temperament inclines you to a natural and blessed reserve, you must be re-educated, as is the little boy in the novel who doesn't want to "play" with the little girl, much to her vindictive chagrin.

Then we have the feminine form, the promotion of children for Social Improvement. Dickens, as always, is instructive. In *Bleak House*, we find the formidable virago-mother Mrs. Pardiggle, the type of evangelical woman on a mission. She sallies forth on preaching and charity ventures to the poor, giving them neither comfort nor hope, while dragging her five sons along as exemplars of virtue. They are meant to be young foot-soldiers in the battle, but Dickens shows us that they would all quickly turn traitor if given half a chance. Their names are advertised in the subscription list that Mrs. Pardiggle's charitable industry sends out for loosening people from their money. "Egbert, my eldest (twelve)," she says, in her righteous womanish pride, "is the boy who sent out his pocket-money, to the amount of five-and-threepence, to the Tockahoopo Indians. Oswald, my second (ten-and-a-half), is the child who contributed two-and-ninepence to the Great National Smithers Testimonial," and so on to the youngest, a child of five, who "has voluntarily enrolled himself in the Infant Bonds of Joy, and is pledged never, through life, to use tobacco in any form."

The wise and benevolent Esther Summerson, through whose eyes we see the Pardiggle family, remarks to herself and to us that the boys, "weazen and shrivelled," "looked absolutely ferocious with discontent." When their mother blithely mentions their voluntary contributions, their faces darken "in a peculiarly vindictive manner," except for "the little recruit into the Infant Bonds of Joy, who was stolidly and evenly miserable." It is not just that Mrs. Pardiggle levies their shillings for the benefit of the Tockahoopo Indians, or, more precisely, for the professional charity-mongers who take their copious shares before the Tockahoopoes get anything, because laborers in the harvest and parasites have to eat too. It is that she turns her motherhood into a political engine, with children for fuel. They are with her constantly. "I am a School lady, I am a Visiting lady, I am a Reading lady, I am a Distributing lady; I am in the local Linen Box Committee, and many general Committees; and my canvassing alone," says she, "is very extensive—perhaps no one's more so."

"Of all tyrannies," writes C. S. Lewis,

> a tyranny sincerely exercised for the good of its victims may be the most oppressive. It would be better to live under robber barons than under omnipotent moral busybodies. The robber baron's cruelty may sometimes sleep, his cupidity may at some point be satiated; but those who torment us for our own good will torment us without end for they do so with the approval of their own conscience.[11]

If I may adjust his observation: once childhood has been enlisted in the armies of politics, any freedom for the household must soon die, and with the bland approval of people who want only the best. Either the children will be made into *agents provocateurs*, spying on their parents and bearing the implicit threat of wicked benevolence descending from the unaccountable and unelected Protectors of Children from on high, or their welfare, real or supposed, will be used as a warrant to destroy, in principle, the authority of parents and the sanctity and independence of the home.

Servility in the name of progress. Frances E. Willard, a leader in the Women's Christian Temperance Union, provides another example of the fervid rhetoric and vague thinking that characterized the politicization of home life in the nineteenth century. It comes from her letter to the editors of *The Century Magazine* in 1883. Miss Willard declares with a boldness by no means temperate that her union's activities have "been from the individual to the home, thence to society, and finally to the Government itself,"[12] without any sense of boundaries or of legitimate restraints upon the power of the national government, as if congressmen should decide when your children should come in for dinner. Already in the air was a call for a *constitutional* measure to deal with a problem essentially local and personal, and the editors of *The Century*, generally friendly to Christian progressives of the time, warn in the same issue that it is the business of legislatures, not the constitution, to enact laws for the common good, and that "anything further destroys its character as a constitution," for "making the constitution a statute-book is to mar its character and to confound things that differ." Their foresight does not extend so far as to guess that Americans would cede to the courts an authority to legislate by divining in state constitutions and the national constitution provisions for statutory law that the people's representatives had never approved. But they do sense the danger. "If a law against the sale of ardent spirits," asks the editor, thinking of a *constitutional measure*, "why not a law against an equal evil, the prostitution of women? Why not a law against gambling, which slays its thousands annually?"[13]

Against all such reservations the ecstatic benevolence of Miss Willard is proof. Her words:

> The W. C. T. U. stands as the exponent, not alone of that return to physical sanity which will follow the downfall of the drink habit, but also of the reign of a religion of the body, which shall correlate with Christ's wholesome, practical, yet blessedly spiritual religion of the soul. "The kingdom of Heaven is within you," shall have a new significance to the clear-eyed, steady-limbed Christians of the future, from whose brain, blood, and brawn the taint of alcohol and nicotine has been eliminated by ages of pure habits and noble heredity. "The body is the temple of the Holy Ghost"

will not then seem so mystical a statement, nor one indicative of a temple so insalubrious as now. "He that destroyeth this temple, him shall God destroy" will be seen to involve no element of vengeance, but to be, instead, the declaration of such boundless love and pity for our race as would not suffer its deterioration to reach the point of absolute failure and irremediable loss. The women of this land have never had such training as our "Topical Studies" furnish, in the laws by which childhood shall set out upon its endless journey with a priceless heritage of powers laid up in store by the tender, sacred foresight of those by whom the young's immortal being was evoked.[14]

A new age, you see; the evolution of mankind to a new and glorious height; children inheriting in their blood the pure habits of their parents; all led by the wise and indefatigable women of the nation, attending lectures and reading studies on health. And, I may say, an age *mechanically produced* by extrinsic legislative action upon the body politic. Suffer the children, rally, carry signs, demand action, pass laws from on high, and sin itself shall be no more.

Folly it was, that bore fruit in the Volstead Act, the proliferation of organized crime, federal police forces to fight the crime, repeal of the Act but not the dismantling of the police forces. And let us not discuss the sallow complexions and sloped shoulders of our ever-indoors children and the sad and lonely habits of depravity to which they have been exposed. Indoors, but not home; far along in decadence, and not taking one step along the journey.

# CHAPTER SIX

## *More Than Small Change*

I n the first volume of his autobiography, *The Infernal Grove*, Malcolm Muggeridge, a conservative and truth-telling man of the Left, recalls his thoughts in 1943 when the Soviet Union broke with Hitler and joined the Allies against Germany. The Left had long been justifying the communist alliance with Hitler as wise, needful, and certainly aimed at the right enemy, the soulless and materialist West. He wondered whether there would be cries of betrayal in the rooms of the *Daily Worker.* He wondered how the Webbs, those bland socialists Sidney and Beatrice, would brave it out. He learned right away that he needn't have wondered. Their adoption of the new Soviet position was as quick and as automatic as if someone had turned a switch. They changed their tune, but in reality, they had not changed at all.

When Catholics pray the Office at Compline, they repeat the words of the psalmist, *Converte nos, Deus, salutaris noster, et averte iram tuam a nobis,* entreating the God of our salvation to turn us about and to turn away from us his wrath. Notice that the prayer is for change, a change that we confess ourselves powerless to bring about on our own. It must be done by God as a gift: He must turn us about, "convert" us, *change* us.

And now it is time to revisit the poem with which I began a previous chapter. The goddess Mutability, a daughter of the Titans dispos-
sessed by Zeus, claims preeminence among the gods and would cast
Jupiter from his throne. What the poet Spenser has in mind is nothing
less than the meaning of change and the governance of the entire
universe, or the lack of any governing power at all. When Mutability
meets Jupiter among the assembled Olympians, she rebuffs both his
threats and his promises of mercy, appealing instead to a deity above
him, the "great God of Nature"—and Jove must submit.

So we find every representative of the natural world—all the
streams, the animals, mankind, and the gods, great and small—assembled for the great trial on a pretty hill in Ireland, waiting for the appearance of Nature, who combines in herself both male and female. She
arrives veiled because her countenance is too brilliant for mortal eyes
to bear, writes Spenser, comparing it to the face of the transfigured
Christ upon Mount Tabor, so dazzling that the apostles "quite their
wits forgot." We are in the presence of a transcendent and everlasting
truth and beauty, and that should alert us that Mutability cannot win
her case.

And yet—when we look about us, what do we see but change? That
is what Mutability alleges in her prosecution of the case, which is
remarkably and perhaps unhelpfully well-ordered. She brings before
us the day and night, the hours, the four seasons, and the twelve
months in progression, each month with its proper work, its zodiacal
sign, and the climate we expect. In other words, it is a progression
properly speaking. A principle is at work beyond the change and within
the change. This is especially evident in Spenser's presentation of what,
to a modern reader, is the final month of the year:

> And after him, came next the chill December:
> Yet he through merry feasting which he made,
> And great bonfires, did not the cold remember;
> His Savior's birth his mind so much did glad:

Upon a shaggy-bearded Goat he rade,
The same wherewith *Dan Jove* in tender years,
They say, was nourished by th'*Idaean* maid;
And in his hand a broad deep bowl he bears,
Of which, he freely drinks an health to all his peers.[1]

That reference to the birth of the Savior is by no means casual. It is central to the whole design, though Mutability herself seems not to be aware of it. That is because her series of months begins not with January but with March. Why March? Christians had the tradition of beginning the year with March, because in March the one genuinely *new* thing in the history of the world happened—the Incarnation of Christ, when Mary said to the angelic messenger, "Behold the handmaid of the Lord; be it unto me according to thy word" (Luke 1:38). At that moment, "the Word was made flesh, and dwelt among us" (John 1:14), to be born nine months later in the stable at Bethlehem. The tradition had sprung, by the way, from the ancient pious belief that the day of a martyr's leaving the world would coincide with the day of his entry into it, and since March 25 was thought to be the date of Christ's death on the Cross (see Augustine, *City of God*, 18.54), on the same date was the Word made flesh, and December 25 would mark his Nativity.

So Mutability's presentation is more powerful than is helpful to her case. It is not simply that things change, but that they have changed regularly and unceasingly and not chaotically, *and* that the history of man is set in the context of an event that transforms it utterly. Both considerations are evident when Nature gives her verdict. All the creatures of the physical world, and the planetary deities themselves, wait with hushed breath to hear what she will say. She does not deny change, nor does she say that mutability applies only to these physical creatures and not to those. Instead she appeals to a principle *beyond change*, which makes sense of change, giving it a stable foundation to act upon, and which directs that change:

I well consider all that ye have said,
And find that all things steadfastness do hate
And changed be; yet being rightly weighed,
They are not changed from their first estate,
But by their change their beings do dilate,
And turning to themselves at length again
Do work their own perfection so by fate:
So over them change doth not rule and reign,
But they reign over change, and do their states maintain.
Cease, therefore, daughter, further to aspire,
But thee content thus to be ruled by me,
For thy decay thou seekst by thy desire;
But time shall come when all shall changed be,
And from thenceforth none no more change shall see.[2]

Nature calls Mutability her "daughter," implying both affection and hierarchical order. Let us not miss the critical points, as these will instruct us about what is and what is not implied by the journey we are on. Change makes sense only in the context of a perduring reality. If you look at the random scattering of points across a television screen tuned to no channel, or if you listen to the skitters of electrical noise on a radio also tuned to nothing, what you observe may be considered as utter change that yields no change at all. One screen tuned to nothing looks like another; one swish of static sounds like another. If there is no underlying reality, a *state*, something *established*, we have no subject for the change, and no way to make sense of any event, if any event may be said to occur at all. For change to exist, there must be *things that change*, and the things, insofar as they are things, are both in change and not in change. They are in, we might say, a constant change, a standing state of change. That is, as Augustine says, the very essence of what it means to be a creature and not the Creator. This is why Nature advises Mutability that she seeks her own decay by her desire. Unless things rule *over change*, *and do their states maintain*, Nature implies, there is no sense to change at all. There is no Mutability.

The second point derives from Christian revelation. Spenser implies it when he compares Nature's glory to that of the transfigured Christ. The Christian does not fear change: but we need to be clear about what change we are talking about. The Christian looks forward to that time that Nature alludes to, "when all shall changed be, / And from thenceforth none no more change shall see." That is both the consummation of change and its transformation into the eternal. So a Christian conservative does not merely affirm the goodness of old forms as against the innovators. He has another view of change altogether: the change that preserves the identity of what is changed and that transforms what is changed into what does not change, in the ever ancient and ever new life of God Himself. "Late have I loved thee," cries Augustine in his *Confessions*, "O beauty so ancient and so new!" (10.27). Why should we waste our time in a spiritual sloth, or material frenzy indistinguishable from sloth, pretending that things that vanish can ever satisfy the human heart? We therefore oppose change that destroys the identity of the subject and that diverts us from the final—the consummating—change to be brought about by God. We oppose change that denies the *pilgrim*, the pilgrimage, and the end. In one sense, we want one kind of change rather than another; in another sense, we want *a more radical change than the progressives can bring about or imagine.*

## Organic Change

First for those changes within time that are natural and genuinely progressive: they advance us along the way we have been traveling and do not destroy us and the enduring realities we love.

In *An Essay on the Development of Christian Doctrine*, Cardinal Newman lays out seven "notes" that indicate that a custom or a belief is a legitimate development of its predecessors and not a corruption.[3]

These criteria are all based on organic and logical unity. To illustrate their general principle, I quote Dr. Horatio Storer, the father of embryology in the United States and the man responsible for many of my readers' being alive now. For the young Dr. Storer, in his embryological investigations, determined that there was an obvious biological continuity between the fertilized ovum and the child, and that at no stage in its development was it anything other than human, alive, and self-organizing. As a matter of biology, it was neither an emergent part of the mother nor a thing that might be resolved back into her. But what about its *humanity*? Storer states what would be obvious enough if sexual intercourse were not so pleasurable and if taking care of the naturally resulting child were not so inconvenient:

> We need not....consider that the movements of the fœtus in utero, and its consequent attitude and position, are signs of an already developed and decided sentience and will, nor is it requisite to suppose them the effect of an almost rational instinct. But that they are wholly independent of the will and the conscience of the mother, and yet, by no means characteristic of organic life, whether hers or its own,— which latter is also by abundant evidence proved independently to exist,—but decidedly animal in their character; that they are not explainable by gravity, despite all the arguments alleged,...nor on any other supposition save that of a special and independent excito-motory system, distinct from that of the mother, brings us directly down to this—the existence of as distinct and independent a nervous centre, self-existing, self-acting, living.
>
> We set aside all the speculations of metaphysicians regarding moral accountability of the fœtus, the "potential man," and its "inanimate vitalities," as useless as they are bewildering. If there be life, then also the existence, however

undeveloped, of an intellectual, moral, and spiritual nature,
the inalienable attribute of humanity, is implied.[4]

Storer does not say that the fetus, even when moving in the womb, exhibits already the function of "sentience and will," nor is he under any illusion about its incipient form. But it is already *animate*, not an accretion of inanimate matter, like an encrustation of coral; it has life, specifically a human life, and therefore it possesses already, "however undeveloped," that "intellectual, moral, and spiritual nature, the inalienable attribute of humanity." It is already that kind of being which, in its gradual and, if given sufficient nutrition and shelter, inevitable development, thinks, chooses, aspires, and adores.

Development, properly speaking, thus unfolds—that is what the word *development* means—powers and potentialities that exist already. Thus the mature tree unfolds and flourishes from the seedling and the sapling; the horse from the foal; the bird from the hatchling in the nest. So it is, says Newman, that development of doctrine, far from being corruption or revolution, displays these characteristics.

First, it preserves the type: "Young birds do not grow into fishes, nor does the child degenerate into the brute, wild or domestic, of which he is by inheritance lord."[5] Such natural change in human institutions can assume a wide variety of appearances while preserving the essence of the thing; but not all changes do preserve the essence. When Pepin the Short, mayor of the palace during the reign of the last feeble Merovingian king, assumed the rule of the kingdom, regardless of whether his action was wise or pious or ambitious, it was "no faithful development of the office he filled, as originally intended and established."[6] A Supreme Court that arrogates to itself the adjudication of cultural questions, for whose discussion and discernment we call for the slow ferment of moral thought, wide experience from men and women of all walks of life, and patient reference to that depository of human wisdom we find in the past, is no longer a court but a super-legislature. It treats not of laws proper, whereof we might expect lawyers to know a great deal, but of moral ideals and pragmatic measures for securing the common good, wherein such lawyers can claim no more wisdom than can any of their subjects (or abjects). That is not development but supplantation. The seedling has not grown into a tree. The tree has been cut down, its stump ground out, and a stone pillar put in its place.

Second, true development preserves a continuity of principles. So the mechanism of voting, central to the establishment of the United States, and naming as voters individual men without regard to their wisdom or their state in life, must inevitably result in universal suffrage. Whether the latter is a good or a bad thing is not the point. Rather it was implied in the beginning, not by the intentions of the Founders or the laws they adopted, but by the principles underlying the laws. When the principles are abandoned, we are dealing not with development but with corruption or death. "Thus the Roman poets," writes Newman, "considered their State in course of ruin because its *prisci mores* and *pietas* were failing."[7] If we consider that the Western world is not a mass of legalisms but a civilization whose moral foundation is Christian, the betrayal of those principles would be ruinous to the civilization as such. To preserve the metaphor of the journey: it would be as if we had veered from the road we were on, with what intention or what end other than some airy utopia no one has seen fit to delineate; or sat down in the middle of the road, or begun to wander without aim, playthings of fortune and chance. This second criterion of the continuity of principles is closely related to Newman's fourth, which is that true development is a playing out of a logical sequence.

Third, the power of assimilation. A living thing takes in nutriments and assimilates them to itself. A living tradition encounters new ideas and new illuminations of truth and grows by them. It becomes more, not less, of what in potential it was before, so long as the new thing is not poisonous to it. "An eclectic, conservative, assimilating, healing, moulding process, a unitive power," writes Newman, "is of the essence, and a third test, of a faithful development."[8]

This third test is related to the fifth and sixth: anticipation of the future and "conservative action" upon the past. With true development we often see, here and there or in embryo, what may come to full fruition far in the future, while at the same time we see, far in the future, the preserved truths and insights of the past: "it is an addition which illustrates, not obscures, corroborates, not corrects, the body of thought from which it proceeds; and this is its characteristic as contrasted with a corruption."[9] When the Pharisees tried to commit Jesus to one of the common positions regarding divorce, Jesus hearkened back behind them to the first principles, saying that although Moses conceded certain measures for divorce because of the hardness of their hearts, "from the beginning it was not so." And Jesus repeated the words of Scripture, that God made them male and female, and for this reason a man was to leave his mother and father and cleave unto his wife, "and they twain shall be one flesh" (Matthew 19:1–9). It is impossible, then, to derive from Jesus' words any position regarding marriage that would deny that intention from the beginning, that God made them male and female. All true developments must "illustrate, not obscure" that original intent, corroborating it, revealing to us ever more clearly and beautifully what it is to be male, what it is to be female, and how the one is by creation itself oriented toward the other in marriage.

Newman's seventh note is also both conservative and forward-marching: "chronic vigour."[10] Mortal diseases often run their course rapidly. The feminism of Christian churches that have ordained women, if we may indulge a medical metaphor, may have been the result of a fatal error already in operation, but if anything, the innovation has accelerated the action of the error, so that now not one of those churches is thriving. We find them exhibiting signs of approaching death not only in the matter of the sexes but in the very worship of the God of the Scriptures himself. Just so, a cancer that begins in the liver may spread to the brain, or a disease of the blood may burden the lungs and fill them with fluid.

Sometimes a principle of health and a principle of destruction oper-
ate in the same body at the same time, and what happens depends upon
which one dominates and overcomes the other. In such cases, we can
look back upon the past and think we see inevitability, but that is an
illusion caused by our failure to imagine a comparable sense of inevitability had the other principle come to dominate. Sixty years ago, in
the American family, the well-developed principle of Christian patri-
archy, which had brought about the ideal of the gentleman father in
control of his sexual passions, loyal to his wife and children and a reliable contributor to church and town, was in combat with the irreconcil-
able principle of individualism, of "freedom" as permission, lack of
restraint, and the drive toward achieving what you want because you
want it. The latter *must have* gained considerable force from feminism
and the sexual revolution, which it nourished in turn, so that now even
soi-disant conservatives can hardly conceive of liberty defined in other
than individualist terms. Such people brandish popguns against the
family-dissolving forces of feminism and the sexual revolution. The
reason why "abstinence" programs, though not useless and foolish as
their enemies charge, are relatively disappointing in their results is that
they assume too many of the wrong principles. You do not abstain from
sexual intercourse before marriage because of *what you want* or *what
you are committed to* but because such activity is wrong. It betrays the
family, the church, and the community. It is a wrong *against others*. It
is not to proceed to the same goal by another path. It is to leave the path
entirely, because your new goal is something other than holiness for the
person and the common good for the family and the community.

*Nostalgia as a Return to the Journey*

Allow me to give an example of a journey that has been slandered
as "mere" nostalgia, against a corruption that was heralded as the next
great advance in human affairs. This corruption fell under several of
Newman's bans. It showed not an assimilation of food but inanition; it

brought forth no latent powers in embryo but smothered many of the natural powers of man and of the culture it purported to lead; it resulted not in dynamic motion but in attrition, enervation, stasis, and death.

The account is given in a collection of essays by Pope John Paul II, fittingly titled *Rise, Let Us Be on Our Way*. Karol Wojtyła, on the evening of his consecration as an auxiliary bishop of Krakow, left on a pilgrimage to Częstochowa, a sacred place for Poland's faith and its history as a free nation. "Here stands the national shrine called Jasna Góra—the Bright Mountain," where was made manifest "the presence of Our Lady in her miraculous image," first during the "terrible Swedish invasion known in history as 'the deluge.' At that time, the shrine, significantly, became a fortress that the attackers could not conquer. The nation interpreted this sign as a promise of victory."[11]

Let us tease out the implications. In 1655, the imperial Swedish army swept through Poland—Poland is not protected by the natural barriers that protect a nation such as Switzerland, or, for that matter, Sweden—and set down before the mountain monastery at Jasna Góra. The Poles were vastly outnumbered. Their provisions were failing. They could expect no assistance from their rulers, who trembled between indecision and capitulation. But the soldiers held out, and heartened by a strange light shining from the mountain, they ambushed the Swedes and routed them.

The story is far more precious to Poles than, say, the story of Washington crossing the Delaware River is to Americans because the very survival of an ancient nation was at stake and the light was an answer to prayers to God and pleas for the protection of the Mother of Christ. Every Pole knows it. Every Pole, said Bishop Wojtyła, makes the pilgrimage to the monastery at Częstochowa. The greatest of all Polish novelists, Henryk Sienkiewicz, immortalized the battle in his trilogy, *With Fire and Sword*, the central part of which is named for the Swedish invasion, "The Deluge." Every Polish boy and girl would read Sienkiewicz. He wrote his novels at a time when Poland, as a political entity, a free nation, was no more, having been partitioned by its ravenous neighbors. Yet Poland did not die because Poland was more than a political institution or a geographical area. It was a living, powerful tradition; it was a religious faith; it was an abiding love for the land, the language, the customs, the holy days. Poland did not die when the Swedes overran the country, slaughtering and pillaging. Poland did not die during the decades of partition, when Sienkiewicz wrote and kept the fire of independence alive. And now Karol Wojtyła went to Częstochowa for the sake of his faith, his people, and their freedom because Poland had been reduced to a satellite of the Soviet empire.

The communist puppets knew about Częstochowa, despised it, but feared what it meant. So the embattled Stefan Cardinal Wyszyński launched a pilgrimage *from Częstochowa* of the icon known as the Black Madonna to every parish and church in Poland. For Catholics, it meant that Mary herself, and the Polish devotion to her, was *on the road, on the way*; and the communists could not abide it. But all their attempts at obstruction served only to strengthen the memory of the Poles and their determination: "When the icon was 'arrested' by the police, the pilgrimage continued with the empty frame, and the message became even more eloquent. The frame with no picture was a silent sign of the lack of religious freedom in Poland. The nation knew it had a right to regain religious freedom and prayed fervently for it. This pilgrimage lasted for almost twenty-five years...."[12]

Think of that. The pilgrimage of the icon lasted for a quarter of a century. Minds riddled with mass entertainment and its ephemera can hardly concentrate on a single thing for a quarter of an hour.

The faith could be hindered, battered, rebuffed, and ridiculed, but the pilgrimage went on. The forces of the future, as they thought themselves, set themselves against a supposedly atavistic faith, a mere tradition, the stubborn survival of medieval customs, the reactionary clinging to a dead past. What actually happened was this: the Soviet empire would soon collapse, and Poland would be free again. Poland would flirt with the dead individualism and secularism of the West, and as yet we do not know the outcome. We who are on the way do not pretend to predict the near future. We know only the goal.

A living Poland, fighting against all odds, would retain and revive her gallant spirit, as when in the sixteenth and seventeenth centuries she shut the doors to an ungrateful Western Europe against invasion by the Turks. A living Poland would go forth in this new world of fallacious promises of liberty, which are actually the snares of license, and not care for the favor of such places as Belgium, dying, or her old enemy Sweden, dying. A frenzy of activity does not imply that you are going anywhere, no more than do the spasms of an epileptic fit. All that the West promises to Poland is the continued disintegration of natural societies such as the family and the irrelevance of localities, even the nation itself. Such disintegration clothes itself in the name of the liberty of the autonomous individual, which turns out to be the license to be sterile in your prime and to die at will in your old age. A Europe that does not respond to that religious call, "Rise, let us be on our way," is a museum of dying cultures or a mausoleum where the remains have withered to the bones. "Sweden does not have a culture," boasted the minister of culture for the government of Sweden.

Now, we will never go on that journey unless we are powerfully moved to do so; it is easier to join the lemmings in the mass phenomena. Nostalgia, as I have been trying to define and describe it, gives us the call. C. S. Lewis knew this *Sehnsucht*, this bittersweet longing that is better than any earthly satisfaction. He felt it as a boy when he heard the story of the handsome god Balder, treacherously slain by Loki, and the gods of Valhalla wailed, "Balder, Balder the good is dead." He knew it was not the *artistry* of the story that appealed to him, since all he had of it was the bare narration, the narrative fact. Something of the "good dream"—or what he would call, in *The Pilgrim's Regress*, "pictures" granted to the pagans by the Landlord God—came to him and planted the seed in his heart. That was the knowledge, bound in a living bond with his love of England, the English countryside, the English language, English folkways, and English literature, that his true home was not here. It is the paradox of a universal desire that, unless God has placed it in us and calls us, would remain without an object—an absurd thing, as many have observed before me. I am hungry; well, there is food. I am curious about the world; well, I have my five senses and a mind, and I can learn. I wish to have children; well, there is a woman, and I marry and we have those children.

It is not that every one of our desires is satisfied, but that every one of our desires has a recognizable object that might satisfy them. Yet we are not satisfied. I recall the beginning of George Herbert's poignant poem "Christmas":

> All after pleasures as I rid one day,
> My horse and I both tir'd, body and mind,
> With full cry of affections, quite astray,
> I put in at the next inn I could find.
> There when I came, whom found I but my dear,
> My dearest Lord, expecting till the grief
> Of pleasures brought me to him, ready there
> To be all passengers' most sweet relief?[13]

The grief of pleasures indeed. One second after satisfaction we find ourselves vaguely disappointed and restless, unless those pleasures lead us toward the transcendent: *Post coitum omne animal triste est.*

But, as I have said, this desire, this *Sehnsucht*, this deep *nostalgia*, is different from the pleasures that bring grief in their wake. "This hunger is better than any other fullness," says Lewis; "this poverty better than all other wealth."[14] It spurs us on to the journey, unless we should stray, which means essentially to cease: "The only fatal error was to pretend that you had passed from desire to fruition, when, in reality, you had found either nothing, or desire itself, or the satisfaction of some different desire."[15] Lewis's pilgrim John, in *The Pilgrim's Regress*, longs for the mysterious island he has seen glimpses of in his happiest and saddest moments, his moments of intense longing, but he is beset on his way by a host of figures who would persuade him that there is no journey to be made. We meet the essential stick-in-the-progressive-mud, Mr. Enlightenment, who tells John that priests "are a shrewd lot" for their religious inventiveness and their cunning in persuading people to believe in the Landlord, and, simultaneously, "simple old souls," "just like children," with "no knowledge of modern science," who "would believe anything they were told."

"How do you know there is no Landlord?" John asks.

Mr. Enlightenment's response is one that all Christians have encountered, though rarely from scientists themselves. It is uttered mostly by people whose spirits are too sluggish to rise and be on their way: "Christopher Columbus, Galileo, the earth is round, invention of printing, gunpowder!"[16]

How many ways men find to excuse their not finding the way, not searching for it, or not taking it when they have found it! Some, Lewis shows, will dally forever with the "brown girls" and brown boys, mistaking their longing for sexual desire. Some devote themselves, in the town of Claptrap, to inventing new machines, without asking exactly where the machines are to take us. Some reject the Enlightenment project entirely and, like savages from the north, look forward to the day when they will drink the progressive's blood from the progressive's skull. Some, like Mr. Broad, dally on the edge of the canyon that separates the pilgrim from the land of his desire, enjoying good food and drink and not bothering overmuch with doctrine. Some are half-hearted hedonists, others are cold-hearted ascetics. Their swarm of activity does not bring them closer to the goal. Deeply envious of those who do make progress, they may have an unacknowledged interest in disillusioning them. The last thing a man who has given up on the journey wants to see is another man energetically on the way. The last thing he wants to feel, for it is his most acute pain, is that old ache, that nostalgia, that call of the journey to the homeland we have always known and never known, long glimpsed and never seen. He will say that all has changed, and so he need not change his ways or his non-ways. He fears the change that would require him to come to his senses, arise from feeding husks to the swine, and say, "I shall return to my Father's house."

## Return to the Future

Let us apply the principle to certain features of culture and realms of human action. I am issuing a nostalgic call to "return to the future," using the title of Sigrid Undset's autobiographical account of her escape from Nazi-occupied Norway across Scandinavia, the Soviet Union, and imperial Japan to the United States with her one surviving son—the

other had died heroically in the first weeks of Norwegian resistance. Undset wrote novels set in medieval Norway not because she believed it was charming and pretty and full of Christian goodness. It was full of violence and confusion, but it was *alive* and going somewhere, whereas Nazism was a parody of life, as was the atheistic Soviet Union; they were to her Norwegian Christians as Tolkien's orcs are to his elves.

We can identify, one by one, several of the fruitless detours of modern man, several ways in which he has wandered off into a far country, to waste his substance and his vigor, and suggest a return to the point of detour, not to remain there, but from that place to go forth on the way.

In this business, we can refer to almost anything. I will begin

Augustus Saint-Gaudens, *Mrs. Schuyler Van Rensselaer (Mariana Griswold)*, 1888 (cast in 1890), courtesy of The Met.

with a work of art. This is a low-relief sculpture, in bronze, of Mariana Griswold Van Rensselaer by the American sculptor with the wonderful French Canadian name, Augustus Saint-Gaudens.

Before I say a word, compare it with a work that would qualify as a great sculpture only a few decades later, *Reclining Figure: Arch Leg* by Henry Moore, a large bronze conglomerate displayed outdoors in Geneva. It looks from the side, or front—it is hard to tell which is which—as if a wiener dog were burying or melting its head into a large ping-pong paddle. Or is it a bowling pin? In the photograph I'm looking at, the most beautiful object is a large evergreen tree beyond the hump of the dog. Moore's title doesn't help me much, except that it causes me to suppose the wiener is the leg. Title or no, the sculpture has no identity, no meaning. It makes no reference to a living culture, or to a place or time, or to a tradition of beliefs. It is equally out of place in Geneva as on the banks of the Ganges.

I do not presume here to pass judgment upon the whole corpus of Henry Moore's work. I object to its primitivism and to a false humanism that will not submit to human perceptions, human feelings, and human concerns. Moore's sculpture is not an evolution from the tradition in which Saint-Gaudens worked. It is a radical break. Moore studied the works of Donatello and the other great sculptors of the Renaissance, but only an art historian would have the knowledge or the patience to tell in what respect there is even a feint at continuity. The work has no roots, and it has borne no *living* fruit: it has nowhere to go, other than to produce other lumps that have likewise no roots and no universe of meaning to which to refer.

Such a thing was inconceivable to the people of Saint-Gaudens's time. But what Saint-Gaudens wrought would not have been inconceivable to the people of Michelangelo's time or to the people of Phidias' time, more than two thousand years before. Notice the classical frame for the bust of Mrs. Van Rensselaer, with the symmetry of the floral design, and the rosettes within the sculpture that echo the flowers in the frame. It is not just a portrait of the woman, but a *presentation* in an architectural setting that is reminiscent of that of a hero or a saint.

Saint-Gaudens had in mind centuries of ecclesiastical portrayals of saints—like the heads of the apostles in the painted lunettes of my boyhood church, now that I think of it. He also had in mind the long tradition of public commemorative sculptures, such as his own splendid memorial to Colonel Robert Gould Shaw and the Massachusetts Fifty-fourth Regiment, made up of African Americans, including two sons of the celebrated man of letters Frederick Douglass; he had been working on that one for several years, and would continue to do so for a long time afterward, until its unveiling in Boston in 1897.

The bust combines gentle features with a calm determination and profound, quiet intelligence. She is dressed so as to emphasize her countenance, and though her tightly bound hair and the braided cloth around her neck suggest Puritan reserve, that same hair, slightly tousled on the forehead, and the rough texture of the clothing suggest action, purpose, openness to new experiences. We would not call her a sprightly girl. Her eyes are sad, and the elongation of those eyes and her nose, like the set of her lips, are well suited to a woman who has recently lost her beloved husband. The inscriptions are in simple block letters. They identify the subject, the artist, and, in Roman numerals, the date. They also place the work, the artist, and the woman in a long tradition of humane learning, for above the bust we find, with the classical alphabet in use during the time of the Caesars, the caption ANIMVS NON OPVS, "the soul, not the work." Perhaps it was Saint-Gaudens's self-effacing attempt to say that his work must fall short of the intention of his soul, to do right by his old friend and patron. Or perhaps it refers to Mrs. Van Rensselaer, who had become one of the finest writers on art and architecture in the English-speaking world, and who had a keen appreciation for the spirit of artists whose hands sometimes trembled in the execution.

Such a work should wring our hearts with regret. Why did we leave that road? A rejection of the rejection is long overdue, and a retracing of steps from the detour. I am no sculptor, so to those who know the specifics I must leave the task of describing all that was lost by the rejection, so that we can return to what made sculptors like Saint-Gaudens possible. It is not just a matter of deciding that you want to be an artist in the vein of Saint-Gaudens or Rodin or a portraitist like Whistler or Sargent, no more than you can merely decide to write poetry in blank verse as did Milton, Wordsworth, Keats, and Tennyson. The knowledge in the fingers takes many long years to acquire, and techniques passed down over many generations are not to be summoned up from the dead by pixie dust and hard-wishing. It is much easier to remain where you are, trying your hand now and then at what will pass for the traditional but is just a gesture in that direction, not full engagement.

But the subject of Saint-Gaudens's work is fascinating and instructive in her own right, and this brings me to a second detour. Consider what a universe separates us from Mariana Griswold Van Rensselaer. Descended from the Puritans who tamed New England, she married into one of the first families of the Dutch patroons who governed New York. She received her education at home till she was seventeen. It appears to have been an education steeped in humane letters and the arts, as she wrote with a clarity, power, concentration, and breadth of reference and knowledge that one would never expect now in a college professor with a doctorate in English. She married fairly young and spent much time living in Europe, about whose art and architecture she began to write for various popular journals of a sort no longer published. I give here a remarkable passage in which she pauses from her sharp-eyed description of artistic works and evaluation of their virtues and failings to meditate upon her feelings as she looks at Lichfield Cathedral, remembering that her own Puritan ancestors had defaced and destroyed so much of its art in the days of Cromwell:

> But here, amidst these cathedrals, what is the Puritan to his
> descendant's thoughts? A rude destroyer of things ancient
> and therefore to be respected; a vandal devastator of things
> rare and beautiful and too precious ever to be replaced; a

brutal scoffer, drinking at the altar, firing his musket at the figure of Christ, parading in priests' vestments through the marketplace, stabling his horses amidst the handiwork of beauty under the roof of God.[17]

We can apply her charge to many a modernist innovation: we have had the fanatical destructiveness of those Puritans in the heat of war but without the Puritan's faith and courage. We have had sick Calvinists without God. Mrs. Van Rensselaer was not a Roman Catholic, as far as I can determine, but it is impossible even to imagine now an author so sensitive and honest as to say that "there were moments in my English journey when I hated the Puritan with a holy hatred and wished that he had never shown his surly face to the world—a wish, however, which included his friend the Anglican, too, as his fellow-fiend in destruction, his fellow-pillager of Catholic rights and destroyer of Catholic charms and graces." Yet here too she refrains from becoming a destroyer in her own right. She does what the politically correct professor will never do. She considers the "enemy" also by his own lights, and as an inheritor and donor of things precious. So she attempts to judge the crimes of the Puritan fairly and to agree with one of her critics that the Puritan "was in fact a worthy personage, thoroughly conscientious after his lights and most serviceable to the best interests of humanity." Says she, "I believe it as I believe in the worth and value of few other human creatures; and I hereby acknowledge that artistic sins and virtues are not those which the recording angel will place at the top of his tablets when he sums up the acts of men either as individuals or as citizens of the world."

The Puritan of old gave Mrs. Van Rensselaer the nation she loved, and she was not to deny the benefit of it, even as she was calling for a renewed study of the works of the past. We can see that this was not merely sentimental, because for her it was a tradition still alive and marvelously productive, as we see when she turns to church architecture in the United States. She emphatically does not want mere attempts to copy what the Europeans had done. Such things would be out of place:

> Look at an ancient example—at Durham imperious on its rock, or at Antwerp soaring from the human habitations that cluster like swallow-nests around its base, and dwarfing even the huge municipal palaces of a later century. Why should we wish to build the like? On our soil, would not such a cathedral be an anachronism of as palpable a sort as would be a Lanfranc or a Becket among the upper shepherds of our flocks?[18]

Everywhere we find her praising the incorporation of ancient skills and motifs into the living culture of American "language," American places, and American stone and wood to build what would be American churches, both Protestant (Trinity Church, Boston) and Catholic (the Paulist church in Manhattan), cathedrals and parish churches (St. Paul's, Stockbridge). To be working in a tradition is to be alive and in change:

> Architectural origins seem strange enough when we try to trace them out. Their history teaches that we may borrow where and when we will—even a plan in one place, features in another, and details in a third. Only—and this is the vital fact that justifies or condemns—we must blend them, so to say, chemically and not mechanically; we must make of them a new body, and not merely a patchwork.[19]

That is the challenge, once we have returned to the living tradition. Return, and begin.

What is true of the false turn in architecture and sculpture may be said of other innovations too, those that brought decay and destruction rather than vigor and development. Ralph Vaughan Williams, combing England for folk melodies never written down that would otherwise soon be lost forever, was no simple-minded antiquarian. He was not "merely" nostalgic. The composer of the *Sinfonia antartica*, with its atonal modulations fit for the mystery and dread of a lifeless land of mountains and ice, cannot justly be accused of sentimentality or of being merely derivative. He aimed to save the old melodies, and he arranged them to be fitted for verses already written as texts for congregational hymns.

Vaughan Williams was something of an agnostic, but not when it came to the long tradition of sacred music in which he worked and to which he contributed most fruitfully. Listen to his *Fantasia on a Theme of Thomas Tallis*—the so-called "Third Mode Melody" by the Elizabethan Catholic composer—and then tell me that the great oak of sacred music had no more sap in it and would bring forth no more acorns for tall trees to come. Why have the churches abandoned it for shabby little political ditties sung to show-tunes or mindless mantras yowled out to the accompaniment of noise? When the Second Vatican Council, in *Sacrosanctum concilium*, declared that Gregorian chant ought to be taught to all the faithful and that the pipe organ had pride of place among instruments for sacred music, that was an invitation to open out to more singers and musicians and congregants the living traditions of centuries so that they could participate more fully in them and composers, taking their cues from those who had gone before, could make the old things new. It was a call to be on the way. That call was misheard, misinterpreted, or ignored, and the new thing put in the place of the tradition has sat like a great mass of tangled metal and rubber, inert and ugly, in the middle of what used to be a choir or a sanctuary.

Or take our schools. Take them, take them away, please. I have noted, in *Out of the Ashes: Rebuilding American Culture*, that a hundred years ago there were twenty-one times as many school boards per thousand students as there are now. That bounty was a healthy thing. It meant that many men and women from all walks of life were directly involved in the oversight of public schools. From that great multitude, parceled out in coherent localities, with all their particulars of place and culture and populace, we might expect direction that was more sensible on the whole than if it had come from a much smaller number of people, from one or two callings (teachers, lawyers), attempting to apply to huge numbers of children indiscriminately the educational dicta handed down from "innovative" teachers' colleges. We might expect, and we did experience, easier cooperation between the school and the churches and regular involvement of businessmen and tradesmen in the education of older children. The school was, I have also written before, a more obvious *physical presence* in the neighborhood, not removed to some faraway and newly cleared portion of woodland, where no one lived, and whither and whence all the children would have to be transported like crates of vegetables. Schools tended to resemble, in their physical form, small town halls, churches, or large homes, not factories.

Again, we are talking about a fruitless detour from the way. I am not saying that our schools in 1900 were in all ways superior to what they are now. In science and mathematics, for the intellectual icing on the cake—for the best of the best students—they were not. Calculus is not to be found in high school math textbooks until recently. Yet let us note one important feature of the old terrain. At the turn of that century, publishers of popular books were marketing large lists specifically for young people, sometimes more specifically for boys or for girls, and though some of the books would stand the test of time and some would not, not one of them was obscene or stupid. The worst of them, like the novels of Marie Corelli, were intelligently bad, like a homely manor house or an ugly dog. For the most part, we are talking about bringing to as many people as possible the bright lights and glory of a great tradition.

I am looking at one such list, "Burt's Home Library," from one of the more prominent of the popularizers of good and great literature, A. L. Burt. It is in the back of my copy of Dickens's *The Old*

*Curiosity Shop.* The company issued reprints of classic works and highly-regarded modern works, in cloth covers, for a relatively low price—$1.25, for each of the 382 books in the list I have at hand. Here is the advertisement:

> Burt's Home Library is a series which includes the standard works of the world's best literature, bound in uniform cloth binding, gilt tops, embracing chiefly selections from writers of the most notable English, American, and Foreign Fiction, together with many important works in the domains of History, Biography, Philosophy, Travel, Poetry and the Essays.
>
> A glance at the following annexed list of titles and authors will endorse the claim that the publishers make for it—that it is the most comprehensive, choice, interesting, and by far the most carefully selected series of standard authors for world-wide reading that has been produced by any publishing house in any country, and that at prices so cheap, and in a style so substantial and pleasing, as to win for it millions of readers and the approval and commendation, not only of the book trade throughout the American continent, but of hundreds of thousands of librarians, clergymen, educators and men of letters interested in the dissemination of instructive, entertaining and thoroughly wholesome reading matter for the masses.

The florid self-praise is merited. The list includes plenty of fiction from first-rate authors, English and otherwise (Dickens, Eliot, Defoe, Fielding, Stevenson, Balzac, Hugo, Dumas, Scott, Melville). There are philosophical essays and meditations (Marcus Aurelius, Emerson, Montaigne, Plato), poetry classical and modern (Keats, Tennyson, Browning, Goldsmith, Homer, Virgil), histories (the Crusades, the Thirty Years' War), biographies (Cromwell, the missionary Livingstone,

Philip II of Spain, Mary Queen of Scots, Pasteur, Lee, Garibaldi), works of science (Darwin, Spencer) and religion (Ernst Renan's *Life of Christ*). You can sail the Pacific with Captain Cook or storm through Mexico with Cortez. You can read of Hannibal and his campaigns against Rome. You can read about what it means to read well with Matthew Arnold and his *Essays in Criticism*. Children can find here, just under "A," *Aesop's Fables, Alice in Wonderland, Andersen's Fairy Tales, Arabian Nights' Entertainment*, and George Macdonald's sweet and haunting *At the Back of the North Wind*, while their parents can read biographies of Alexander the Great, Alfred the Great, and Benedict Arnold.

Those who compiled the list assumed what everyone at the time assumed. Given the opportunity, people of the lower and middle classes, who were divided from the upper classes by means and not by native intelligence, would be as likely to read Virgil as were the people who sent their scions to Deerfield and Groton, not to mention such genuinely and tremendously popular authors as Dickens and George Eliot. They were correct in that assumption, because otherwise they would have folded their tent, rather than going strong for sixty years before selling their operation to the larger Doubleday. Nor were they alone. Everywhere you turned, publishers were doing the same sort of thing.

It is no exaggeration to say that if you read a quarter of the books on Burt's list, you would have a better grounding in arts and letters than most college professors have now.

But just when books were about to become even easier to procure, at a price that would be a fraction of what Burt's had to charge, our schools and libraries gave the whole thing over. I have countless discards from such places, nor were the titles replaced by newer editions. We could without any considerable expense—indeed at considerably more modest expense than is required to buy the hardcover political and entertainment garbage and slick and sleazy romances that stock our libraries now—have in every school in the country a small library ten times the size of Burt's list. Yet we do not because we fell from the way. It is not just that children will no longer read *Little Dorrit*. Their parents and teachers will not, either. Not because they lack the time. They are intellectual and cultural tumbleweeds: no roots.

What I say about school libraries goes also for textbooks. They used to work from a tradition that was energetic, fruitful, intelligent, and alive. The McGuffey readers, compiled by a sensitive and intelligent and progressive Christian, gave birth in the early twentieth century to textbooks that were stocked with more, not less, of the literature that their founder loved. The grammar books of the 1910s were not encrusted with trivial distinctions between adverbs of manner and adverbs of means, supposing those to be trivial; they were compiled by intelligent educators who tried to accommodate new understandings of grammar to the needs of children at the ages in which they would be using the books. We were seeing more, not less, of what a clear understanding of the structure of language could do. The smaller children were taught phonetically, the plainly reasonable way for children to encounter an alphabet. Consider that whenever Christian monks came to a new land whose people had no writing, they would adapt or invent an alphabet for the needs of the language, taking care to produce a system of signs so that the people could "see" what they heard.

So phonetics too was abandoned. Interesting textbooks on grammar, for grammar school children, disappear in the mid-century, the readers grow quickly insipid and dull, the look-say method replaces phonetics, Johnny finds that he can't read, and, some decades later, it is as rare to find a college student who can parse a good English sentence as it is to find a college professor who can write one.

The point, again, is not simply that the new was bad and the old was good. The new was not a development from the old. It did not improve upon a tradition. It abandoned it. Look-say was not a development of phonetics. It was its betrayal. Learning the grammar of English in such a way as to prepare you to be able to learn the grammar of other languages did not come to fruition in learning no

grammar at all or spending years learning no more in another language than how to ask where the toilets are. What we want is a return
to the living thing that was still bearing much fruit. What we have
instead is the stasis of non-entity. Ultimately one student who doesn't
know any grammar and has a hard time reading Dickens is much like
any other. Ignorance in this sense is like chaos. How do you distinguish between mud and mud?

Have at it, then. Was the rock music of the 1950s a development of
or a deterioration from the popular music of the big bands? There are
ways to answer the question that are not simply subjective. Did that
music develop from and work with and build upon the complex modulations of Benny Goodman and Glenn Miller and the dozens of others? Did that music unite old and young? Every single people until our
own day has had the experience of watching very young children begin
to learn the old dances to the old music, with flushed cheeks and fum-
bling steps and, in the boys, unwilling sweat, while their grandparents
do the steps they have known for sixty years, and if they tremble it is
with glee and age. What happened to that? Music stores, once quite
common, used to do much of their business in sheet music, which
implies that the music could be registered in that way and passed along
through the generations, and that there were plenty of people who
could read it. What happened? What of the musical theater, and opera
houses in every medium-sized city? Jenny Lind earned her fame in the
United States by traveling from place to place and singing in front of
large audiences of people who could appreciate what she was doing.
Now we can watch television and listen to recordings of opera, but
still—who does? Whose ear has been trained by the good strong soil
of folk music to appreciate its flourishing and its transformation in
Dvorak, Debussy, Grieg, and Copland?

In the early days of television, we had a lot of banal and silly and
otherwise innocent stuff, but also quite a variety of programs intended
to bring the playhouse to ordinary people who did not live near the
cities, and the plays on offer were sometimes written by the most

prominent playwrights of the time. That had a run of about ten years, and then it was over. What happened to the travel down that road?

Before high tax rates gave companies the incentive to include non-taxable medical insurance benefits in their compensation packages, people had gotten together to form their own insurance cooperatives, often associated with fraternal and other beneficent societies. Was not the link of insurance to employment quite adventitious and unproductive? It foreclosed further development in variety, given how one group of people might see advantages in, let us say, hiring a doctor for their exclusive use, while another group might instead pool resources for ordinary expenses and commit by pledges of certain amounts to defray the extraordinary. Was the tremendously large farm, workable only by means of huge mortgages on land and equipment, a development of, or a deviation from, the small family farm, and in either case did it have to happen, or was it rather a result of policies handed down from the national government? Must there always be an inevitable movement away from variety and local initiative? Why should that be so?

And what of that national government? I note the editors for *The Century* in 1884 were uneasy about it. Their reason is quietly astonishing. They worry that the nation has become too apathetic about what kind of man will be elected president later that year. Let us put it in context. It had not been twenty years since Appomattox. It had been seven years since Hayes declared an end to Reconstruction. Millions of men were still alive who had taken up arms against their countrymen, even against their own kin. The election itself, wherein Grover Cleveland would defeat the anti-Catholic James G. Blaine by the slenderest of margins, was bitter enough. Yet there was, according to the editor, nothing like the frenzied preoccupation with that national government that we see everywhere among us now. I take it that if your teachers are terrified about who the next principal may be, then whether they have cause to be so or not, the office of the principal is far too powerful, and the office of the teacher has withered away. We are talking then about the simultaneous growth of one kind of government and the atrophy of self-government in all its innumerable, diverse, local, and personal forms. That is not progress, unless you are betting on the cancer.

My readers will bring their own experiences to the general question. I say that the disappearance of entire genres of art, music, and poetry, with the atrophy of local and personal participation in them, suggests not development but decay. The paradox of modernity is just this: it refuses to define progress in any way accordant with the nature of fallen man and therefore rejects the hard-won wisdom of our forebears, thereby rejecting the foundations upon which alone we can build. To be more truly modern we must be less the modernist. To have real development we must preserve the life of what is to come to flower. We must now acknowledge that for all our wealth and power, we have merely deviated from the journey and gone nowhere, fast. Men in previous generations have had the exigencies of survival and of living in real communities to keep them from going as destructively wrong as we have gone, so quickly and in so many ways.

## Ideology in the Bottom of the Sack

I suppose I must hear that certain social innovations in the last century are required by simple justice. Since I hold no brief against organic development of genuine human goods, I am not required to champion the vices of our grandparents just because I do champion their virtues. We must stipulate that all virtue is a power, and vice literally *vitiates*: so that our grandparents would have been truer to themselves, not traitors, had they behaved with vigorous and manly justice toward African Americans, to take the obvious example from the United States. It is as Plato says—no one can behave unjustly toward others without harming himself in the act.

But those same African Americans have been employed as ideological pack-mules. One group after another has heaped its luggage atop their backs, even while the injustice that the blacks did most grossly suffer has been elided. Their actual condition in the present is largely ignored by right and left because it touches upon moral questions that we prefer not to address: it touches upon the lotos. The absurdity of laws that made blacks sleep in shabby motels while their white counterparts, or their white inferiors, swanked around in a Hilton could be seen a thousand miles away, and no one now should dare to justify them. Such laws served no legitimate human purpose, and though ethnic discrimination is common enough across the world (consider the iron caste system of old India), the peculiarly racial form it took in the United States was itself an ideological detour, a swerve, and those who justified it employed arguments from the misapplied biology of the day. Hence it is no surprise that Woodrow Wilson was both an arch-progressive and an arrant racist. He thought he had "history" on his side.

Justice is one thing. Feminism is another. It is an ideological cul-de-sac. It leads nowhere. If we say that people ought to be treated fairly, we are recognizing a requirement of justice. If we say that our expectations regarding men and women ought to be identical, we are running athwart the biology of the sexes and, I believe, athwart the health of the family as an institution. The early feminists fought for suffrage on two grounds: it was a matter of justice, and it would redound to the benefit of society because women were more virtuous than men were. Women were to bring the feminine genius to all things and transform them forever. We may call it the Verena Tarrant Syndrome, after the breathless ingenue of Henry James's *The Bostonians*. The following comes from her debut as a public speaker before a crowd of women and some men who go along for the ride:

> "Do you know how you strike me? You strike me as men who are starving to death while they have a cupboard at home, all full of bread and meat and wine; or as blind, demented beings who let themselves be cast into a debtor's prison, while in their pocket they have the key of vaults and treasure-chests heaped up with gold and silver. The meat

and wine, the gold and silver," Verena went on, "are simply the suppressed and wasted force, the precious sovereign remedy, of which society insanely deprives itself—the genius, the intelligence, the inspiration of women. It is dying, inch by inch, in the midst of old superstitions which it invokes in vain and yet it has the elixir of life in its hands. Let it drink but a draught and it will bloom once more; it will be refreshed, radiant; it will find its youth again. The heart, the heart is cold, and nothing but the touch of woman can warm it, make it act. We are the Heart of humanity, and let us have the courage to insist on it! The public life of the world will move in the same barren, mechanical, vicious circle—the circle of egotism, cruelty, ferocity, jealousy, greed, of blind striving to do things only for *some*, at the cost of others, instead of trying to do everything for all."[20]

It is hardly necessary, I think, to amass arguments to show that not one of these lofty predictions has come true. There is no *Herland*, the egalitarian, woman-led utopia dreamed up by James's near contemporary Charlotte Perkins Gilman. Feminists themselves do not speak of woman as "the Heart of humanity" but are instead adamant about the prime directive of a culture of narcissism: that the individual's self-actualization, to use the ugly psycho-lingo, takes precedence over all other considerations, including the life of an unborn child in the womb, let alone the institution of marriage and the good of men. Verena Tarrant proposes to help men, those poor deluded creatures. Our feminists, scoffing at the idea of considering that good at all, look forward to a day when children will be manufactured *en masse* without men and without conjugal love. In other words, they have, as the fallen human beings we all are, punched their tickets for admission to what Miss Tarrant calls "the circle of egotism, cruelty, ferocity, jealousy, greed," and so forth.

No, the history of the twentieth century, awash in blood, bore out none of *those* feminist hopes. We have enjoyed no flowering of arts and letters, even as our colleges and universities have exploded in numbers, wealth, and the burden they levy upon hapless parents. The family, the foundation of any society, is frail and sickly, and Western nations have not the hope and energy to replace one generation with another.

I lay some of the blame not on women who pursue arts and letters but on the innovation, feminism, that leads so many of them into fruitless endeavors. How could Mariana Griswold Van Rensselaer have been *improved* by feminist theology and pseudo-theology? She already was, after the heyday of John Ruskin, the greatest English-speaking architectural promoter and the champion not of individual artists alone but of whole architectural firms. The nineteenth century gave us the greatest women novelists in English: Jane Austen, the Brontë sisters, and George Eliot; the splendid children's storyteller and illustrator Beatrix Potter; and the woman who, for my money, is the greatest female painter in history, Mary Cassatt. By the 1930s and 1940s, there were women in my academic field, Renaissance literature, whose work should endure as long as people read the poets about whom they wrote: Josephine Waters Bennett, Helen Vendler, Rosemond Tuve. Not one of them was a career feminist.

What has the ideology of feminism accomplished? First, it has riddled the family with confusion, making millions of women feel inadequate unless they work outside the home, even when by their own testimony they would prefer to do less of that or none at all. Second, it has funneled women's work in arts and letters into the narrow channel of an ideology, which is a death sentence. (Does anybody read Soviet sociology now?) Third, it has poisoned the relations of men and women themselves, so that now it is almost inconceivable that a woman can write in praise of the male sex and not be attacked for it. And fourth, it has introduced into the body politic the additional confusions of pathological sexual "identity," especially harmful to boys growing up without a father in the home and without any strong males in their lives to serve as patterns of masculine strength and purpose and love.

The intellectual work has been, after such women as I have mentioned, utterly disappointing. I will take the field of literary criticism as paradigmatic. Writes the literary scholar John Ellis:

> Typically, work by feminist critics is shaped so completely
> by the notion of patriarchy that an intelligent contribution
> to the understanding of literature becomes almost impossible. The greatest problem is anachronism: when feminists
> use literature of the past only to find evidence of patriarchal
> oppression, or of resistance thereto, they are in effect taking
> the condition of modern life as the universal standard. The
> result is that their work becomes irrelevant to literature
> produced by societies whose conditions they have fundamentally misunderstood.[21]

Such an attitude is, ahem, *patronizing* and *colonialist* in the worst sense, evincing a complete unwillingness to understand a culture on its terms rather than ours. It is Mrs. Pardiggle again, but with a difference: a Puritanism of social decay, without God, beholden to the contemporary Western mammon of money and ambition. Imagine a veritable army of lady missionaries determined to make the natives into tea-and-scones Englishmen and women, and then replace the tea and scones with sexual "independence" and the worship of autonomy generally. The result is not flourishing but uniformity and stagnation:

> When the feminist critic's attention is turned to female
> characters in great books, the results are just as predictable.
> It is easy enough to see the theory of a malevolent patriarchy
> as the basis for commentary on how Ophelia or Desdemona
> or Cordelia is mistreated, or how *The Taming of the Shrew*
> is full of misogynistic prejudice. But quite apart from the

fact that this approach applies a historically unrealistic theory of relations between the sexes, it also applies indiscriminately a preconceived idea as to what will be important....
[T]he critic's obsessions determine in advance what is going
to be important for a particular work.[22]

For this, we are sacrificing quite a great deal, among which is the
possibility that we will see the likes of George Eliot again any time
soon. Here too we are looking at a much-touted innovation that stunts
the growth of what it purported to advance, and an expensive innovation, to boot. It is like adding to a house a library whose leaky roof ruins
the books, whose flimsy structure compromises the rest of the house,
and whose expense ruins the householders. One may also ask why, if
the generation of our great-grandparents was so evil, the sexes seem
to have gotten along fairly well and women of letters were common,
along with women whose erudition enabled them to read philosophical, cultural, and literary articles that for their breadth of reference and
careful thought would stump most college professors now, let alone
students.

A dead end. You make no progress milling around in a cul-de-sac.

### We Shall All Be Changed

I have said that human nature has not changed, and that whatever
moral progress we make has been slow and fitful and uncertain. Yet I
make one exception to this rule. It is not simply, I say, the most important event in the history of mankind. I believe that it is the definitive
event; and it is not something that human beings are themselves
responsible for.

Robert Browning illustrates it for us in the person of his Karshish,
an itinerant physician and gatherer of herbs, local remedies, and medic-
inal lore, making his careful and observant way through Palestine in

the middle of the first century. There he meets a man who was supposedly raised from the dead by someone who, as Karshish assumes, must
have been a member of his sacred brotherhood—a fellow physician. The
good physician's methods must have dazzled the credulous people,
whether he wanted them to or not, and they turned him into a legend;
while at the same time he brought down on his own head the hatred
and superstition of the local religious leaders, who destroyed him. So
Karshish interprets it, and so he writes in a letter to his friend Abib in
the poem with the delightful name, "An Epistle Containing the Strange
Medical Experience of Karshish, the Arab Physician."

Yet Karshish, interviewing the man who had been cured, finds him
strangely reticent on the subject of his death and revival and strangely
unconcerned with the wars and rumors of war all about him. Karshish
tries to rouse him with the threats of Rome, but this man called Lazarus is unmoved:

> "How, beast," said I, "this stolid carelessness
> Sufficeth thee, when Rome is on her march
> To stamp out like a little spark thy town,
> Thy tribe, thy crazy tale and thee at once?"
> He merely looked with his large eyes on me.

Those who despise it will call it naiveté, a simple-minded carelessness. I wonder what they would make of Father Christian de Chergé,
the abbot of a group of Trappist monks living in the Atlas Mountains
in Algeria who devoted his life to performing good works among his
Muslim neighbors. Dom Christian prayed for them always and had
a presentiment of his death shortly before he and his brothers were
butchered by a band of radicals. His last letter advises the brothers to
keep their faith and their love of their murderers, who, like those who
put Jesus to death, knew not what they were doing. The proof of the
*new thing in the world* is that we cannot imagine that depth of divine

love, which has never been made manifest by any other group in the world, no matter how old and venerable and benevolent and worthy.

Secular man can be a tender humanitarian, but as Walker Percy puts it in *The Thanatos Syndrome*, tenderness of that sort leads to the gas chamber. Secular man can make a great show of strewing money, usually appropriated from other people, like confetti, much to the advertisement of himself and little to the material purpose—nothing at all to the human and spiritual purpose. There is no Dom Christian among the Muslims, nor among the hedonists of the West. There never was, and there never will be, outside of the utterly transforming power of *the new thing in the world*.

But let us return to Karshish. He anticipates the conclusion of his friend Abib, to whom he is addressing his letter. There must be something wrong with the fellow's emotional constitution. But no, that is not the case:

> The man is apathetic, you deduce?
> Contrariwise, he loves both old and young,
> Able and weak, affects the very brutes
> And birds—how say I? flowers of the field—
> As a wise workman recognizes tools
> In a master's workshop, loving what they make. Thus is the
>     man as harmless as a lamb.
> Is he then a smiling, vacant imbecile? No, not that either:
> Only impatient, let him do his best,
> At ignorance and carelessness and sin—
> An indignation which is promptly curbed:
> As when in certain travels I have feigned
> To be an ignoramus in our art
> According to some preconceived design,
> And happed to hear the land's practitioners,
> Steeped in conceit sublimed by ignorance,

Prattle fantastically on disease,
Its cause and cure—and I must hold my peace!

Karshish here "projects" upon Lazarus his own sense of superiority, but we can glean from his words a meaning whereof Browning suggests that the physician is now and then aware. Lazarus is cut to the quick by human evil and folly, but then he cools his temper right away, recalling that he is dealing with sinners, and that Jesus came to save even such, and forgave them from the Cross. Karshish imagines that Lazarus is like a canny doctor who keeps his own counsel, and it may be that when he was speaking to Lazarus with that touch of harshness, Lazarus did that same thing that Karshish does when he overhears people chattering about disease, of which they know nothing. Lazarus is the physician, and Karshish may or may not suspect it.

But how can this be? Karshish saves the most astonishing feature of the story for the last. It is that this Lazarus regards the man who cured him as—Karshish can hardly write the words, begging pardon from Abib as he does so—"the creator and sustainer of the world"! It is but the message of Saint John, from whose gospel we read the account of the raising of Lazarus from the tomb:

He was in the world, and the world was made by him, and
the world knew him not.
He came unto his own, and his own received him not.
But as many as received him, to them gave he power to
become the sons of God, even to them that believe on
his name:
Which were born, not of blood, nor of the will of the flesh,
nor of the will of man, but of God.
And the Word was made flesh, and dwelt among us, (and
we beheld his glory, the glory as of the only begotten of
the Father,) full of grace and truth. (John 1:10–14)

Browning understands that this claim is *not like* anything that came before or that has come since. Karshish, concluding his letter, puts it this way:

> The very God! think, Abib; dost thou think?
> So, the All-Great, were the All-Loving too—
> So, through the thunder comes a human voice
> Saying, "O heart I made, a heart beats here!
> Face, my hands fashioned, see it in myself!
> Thou hast no power nor mayst conceive of mine,
> But love I gave thee, with myself to love,
> And thou must love me who have died for thee!"
> The madman saith He said so: it is strange.

Every atom of my being is not only blessed by the God who made it but, in the Incarnation, suffused with meaning. If Christ was who he said, then there is nothing in all of creation that we may merely scorn. The body is holy because he dwelt therein. The very lilies of the field are blessed because they have sprung from the dust that was trod by his feet, and they caught his eye on that mountain when he preached the truths we all know in our hearts but have all denied. No more can we go behind Christ and live as if we were pagans in the violent childhood of man or sages in the dim and sad old age of the pagan world. If Christ was who he said, then not the slightest impulse of a human heart is for naught. One touch transforms the world, not as in the magic of a pagan deity and not as in the fevered dreams of those who have only technology to worship, but intimately, working quietly from within, for the kingdom of God is like those three measures of yeast that the woman mingled in with her dough, unseen, but bringing about what the world has never seen before. The world, as the world, can bring forth a proud hero now and again, like Regulus, or a cold and ruthlessly efficient statesman, like Augustus. As the world, it cannot bring forth, it had never brought forth, it had never conceived of the possibility of bringing forth, a single saint.

This new thing in the world turns a small and well-liked Albanian nun doing pleasantly good work at a girls' school in India into the tireless Mother Teresa, working among the detritus of an ancient and intelligent civilization. "I wouldn't do that for a million dollars," said a reporter as he watched her dress the stinking and suppurating sores of a man dying in a ditch. "Neither would I," said Mother Teresa.

This new thing in the world sends Isaac Jogues back to the American Indians who had mangled him to be martyred. One of the men who murdered him was later baptized and took as his name Isaac Jogues, and he too was martyred. The great historian Francis Parkman, no friend to the Jesuit missions, duly admires the courage, attributing it in part to the fanaticism of Rome and suggesting that, take it all in all, the Puritans' indifference to the Indians was the superior course. Yet we have seen from Mrs. Jackson the miracles that the same supposed fanatics could achieve among the more severe Spanish in a climate just slightly less forbidding than that of the Great Lakes and the Saint Lawrence River Valley. Where does the world, of its own, give birth to such love of enemies, even unto death?

The world rather gives birth to enmity. Says Saint Augustine of the city of man, "Each individual in this community is driven by his passions to pursue his private purposes," his "dreams" as we sentimentally call them now. But these objects "are such that no one person (let alone, the world community) can ever be wholly satisfied" because we are made by God, for God, and "nothing but Absolute Being can satisfy human nature." That means that "the city of man remains in a chronic condition of civil war" (*City of God*, 18.2). We see this sad truth borne out in the relentless political unrest of our time. There is no Sabbath to relieve us of our laborious enmity, as there is no secular sacrament to heal our exhausted spirits and nourish us after the depletion wrought by ambition and lust. Enmity is the old story; even great patriots have hated one another, as Quintus Fabius Maximus hated Scipio Africanus, as Jefferson hated Hamilton, and as Theodore Roosevelt turned with a vengeance against his old friend William Howard Taft, flinging the door open for Woodrow Wilson, that coldly precise intellectual with a large capacity for hating everything.

Wilson was a "progressive," and therefore he forgot the new thing in the world, setting the world up for the bloodiest war in its long and miserable history. He set it up for the same old story. We do not have Christ without Christ. The Russians traded the mild and reform-minded Tsar Nicholas for Lenin, a paragon of intellectual and political evil, and reduced themselves to political imprisonment for the next eighty years—to serfdom even in the cities. The Mexicans turned Catholic priests into outlaws and endured a decade of misery.

We have forgotten, not because we were strong but because remembering the new thing in the world makes claims on us, calls forth our strength, and we prefer to slide and slouch instead. The faith is too heroic for our flaccid souls. We thought we could live off its patrimony forever. Therefore, we ceased to grow. We did not develop. We honored no saints, and we knew no dawn. Forget saints—we do not raise up even the cultural dwelling places where saints might be nourished. For this new thing in the world graced Europe with the great cathedrals, whose beauty is still unrivaled, and invented the university, an institution that is still among us though in debased form, having been torn from its religious roots. Oh, there were formal schools here and there in the ancient world, yet nothing to unite them, much less to induce people from all over Europe to send likely lads there to study all that might be studied, regardless of the wealth or the political importance of their parents, then to be licensed to teach in their own right, wherever the Cross was raised.

The modern world is the rich and irresponsible, wise and stupid daughter of this event. Forgetting what and who made it so, the world now purports to go on without spiritual roots or spiritual aim, as if the Word had never been made flesh at all. And we are rapidly losing any sense of the holiness of our own flesh. We are hedonists without plea-sure; carnal men and women, ignorant of their skin; of the world, but not in it; incoherent in our madness, and consistent only in our inabil-ity to follow a single principle to its conclusion.

Back to the road, modernist lotos-eaters.

# CHAPTER SEVEN

# Back to the Family

T he fundamental institution of social life is the family. If it is
   healthy, the body politic may perhaps be healthy too. If it is in
   decay, the body politic will be riddled with disease, and this is
true even if that body politic is the agent of the family's decay, appearing—appearing!—to thrive by robbing the family of its authority, its
influence, and its very life. Jabba the State may be very big, with a
hearty appetite for wealth and human flesh, but we could hardly call
it healthy.

I will hear again that I want us to return to a Golden Age that never
existed, when families were strong, headed by father-leaders (patri-
archs), and when most women stayed home and baked cookies. That
is nonsense. What I want is this: *not to live in an age of stunting and
decay*. A true development of the family would render it more powerful, not less; a force to be reckoned with in every feature of social and
political life, not invisible; muscular in its production and preservation
of culture, not weak-kneed and tamely submitting to be fed poisoned
pablum by the mass entertainment industry; firmly and forthrightly
the bearer of its own rights, not denied those rights by those Siamese
twins of decadence, statism and individualism; clearly the root and the
aim of persons in their true sexual identity as male and female, not set

aside for supposedly more important things, such as years of genital hedonism as the lubrication of mammon's machine. It would be rich in children, not poor and grudging. It would be the soil wherein we learn, throughout our lives, what it is to be charitable, brave, true, self-denying, patient, and pious, even though, or especially because, we are all sinners on a journey to death and judgment.

I want not a return to a *status quo ante*, but the recovery of a once living and thriving thing. The families of our grandparents are to be admired not because they were perfect but because they were very much *alive* and, potentially, on the way. Their virtues can be made manifest again in these new circumstances. They had homes, not flophouses, and they were pilgrims, not mudded wanderers, mulling round about and getting nowhere.

### A Lot of Leaves, No Fruit

Consider this parable of Jesus:

> A certain man had a fig tree planted in his vineyard; and he came and sought fruit thereon, and found none.
> Then he said unto the dresser of his vineyard, Behold, these three years I come seeking fruit on this fig tree, and find none: cut it down; why cumbereth it the ground?
> And he answering said unto him, Lord, let it alone this year also, till I shall dig about it, and dung it.
> And if it bear fruit, well: and if not, then after that thou shalt cut it down. (Luke 13:6–9)

We have borne more than four years not of tending to the family but of putting it on a starvation diet. We have supposed that the autonomy of individuals and the liberation of large state forces would lead to great things. They have not done so. There may be a lot of leaves, but there is no fruit.

I can say so in the most obvious sense: there are few children. The begetting and rearing of children is not instrumental to human goods; it is the good for which almost every other one of our activities is or ought to be instrumental. To cite Péguy again, writing in a saner time than ours, no one works except on behalf of his children. They are our prime physical and cultural bonds to the past and the future. Taken as a whole, any way of life that is poor in children is poor indeed, and any political innovation that leads to the birth of fewer children is like an induced sterility in culture itself; it is a dampening of human hope, in both its common and its theological sense. Herod did not want simply to kill a baby boy. He wanted to kill hope itself, embodied in the child, the long-expected Messiah.

Once we put it that way, we see that the "freedom" of the sexual revolution is not a liberating power but a self-administered vitiation. Let us examine the ways in which this is so. The Western nations are so poor in children that they are in the midst of cultural suicide. Marriages are rarer than ever, and the children that ought to bind mother and father together more closely are often lacking by design, not by the accidents of biology. Young people are taught about the genital action of sexual intercourse but not about what it means. They are not encouraged to see that the coming together of the sexes, male and female, is *essentially and not accidentally* the child-making thing, with each sex bringing to the other his or her precious strands of the immemorial history of mankind, including mother and father, brothers and sisters, and ancestors far back into the forgotten past. The "ideal" proposed to young people instead has no vista beyond the pleasure of the act. It is constricted; another cul-de-sac. Male and female then bring to one another no precious and sacred gifts; they are instead perceived as threats to all-important autonomy. It is believed better to be sterile and loose, like a nearly uprooted tree, than to be fruitful and bound to the life-giving soil.

We can see the vitiation also in the "gender identity" movement, whose incoherence suggests an autoimmune attack by the body upon itself. It is as if the sexual body were the thing to be made to flourish and at the same time the thing to kill at all costs. Almost in the same breath, we deny that there is any reality to masculine and feminine nature *and* insist upon a biological impossibility—namely, that a man can be trapped in a woman's body, or vice versa—that our premises have rendered a logical impossibility. The result has not been deeper meditation upon the beauty of being masculine and feminine but a compulsion to play along with someone's cartoon imagination of what it might be like to belong to the opposite sex, or to play along with a mad denial of sex itself, as everyone is supposed to occupy a position along a spectrum or is supposed to be "fluid." In biological reality, except for exceedingly rare cases of a genetic defect, there is no spectrum and no fluidity. We do not find, biologically, that there are millions of people occupying a spectrum between having male organs and having female organs. We do not find on every street corner a man with one developed mammary or a woman with one testicle.

The call to make homosexual relations legitimate, even ideal, is likewise a willful denial of sexual reality—willed sterility. It portends not growth but the refusal to grow. It is a primitivism of the individual life, a peculiar version of the so-called Peter Pan syndrome. The boy, often on account of some trauma in youth, wants to remain with the boys and not grow into his masculine nature, which is made for women and for the begetting of children. It is a form of arrested development. (I mean here not to insult but to describe the phenomenon with some biological and anthropological precision.) The human race cannot thrive by it. It leads nowhere. The girl, often on account of bad treatment she has received from boys and men, wants to remain with the girls, not growing into her feminine nature, which is made for men and for the conceiving and bearing of children. It is a sexual slumber party. It leads nowhere.

I notice also—it is hard not to notice it—that those churches which have accepted the New Sterility have handed over their charism as churches. Aldous Huxley, in *Brave New World*, was a shrewder theologian than the Anglican prelates who met at Lambeth in 1930. They retreated from a Christian understanding of the inner meaning of sexual intercourse, allowing—for grave reasons only, naturally—that married couples could legitimately opt for sterility in the child-making thing, to filch the pleasure from the act and rob it of meaning. Huxley saw where this decision would lead, as conclusions follow inexorably from the premises. In his novel, we have the head of the Anglican Church reduced to a figurehead in a funny costume, the Arch-High Songster of Canterbury. Dead end. No life, no pilgrimage. If anything may rightly be accused of "mere" nostalgia, of the antiquarian, it is the sweetish feeling of niceness that some few people attach to the idea of church. The worship of the dread God of the universe is, in such places, a hobby for old church ladies. It is as sterile as they are.

The sexual revolution is no more a development than are gelding and spaying. There is no future to it. It stifles the future in the womb.

## Get Thee Behind Me, Satan

I will now hear the objection that this autonomy I decry is necessary for a person's development. Quite the contrary. We human persons grow by the gift, not by hoarding; by being fruitful, not by sterility. Self-hoarding stunts our growth. It is a lie. It is based upon a misapprehension of what it means to be a human person.

Walker Percy, in *Lost in the Cosmos*, describes those who aspire to autonomy:

> The self sees itself as a sovereign and individual consciousness, liberated by education from the traditional bonds of religion, by democracy from the structures of class, by technology from the drudgery of poverty, and by self-knowledge from the tyranny of the unconscious—and therefore free to pursue its own destiny without God.[1]

But that turns out to be like the freedom of someone falling from the window ledge of his office on the eightieth story, his last connection to earth and mankind. Or like the ceaseless and futile activity that characterizes the damned in Dante's *Inferno*, as in the circle of the lecherous, tossed for all eternity in a tempest that is the objective correlative of their surrendering reason to desire:

> And as a flock of starlings winter-beaten
> founder upon their wings in widening turns,
> so did that whirlwind whip those evil souls,
> Flinging them here and there and up and down;
> nor were they ever comforted by hope—
> no hope for rest, or even lesser pain.[2]

Ceaseless motion that is stasis; a mockery of the steadfastness in faith, hope, and love that advances us along the way. It is everywhere in the *Inferno*, and it grows more mindless and inhuman and impersonal the farther down we go. For the human being is a person, and to be a person is to have a face, that is, to be toward and for the rest of the created world, other persons, and God.

Christians thus believe that it was fit for the incarnate Word to be born within the sheltering haven of the family and then to raise marriage to a position more honorable than man had ever conceived—man, who had fallen prey to his passions and his vain imaginations. So writes Pope Leo XIII about the teachings of Christ:

> He ennobled the marriage in Cana of Galilee by His presence, and made it memorable by the first of His miracles which He wrought; and for this reason, even from that day forth, it seemed as if the beginnings of new holiness had been conferred upon human marriages. Later on He brought back matrimony to the nobility of its primeval origin, by condemning the customs of the Jews in their abuse of the

plurality of wives and of the power of giving bills of divorce; and still more by commanding most strictly that no one should dare to dissolve that union which God Himself had sanctioned by a bond perpetual. (*Arcanum divinae*, February 10, 1880)

"It is not good for the man to be alone," said God, and he made for Adam and from Adam the first woman (Genesis 2:18–24). For God had himself used the first person *plural* when he said, "Let us make man in our image" (Genesis 1:26), man who is both the individual person and the human race. We cannot be human without love, and love by its nature seeks the eternal, not the passing moment. It does not flit about from place to place, but builds, tends, and beautifies its home, the home that is an earnest of the heavenly Jerusalem.

What happens to man when he is severed from both his bodily and his spiritual nature? He does not gain liberty, which is to the moral life what health is to the body, the freedom to act in concord with his nature for ends that are truly human and that therefore direct him toward the divine. That is why we can understand Virgil's plea for the pilgrim Dante at the bottom of the mount of Purgatory. *Libertà va cercando*, says he to his fellow Roman, the severe moralist Cato: "He seeks his freedom."[3] Such a quest would make no sense if by freedom we meant choosing merely what you like and therefore being trammeled up in self-will; that kind of false freedom is available to us at every moment. No, we do not grow strong that way. We become like Thomas Wolfe's ironically named character Eugene, "well born," with no roots and no nourishment. So he turns to sexual action either in the boredom of lust or the frenzy of a search for his very self.

For such a person, says Walker Percy, "the pleasure of a sexual encounter derives not only from physical gratification but also from the demonstration to oneself that, despite one's own ghostliness, one is, for the moment at least, a sexual being. Amazing! Indeed, the most amazing of all the creatures of the Cosmos: a ghost with an erection!"[4] Such an evanescent sense of the self is perfectly consistent with narcissism. We gaze into that reflecting pool not exactly in delight of what we see there but in the uneasy worry that there may not be anything to see there at all. The narcissist is in love with a ghost. The autonomous self, detached from the bonds of family in all its powers and hierarchies, from the family of mother and father and children to that great *societas domestica* of all the saints, is a ghost, and betrays the insubstantiality and the ceaseless repetitive haunting and fluttering of the ghost. Fifty shades of grey, indeed—grey skies everywhere, and the human soul weak, prone to the psychological manipulations of the mass phenomena, unheroically unhappy, unsociable, lonesome, and grey.

Satan, offering all the kingdoms and pleasures of the world, delivers an exhausted whore in the back end of an abandoned warehouse in Newark. Get thee hence, fool.

### Safety Kills

How do I love thee? Let me count the ways.
I love thee to the depth and breadth and height
My soul can reach, when feeling out of sight
For the ends of being and ideal grace.
I love thee to the level of every day's
Most quiet need, by sun and candle-light.
I love thee freely, as men strive for right.
I love thee purely, as they turn from praise.
I love thee with the passion put to use
In my old griefs, and with my childhood's faith.
I love thee with a love I seemed to lose
With my lost saints. I love thee with the breath,
Smiles, tears, of all my life; and, if God choose,
I shall but love thee better after death.
—Elizabeth Barrett Browning, Sonnet 43, *Sonnets from the Portuguese*

Behold one of the most popular poems ever written. I give it not because I think it is one of the *best* love sonnets, though it is very fine indeed. I give it because it shows us what the people of Mrs. Browning's time looked upon as a perfect expression of perfect love between a married man and woman. It speaks to us about the supposedly prudish Victorians.

What we notice here is that the passion of her intensely personal wedded love is far-reaching in all kinds of ways. It is spiritual, as it directs her soul to the profundities of being itself and "ideal grace." It is a love of home and the ordinary things of the day. It is free, and its freedom is bound up with striving for virtue. It is pure, and not a matter of a mercenary exchange, even if the reward is praise. She loves her husband with all the passion that once troubled her in her "old griefs" and with the simplicity and trust of a child. Every breath she draws, every smile, every tear she sheds is an act of love here and now, and if the good Lord should grant it, she will love her husband "better after death."

Such poetry was not at all unusual. Christian poets have in fact been celebrating in song the love of man and woman for many hundreds of years, with mirth, bawdy humor, magical romance, quiet faith, and passionate pleading. If we no longer do so, we are the odd ones. Nor do we need to look only at the works of the professionals. Folk songs testify most eloquently. Here is a splendidly sad one, written in Italy a hundred years ago. The singer cries out to his departing beloved, begging her to look upon the blue sea from the cliffs of Sorrento, as she is leaving the heart that loves her so much that he cannot bear to live without her:

> *E tu dice: "Io parto, addio!"*
> *T'alluntane da stu core,*
> *Da la terra de ll'ammore,*
> *tiene 'o core 'e nun turnà?*
> *Ma nun mme lassà,*

*nun darme stu turmiento:*
*Torna a Surriento,*
*famme campà!*

And you say, "I'm leaving, goodbye,"
Going far away from this heart of mine,
Far from the land of love—
How can you have the heart not to return?
But do not leave me,
Do not give me this anguish:
Come back to Sorrento,
Let me live once more!

No one who has heard the Neapolitan words sung in their strange and haunting melody can doubt that this song, "Come Back to Sorrento," has the power to make us feel what it may be like to know that your beloved is leaving, that you will not see her again, and that all the beauty and the joy of life will depart with her. It will not do at all to say that such feelings are "inappropriate" or beneath the dignity of someone who should instead be making his way in the world. Let not people whose hearts beat slow and cold, whose love is reckoned up in material advantages, prescribe for the rest of humanity. Let not the cripple cast aspersions on the race.

We can best judge of the hearts of a people by what it takes as ordinary, and for that we need not always turn to excellent poets and artists. We can turn to the great good in the middle, available to everyone. Let me give as an example a song by a woman composer of some note, Virginia Gabriel, with lyrics by one E. A. Warden, whom I have not been able to identify. The song was printed in the June 1869 number of *Arthur's Home Magazine*, a sort of *The Century* for housewives, which included among its plentiful literary offerings essays on medicine, on the making and mending of clothes, on the growing, storing, and preparing of food, and on the Christian faith. It also included printed music, scored for piano and voice. Here is the second and final stanza of one entry, "Say Thou Art Mine":

Say thou art mine; my heart could claim
No purer spirit for its mate;
I do not long for wealth or fame,
No joy so deep, no wealth so great,
But deeper in its changeless truth,
And stronger in its gentle power,
The love that smiles upon our youth,
And makes thee mine, my gentle flower.
*Refrain:*
Oh, say thou art mine, I'll cherish thee,
And prize thy happiness above all else on earth,
Then smile on me, and bless me with thy priceless love.

What we have here, in the both homely and decorative language of the time, is grandly adventurous. The poet does not care for money or notoriety, those stodgy settlements. He does not seek to delay his love in order to gain better prospects at work. He does not adopt a cold temperance in love, subordinating it to low and petty aims, or to the shabby exhaustion of a nervous will. He is young and bold and looks forward to a life of complete devotion, complete self-giving, in return for his beloved's gift of her own "priceless love." To return to relations between the sexes in which it was even conceivable that men and women would want to sing such a song—that a man would write the words and a woman would set the music—is, again, not to retreat to a drawing room with lace curtains and portraits of double-chinned forebears, filmed over with candle-smoke and grease. It is to return, weary of aimlessness and meaningless motion, to a powerful central current of the great river of married love.

We prefer "safe sex," that timid, puling little oxymoron. We prefer the mechanism of the "hookup," a sweating-off of energy, like a sauna

after riding an exercise bicycle for an hour. We prefer hedges, plenty of
exits, sprinkler systems, and fire extinguishers. Our banality shows not
a freedom with sex but a pallor of spirit, a near-numbness to its beauty
and power. We are like people who cannot bear the grand and soul-
stirring power of the words of Jesus, that the two shall be one, but pore
over dirty pictures scratched on a lavatory wall. No steak, but spam.

It is time to raise people again who have the heart for that loving
pilgrimage of old.

### Let Boys Be Men

I take it as obvious that if we are going to have strong marriages
we must have strong men, and that means we will have to see to the
generous, healthy, and hopeful raising of boys.

I trust I need not make the case that boys are in a bad way. My
opponents themselves say so, though not in words I would use. They
say that boys in our time are shiftless, cruel, dishonest, and contemptuous of women. If that is true, then by their own testimony, the liberals who are in *complete control of our schools and the media* have failed
miserably to raise boys to be good men. We cannot here point to a
development, an advance along the way. Instead we have frustration,
even a concerted refusal to give boys the intellectual and moral nourishment they need. It is like castration—and behold, the castration of
confused and unhappy boys has now become a veritable fashion of the
"progressive" world, a world of madness, incoherence, and sterility.

With all our wealth, there should be a flourishing of manhood, the
activities of boys reaching more broadly into the world, not pent up in
a pigsty, boys' peculiar gifts, freely encouraged, earning greater esteem
and gratitude. Yet a boy who is not athletic can go through twelve years
of schooling and another four years of college and not once hear that,
simply because he is male, he has something special to bring to the
world. The Aztecs used to cut the hearts out of prisoners of war whom
they sacrificed to their sun god. Nothing is new under that sun.

Let me say categorically that the notion that one sex is primarily responsible for evil—whether it is Islam with its hell full of women or feminism with its hell full of men—is a delusion. Anyone who wishes to know what is wrong the world need only consult a mirror. I am also unpersuaded that our culture, of all the cultures in the history of the world, has gotten the relations between the sexes right. Again, liberals themselves, with their complaints and accusations, say as much. Do I want to return to the days when a woman could not own a credit card? No more than I want to return to the days when there were no credit cards to own. That is not the point. I want to return to something that was alive and thriving, because only a living thing can properly be said to progress.

Hence we must see to the boys. And the girls? Undoubtedly. But what can I say about that in a time of rankling suspicion between the sexes? That is not my place. I will leave that instruction to good and wise women. I have learned by experience that as soon as a man utters a word that is critical of the way women lead their wandering lives now, despite his having uttered a hundred words that are critical of the wandering lives of contemporary men, he will be accused of misogyny, and all further discussion comes to an end. Then I will write about boys here, briefly.

Suppose your objective is to inspire a boy with a hunger to learn things. There is nothing political about it. You want to light the fire within. What do you do? I can tell you immediately what you do *not* do. You do not assume that he is going to enjoy what his sister does. Pay attention. Not every boy I meet is interested in military history. Most are not, but every child I have met who was so interested was a boy. Not every boy memorizes, out of sheer fascination, sheets of sports statistics. Most do not, but every child I have met who did that was a boy. Not every boy gazes lovingly at a four-square-foot street map of his home town, as I did when I was seven. Most do not, but every atlas-scanner I have met, everyone whose road map was a prized possession, was a boy. Just as in physical training you would go with and not against a boy's natural bodily strengths, so you should go with and not against his ways of learning and the things he wants to learn about.

We do not have to invent anything. We have only to retrieve what has been invented.

I open, at random, *The American Boy's Handy Book* by Daniel Carter Beard (1850–1941). The dates of his life are telling. He lived through the Civil War, the Industrial Revolution, a world war, and the Great Depression. He was already near old age when that once boyish and now deeply confused organization called the Boy Scouts came to the United States to strengthen boys' bodies and raise up their minds and souls. Beard was himself a great part of that arrival, writing and illustrating articles for *Boys' Life* from its inception in 1911. He appealed to the boy that is still alive, though too often dormant, in every man.

At random, then: "The Water-Telescope":

Nearly three-fourths of the whole world is covered by water. Old Isaak Walton in his quaint book says that this vast expanse of territory is "Nature's storehouse, in which she locks up all her wonders." The previous chapters on fresh water and marine aquariums have already shown how a portion of the "wonders" may be kept in your own house, in what might be termed little glass side-shows to the great marine menagerie. This chapter will tell you how to make an instrument through which you can peep under the watery tent of the big show itself, and see the curiosities swimming about in their native haunts.

The water-telescope is not made of aqueous fluid, as its name might imply, but is a contrivance made of wood or metal, through which, when one end is partly submerged, objects beneath the water can be plainly seen that would otherwise be invisible.[5]

Apparently Beard thought that the boys would understand the terms "marine menagerie" and the jocularly overdone "aqueous fluid." He took for granted that they had gone to circuses and could pick up the allusion to the big show and the side shows and that at least some of them would have heard of Walton's *The Compleat Angler*. More, he assumes that they would *want* to see things underwater from above, and that means that he assumes they would often be in a place where they might have the opportunity: fooling around in a pond or on a lake, or in a boat on a lagoon or bay. The construction he describes requires sawing, nailing, puttying, and soldering. Consider how many skills are ancillary to the sheer wonder of looking at the strange fish below.

Again at random, from the chapter "Dogs: What They are Good For, and How to Train Them":

> The pointer or setter you may commence to teach to "stand," at a very early age, using first a piece of meat, praising and petting him when he does well, and reprimanding him when required. Do not tire your pup out, but if he does well once let him play and sleep before trying again. As he grows older, replace the meat with a dead bird.[6]

Beard is careful to tell the boy that though he must be a firm teacher, he must also realize that all kinds of differences are to be found among breeds and among the individuals within a breed, varying considerably "in intelligence, amiability, and all those little traits that go to make up a dog's character." Yet he has clearly in mind a relationship between the boy and the dog that is close, affectionate, and productive. They get things done together. Since the boy will be using the pointer or setter as a bird dog or small-game hunter, he will be trained in the use of a shotgun for procuring food. Against such a pastime only a vegetarian can reasonably object.

Boys may learn how to build eighteen kinds of kites, how to make their own fishing tackle, how to build boats and canoes, how to rig the boats, how to rear and tame wild birds, how to build snow forts, how to make puppets for a puppet show, how to make costumes for the masquerades and other theatrical productions fit for indoors in the winter, and on and on. Some of his suggestions are eye-opening for their sophistication and for his assumption that they are not merely girlish pastimes. Beard describes a "Literary Sketch Club," which

> has been tried and has proved very successful, the original club having prospered through three winters, and still boasts of some thirty enthusiastic members. The idea of the club is that each member illustrate the same subject (previously selected) in any way he thinks fit—the artists, if there be any present, by a drawing or painting on the subject; a member who sings may select, adapt, or originate a song that will express his idea of the subject. Instrumental music may be made to tell the story; short sketches, in prose or poetry, original essays, or selections carefully made from good authors; in fact, there is scarcely any one who cannot illustrate the subject in some way that will add to the entertainment of the evening.[7]

At which we must gape in wonder. Here Beard takes for granted that boys will write poetry or sing or play musical instruments or paint. There were no video games. The things that have been done can be done again. But if we believe that they can be done again *while we continue to deny reality*—assuming boys are girls and that boys in the company of girls will behave just as they might when they are alone with one another—then we are lying to ourselves and hurting the boys. And our denial of reality forces women, who might have had their easy pick of many good men suing for their affection, to undertake the difficult search for a good man to marry.

What Beard describes was no fluke. The crucial thing, now largely dismissed, is to get the boys together at times—*at times!*—apart from their sisters and to do boyish literary things in a boyish way. Here is a description, by one Eliot McCormick, of another literary club several decades before Beard wrote his book. The "Newspaper Club" met every two weeks, its exercises comprising "readings, essays, declamation and debates, and the presentation by some previously appointed member of the current events of the fortnight gleaned from the newspapers." One of the exercises was boldly competitive. The boys were given a long list of historical questions, a prize promised to the one who could answer the most questions two weeks later. McCormick was concerned that too many boys were reading dime novels that were at best empty and at worst vicious. He did not like the "vile" novels of Zola; Lord only knows what he would say about "young adult" fiction now. So he describes the boys' activity, when motivated by the spirit of a contest:

> Difficult as [the questions] were, the boys attacked them
> with undismayed courage, took them to their teachers and
> friends, involved the assistance of editors and library men,
> besieged the Brooklyn, the Astor, and the Historical Society
> libraries, made the librarians' lives a burden, and in every
> possible way sought to obtain the answers. It is no exag-
> geration to say that for a fortnight the questions were the
> uppermost thought in their minds; and not so much for the
> sake of the prize as from an ambitious desire to excel in the
> competition. The president was simply amazed. Boys who
> were not naturally studious spent hours over books which
> they had never opened before in their lives; others who were
> fond of reading left fiction for history and biography.[8]

What was done once can be done again. I have seen it done again: as for instance in the remarkable Riverside Center for Imaginative Learning in Illinois, run by men who have remained blessedly boyish at heart and who therefore can broaden a boy's interests to include drama for those who are shy, carpentry for those who are at first skittish around tools, and the reading of great books for those who are like most adults nowadays and do not know that there are any great books to begin with. Development does not imply dilapidation, debility, and decay. If the interests of boys are far more circumscribed than they once were, if more and more boys never emerge from the fog of apathy, let alone alienation and seething hatred, then we cannot talk about progress but about futility and inaction. To "progress" in quicksand is to sink further. Daniel Carter Beard holds out a pole for the man stuck fast so he can free himself and get on with his journey.

What we say of the boy's physical and intellectual interests we may say of his moral development also. Any decent boy can be raised with the high aim of protecting his mother, and by age eleven or twelve, when he begins to exceed his mother in strength and agility, his moral duty to protect her is more than a pleasant fiction. If he can be raised to do that, then he can be raised to protect women in general. Any decent boy, looking upon the serious piety of a devout, gentle, and intelligent father, can be raised with a vision of manhood embodied in piety, not grossness, vulgarity, debauchery, and irreligion. It used to be done. It can be done again. If we can raise gentlemen to protect ladies, for the good of everyone, we can raise ladies who will expect such protection and appreciate it. I am not talking about utopia. I am talking about ordinary life.

What will men of the future think of our castration of boys, now in the most literal sense? It rivals the most perverted of human cruelties. Somewhere in the everlasting bonfire, Josef Mengele is laughing.

### Where Has All the Silence Gone?

"And he went down with them and came to Nazareth," writes Saint Luke of the boy Jesus, "and was subject to them; and his mother kept all these things carefully in her heart" (2:51). The gospel writers, chroniclers as they were, did not pry into the private life of Jesus, and what few glimpses we have suggest a life full of rich and fruitful silence. The same Jesus who is to be found among enormous crowds on the plains or on a hillside overlooking the sea, who was accused of eating and drinking among publicans and sinners, and who had a keen eye for the outcast and the suffering regularly retreats for long periods of prayer, with a few of his friends or alone. Yet we never sense that Jesus enjoyed aloneness for its own sake but rather to draw nearer to the Father. He was then exchanging one kind of communion for another, or drawing on his communion with the Father to draw closer to his disciples and to mankind. Christian artists and mystics have reasonably supposed that Jesus learned his habits of conversation and silence, of action and prayer, in the home at Nazareth.

Talk is cheap, it is said, and rightly so. Much talk makes what is said seem cheap; a glass cube will seem to shine brighter than a diamond; it is the weakest sergeant who must always shout; a tattoo causes the eye of the beholder to turn aside in embarrassment. As a cancer is to healthy tissue, both its destroyer and its cheap and deformed imitation, so are the noise and the loneliness of the world to the conversation and silence in the home. We may say that a friend is one before whom you would feel comfortable saying anything, and that is true as far as it goes, but it does not go far enough. Intimacy implies that you may be comfortable saying nothing at all, but merely to take a quiet and rich delight in the felt presence of those you love. In silence does the tree grow tall and strong.

The moments I recall most clearly from my early childhood do not involve bustle. I am lying on the floor of our small living room, drawing pictures and writing stories on pieces of cardboard that came back with my father's shirts from the laundry. My mother is in the kitchen, ten feet away, preparing something for lunch, humming and singing. My baby sister is asleep in her crib. These are the moments that C. S. Lewis's tempter Screwtape says are most dangerous for the cause of hell. "You allowed him," writes the infernal uncle to his incompetent nephew Wormwood, speaking of the man they are trying to tempt to his eternal loss, "to walk down to the old mill and have tea there—a walk through country he really likes, and taken alone."[9] This colossal blunder is the living and human counterpart of another that Wormwood would make later on, that of allowing the patient to meet a young Christian woman, sprightly, innocent, witty, and pure, "yet ready to fall into this booby's arms like any other breeding animal."[10] How far, this ready physicality, this genuine feminine passion, from the cold reserve of the men and women of our time, hedonists in principle and starved in fact!

Perhaps the sound that Satan hates the most is that of children laughing. Or maybe that of old people laughing along with children. Or the merriment of people enjoying, as Screwtape calls it, "that detestable art which the humans call Music," akin to what occurs in Heaven, "a meaningless acceleration in the rhythm of celestial experience, quite opaque to us,"[11] for in Hell it is as in Hollywood, by the testimony of one who should know: "[A]ll has been occupied by Noise—Noise, the grand dynamism, the audible expression of all that is exultant, ruthless, and virile—Noise which alone defends us from silly qualms, despairing scruples, and impossible desires."[12]

If there is news in Hell, it is all the politics of war, graft, vote-buying, soul-cramping, and scandal, and if there is entertainment, it is all loud, brash, salacious, relentless, and a most effectual battery against the human soul. But as Max Picard suggests poetically but no less perceptively in *The World of Silence*, noise is opposed to silence not as presence is to absence, but as absence is to presence. Noise is for crowds of people reduced to atoms of self-will and self-protectiveness colliding against one another in an empty secular space. We hear nothing in noise that we should like to remember when we are old or that brings back to us the scenes of our childhood. Our feelings are harried and necessarily impersonal. We are absent to one another, anonymous and faceless. The richness of "communal silence"—Josef Pieper's fine term, from *In Search of the Sacred*—binds people together in a way that they themselves would find hard to put in words, as when my students and my colleagues and I pray quietly in our college chapel before Mass, and I am aware of them more keenly as persons than I am at any other time. We are for one another and with one another, in the sight of God.

The family and the home are sites of bold and easygoing play, of raucous argument that need not result in enmity, and of silence that is not icy or drab but warm and fostering, like the good earth beneath our feet.

## Except Ye Become as Little Children

As we have forgotten the family, so have we forgotten children. It is a spiritual dementia. Let me then try to remember, and to bring back to the reader's remembrance, what intimations of home and eternity the child may bring.

One night from my youth stands out bold in my memory. It was winter, and our dead-end street—dead-end for cars but not for people walking far into the woods—was covered with powdery snow, as were the hills round about. And I and a couple of my cousins took our sleds to the top of the wooded hill above our grandparents' house, riding a winding footpath down it, through the yard and into the street, into the bright light of the lamps on the telephone pole above. It was intensely cold, that good sharp cold that is exhilarating when you are dry and wrapped up well. I was eight, and while I was sledding a melody ran through my mind, one that the nun at our school had introduced to the children, hoping that they would sing it at Mass and thus teach it to the parents. I had not known it at the time, but the melody was more than four hundred years old and was composed across the ocean, in Germany: "Ein' Feste Burg"—"A Mighty Fortress Is Our God."

And the disciples were footsore, and the sun was slanting late in the afternoon. They and Jesus came to a small village on the coast of Judea. They were going to stay at the home of one of his followers, but before they could rest, the women of the village came to him bringing their children. And the disciples, weary and wanting to seem important, and all the wearier in their importance, began to rebuke the women because, after all, the Master had traveled a long way. But the Lord brightened at the sight of the children and spoke sharply to his disciples: "Suffer the little children to come unto me, and forbid them not: for of such is the kingdom of God." And he added the mysterious warning that unless we welcome the kingdom of God as would a little child, we shall find no way to enter in. "And he took them up in his arms, put his hands upon them, and blessed them" (Mark 10:13–16).

But Silas Marner hardened in his dislike of his fellow human beings, who had slandered him and driven him into exile. Far away from his village he found a hovel, no home, and there he plied his trade as a weaver, earning his food, speaking very little to anyone, collecting his gold and counting the coins as if they were the sole proof of his worth, never mingling among his neighbors to pray and to sing to God. And he had no home, and he went forth on no journey, and there he would have remained to the day he died, shut up in the vault of his resentment and despair, except that one night he found something gold gleaming in the snow outside of his place. It was the gold hair of a baby girl, left there for death, or for the mysterious workings of God, the God who has been known to hide in the darkest corners of all, those in the human heart. Silas took up the child and cared for her, and under the ice of his heart the seed broke open its shell and came to life.

And another memory is seared into my mind. Older now, I had stopped at a seamy little grocery store to get a carton of orange juice. I was in the middle of my paper route and was thirsty. A friend of mine, a couple of years younger, led me into the back room, where boys smoked cigarettes and shot pool. And there on the wall was a big picture of a naked woman photographed from the back, answering a doorbell and giving a smutty answer to the surprised man standing there. I had never seen anything at once so disappointing, shameful, and sad. Three years later I would not find it sad. I would have "grown," and that would in large part obscure the truth I had known when I was innocent. But that picture was mere innocence and purity itself by comparison with what children are given to gaze at by their own teachers in our schools now; children old and stupid before their time. "When ignorance is bliss," wrote the poet Thomas Gray, looking out at schoolboys playing on the fields of Eton, "'tis folly to be wise." He had no idea that man would come to rub out the ignorance, ruin the bliss, yet impart no wisdom, making the poor children more foolish than ever.

The local country boy and the orphan girl found what was inside the walls overgrown with brush. It was a secret garden, and there they found strange books with filthy pictures in them, and they snorted and laughed, and imitated what they found, and passed along the wisdom to their playfellows, particularly the little crippled boy who kept to his bed in the manor house. That is the modern version of the story. What an advancement over what the homesick Frances Hodgson Burnett actually wrote.

"Unless you become as little children, you shall not enter the kingdom of heaven." That is a stern warning. How can we understand it in our time? Not at all, so long as we remain in the imprisoning grooves of sexual "progress." I will end here with a beginning. It comes from *The Angel in the House* (1856) by the long-neglected poet Coventry Patmore, whose theme was homely love and a Christian man's admiration for a virtuous and comely woman. Here he describes, in the first person, the moments leading up to the wedding night, after all the guests have gone:

> As souls, ambitious, but low-born,
> If raised past hope by luck or wit,
> All pride of place will proudly scorn,
> And live as they'd been used to it,
> So we two wore our strange estate:
> Familiar, unaffected, free,

We talk'd, until the dusk grew late,
Of this and that; but, after tea,
As doubtful if a lot so sweet
As ours was ours in very sooth,
Like children, to promote conceit,
We feign'd that it was not the truth;
And she assumed the maiden coy,
And I adored remorseless charms,
And then we clapp'd our hands for joy,
And ran into each other's arms.

The lovers in that passage are both more innocent than we can imagine and more powerfully and boldly mature. They are about to embark on the great adventure of marriage, making the home that will be their haven on earth, and those two, the adventure and the home, are one. Be brave, my reader, and do not fear the haven and the adventure.

# CHAPTER EIGHT

## O Grave, Where Is Thy Victory?

The Indian Ocean, off the coast of Madagascar, in time of war. A middle-aged British soldier, assigned to counterespionage; an evening of debauchery. It was a requirement of the job. He had to keep an eye on his Italian and German counterparts. After it all, he was filled with disgust for himself, his life, and the world. He drove his car to the beach. He began to walk far out into the water, intending never to return. It took some time, but finally he had to swim, and so he did, farther out, sensing that he could sleep in this water, as in a sweet bed after much trouble and disappointment. Then, as he writes,

> suddenly, without thinking or deciding, he started swimming back to shore. He was very tired, and kept feeling as if he was in his depth again, and wasn't; so he shouted foolishly for help, and kept his eyes fixed on the lights of Peter's Cafe and Costa da Sol.
>
> They were lights of the world; they were the lights of his home, his habitat, where he belonged. He must reach them. There followed an overwhelming joy such as he had never experienced before, an ecstasy. *In some mysterious way it*

*became clear to him that there was no darkness, only the pos-*
*sibility of losing sight of a light which shone eternally;* that our
clumsy appetites are no more than the blind reaching of a
newly born child after the teat through which to suck the
milk of life; that our sufferings, our affliction, are part of a
drama—an essential, even an ecstatic, part—endlessly
revolving round the two great propositions of good and evil,
of light and darkness.[1]

Those are the words of Malcolm Muggeridge, in his eighty-fifth
year, looking back upon his journey in the world that was his exile and
the world that was his home. What called the man back to life? It was
not, in that moment, his memory of love, his pride in his work, his
anticipation of children and grandchildren. It was nothing so sweet,
"but just the lights of a sleazy cafe looking over the sea; a noisy haunt
of mortal men and women; St. Teresa of Avila's second-class hotel."[2]

The world around us is not to be loved because it is great and glorious and a heaven in the making. It is that Earthly Inn. For "the true
wonder of life is indeed its ordinariness rather than an imaginary
extraordinariness. God did not come among us trailing clouds of glory,
incarnate." He had no formal schooling, he spoke to children, who
understood him more readily than their parents did; he chose the lowly
for his apostles, "and even then, one of the chosen twelve proves to be
a crook, and the rest ran away."

Perhaps we can love the second-class hotel only if we remember
that we are second-class creatures, mostly foolish, often wicked, usually
lost, hard to teach, and resentful of the teaching, like the mongrel with
one floppy ear or the boy in the class who spends his best minutes
dreaming of a field on the other side of the window and before whose
eyes the letters on the page play hooky too and go swimming.

Muggeridge called his book *Confessions of a Twentieth-Century
Pilgrim*, and justly so. If we are on a journey home—a real home and
not some philosophical abstraction, the home where dwells the Word

incarnate, "both God and man, son both of God and man," as Milton puts it—then the home on earth that is a way station on the road to our true and final home claims our gratitude even more, because it was there that we learned first whence we have come and where we long to return. Moments of illumination flash upon us, and we long to have them again, but we can do so only if we proceed along the pilgrimage.

Muggeridge quotes the poet William Cowper, a man who knew both joy and deep sadness:

> What peaceful hours I once enjoyed!
> How sweet their memory still!
> But they have left an aching void,
> The world can never fill.
> Return, O holy Dove, return,
> Sweet messenger of rest;
> I hate the sins that made Thee mourn,
> And drove Thee from my breast.[3]

Cowper longs for "a closer walk with God," and we must acknowledge the force of that verbal noun. He does not mean, and Muggeridge does not understand him to mean, that if we follow the laws of God, all shall be well with us here, and we shall never know suffering, humiliation, and loss. We must *walk*. No pilgrim, no progress. The pilgrim knows and loves the home he leaves and the home he seeks. His is the ultimate nostalgia, the ultimate heartache for the return. He can say, confidently, with the psalmist, "yea, though I walk through the valley of the shadow of death, I shall fear no evil, for thou art with me" (Psalm 23:4) and can beg the Lord for the grace to take up his cross and follow where he goes.

It is not merely a movement from one point to another, or from an earth to be shrugged away to a heaven that has nothing to do with earth. The Word became flesh and dwelt among us, and he is the still center of all that turns in heaven and on earth. The pilgrimage is not an escape from but a plunge into the fullness of life, for Christ rose not as a specter or a disembodied soul but in the flesh. The bodily resurrection was the single doctrine of Christianity least likely to recommend itself to the philosophers of the time, as Christ's assertion that his kingdom "was not of this world" was least likely to recommend itself to the Jewish patriots of the time. But upon that doctrine, upon man's adoration of the God who humbled himself to take on human flesh and exalted that flesh eternally, is built all that in Christian culture and civilization is good and true and beautiful:

> And I saw a new heaven and a new earth: for the first heaven and the first earth were passed away; and there was no more sea.
> And I John saw the holy city, new Jerusalem, coming down from God out of heaven, prepared as a bride adorned for her husband.
> And I heard a great voice out of heaven saying, Behold, the tabernacle of God is with men, and he will dwell with them, and they shall be his people, and God himself shall be with them, and be their God. (Revelation 21:1–3)

A new heaven and a new earth: and the two live together, as "in the beginning God created the heavens and the earth" (Genesis 1:1).

If we believe this, then nothing on earth is beneath our notice, for we are given light and life, writes Muggeridge, by the "universal spirit of love which informs, animates, illuminates all creation, from the tiniest particle of insentient matter to the radiance of God's very throne."[4] Everything in that creation is an expression of God, a word we may listen to. The whole world then speaks of what it is and what it is not, of the God who made it and the God who brings it to its consummation, for "it is he that hath made us, and not we ourselves" (Psalm 100:3), and "the whole creation groaneth and travaileth in pain together," awaiting "the glorious liberty of the children of God"

(Romans 8:22, 21). The pilgrim alone knows that his good and humble home perched on a hillside is an allegory of heaven, and not so by the arbitrary choice of the allegorist, but by its essence and our essence, as made by the God who speaks to us through those essences. In the heart and mind of the pilgrim, everything is full to bursting with the dangerous and dashing bravura of the Maker in which Gerard Manley Hopkins revels:

> No wonder of it: sheer plod makes plough-down sillion
> Shine, and blue-bleak embers, ah my dear,
> Fall, gall themselves, and gash gold-vermilion.[5]

No pilgrim, I say, no progress. The old is worn out. The most common product in a world that has forgotten the pilgrimage, that worships a "progress" it defines in worldly terms if it defines it at all, is garbage: things made to become garbage and to be cast away as garbage. Old books are cast off because no one reads them because they are old. Old people are cast off because no one heeds them because they are old. Children who are not wanted—as if the most precious gift from the hand of God were nothing but scraps of costume jewelry—are cast off. History is bunk, as Henry Ford said. Garbage—mountains of it. I have found books in our town's garbage station that should be in a library, and some of them used to be in the library, until they were cast aside, unread, for garbage.

Here is the paradox. They who long for heaven cherish the home. They who are on the way look with kindly favor and forgiveness upon the homely places along that way where they have taken nourishment and lived and loved and suffered and died. They who adore progress and look for perfection upon earth can at best tolerate those places. At worst, they despise them and want to clear them away because they speak of human folly, imperfection, and transience. The pilgrim understands Jacob, who, waking from his dream upon the plains of Luz, built a small altar there, to which he gave a holy name, "Bethel," the house of God (Genesis 28:19). They understand both the ordinary and the holy, the holy sometimes hidden within the ordinary.

They who worship progress pulverize. No place speaks to them, because there is no allegory and no holy God made manifest by the allegory; their ears are clotted with the wax of the hour. Is it so surprising, then, that the sons of Saint Benedict would at once devote their lives to prayer and to make and love places where there had been but barrens and wilderness before? The pilgrim understands the vow of stability; the restless wanderer hardly attains a place but he then wants to leave it.

That is because the pilgrim has in his mind the words of Jesus, that he who would save his life must lose it. The progressive looks forward to a time when pills and prostheses will prolong human life for additional decades or centuries of aimless and pointless years. For the pilgrim, that would be like being sentenced to a prison or a haven for pensioners in Florida, watching television, playing shuffleboard, and boasting that not all the flesh on the body merely hangs. The steadfast pilgrim has somewhere to love and somewhere to go. Home is like home.

*Into Thy Hands, O Lord*

Imagine a dying man, surrounded by his friends. There is no noise of medical monitors. There are no anonymous nurses and orderlies bustling about his chassis. Looking round, he sees some of his fellows in the infirmary in better health than he is. He sees the simple articles of their lives of prayer: a crucifix, a stoup of holy water, an earthy icon hanging from the wooden planks of the wall. Through the window, he can hear the bells calling his brother monks to prayer, seven times a day.

It had not always been so. He was an illiterate keeper of the cattle for the monastery, one among many. One evening the cowherds gathered for some food and beer and song, as they commonly did, and the harp went round from one man to the next. Each was to sing a song of the old war heroes, songs he had heard his parents and grandparents sing when he was a child. But this man did not know any song to sing, or perhaps his conscience was uneasy about it, since he was a baptized Christian. So he excused himself and went to the shed to see to the cattle before retiring. He fell asleep, and an angel of the Lord appeared to him and encouraged him to sing. He woke with a hymn in his memory, composed to the glory of God in the same ancient meter and the same poetic language that his forebears had used for centuries. Then all was changed. The monks welcomed this man—Caedmon was his name—into their monastery, and the Venerable Bede tells us that from then on, though he never learned to read or write, he took the lessons from Scripture and from the lives of the saints that the monks taught him, and he ruminated upon them, transforming them into heroic poetry.

On the evening of his death, Caedmon called his fellow monks around him and asked if any of them held anything against him. Nothing at all, they said, and he was glad and replied that he too was at peace with them and with all Christian men. As the evening wore on, he asked for the waybread—the bread for the journey, for that is what *viaticum* means. They were surprised, because he had been there for only two weeks, and it did not seem to them that his journey-forth—his *utgang*—was near. But they brought it to him, and he received it, and shut his eyes in perfect calm and content. That was when the brethren had risen in the dark to sing the morning-song to the Lord. Caedmon went forth on that night, bravely and calmly.

Sigrid Undset, in her novel of medieval Norway, *Kristin Lavransdatter*, portrays for us such a death. The good farmer Lavrans, pious in his works, a man of powerful build and usually gentle words, honest and brave, is nearing the end of his life. There is nothing sentimental about this end. He and his wife, Ragnfrid, have spent most of their marriage misunderstanding one another and not loving one another well enough. His favorite daughter, Kristin, has brought shame upon

him, marrying a man not of his choosing and getting a child by him
while she was betrothed to someone else. Many of his neighbors envy
him for his piety. But now he lies on his bed in the great hall he built,
whose planks he pegged together with his own hands, waiting for
death. Over the course of a day or so his friends and neighbors and kin
come by to say farewell and to assure him that he owes them nothing.
He lies in pain, coming in and out of consciousness.

At the crisis, they call for the parish priest, Lavrans's old friend Sira
Eirik, a priest in a Viking mold if ever there was one—hot tempered
and severe, not above keeping a concubine in those half-pagan days
but devoted to the Church and sure in his ways. Sira Eirik keeps watch
over the dying man and gives him the anointing and the waybread,
and when the clutches of death shake the man's frame for the last time,
he holds up Lavrans's head and back with one arm, while in his other
hand he holds before his friend's eyes the crucifix. They pray together
the words of Jesus upon the cross: *In manus tuas, Domine, commendo
spiritum meum*: "Into your hands, O Lord, I commend my spirit."

What happens when we do not understand our journey into
depth—Saint Bonaventure's *Itinerarium mentis in Deum*, the mind's
journey into God? Notice the preposition, *into*. For God is the Being
who circumscribes all things and creates them by circumscribing,
while he himself is not circumscribed. There is no fathoming God. He
does not possess characteristics as contingent beings do. To know God
is to know that all your knowledge of him is as nothing, and the more
deeply you are immersed in the divine life, the more you know your
insignificance. You are no more than a mustard seed, the smallest of
all the seeds, yet in that smallest of the seeds dwells the kingdom of
God and all the cherubim and seraphim singing his glory.

What happens when we know no depth? We try to make up for it
in the dimensions we do know. We try to make up for it in length. We
fall into an idle vitalism, as if the purpose of human life were to extend
it as long as possible. But since long life without health and a sharp
mind is but length of irritation and vagary, we end up reckoning our

last years as weary, and so it is that many people seek an end of it all, for as far as they know, they have reached the end already. They are going on no pilgrimage, they are not returning home. They have no more opportunities for the here-and-there traffic of this life. They cannot go to the Grand Canyon, that great crack in the ground, so they will go to the grave instead. The car has idled too long. Turn the key and shut off the engine.

### Daily Dying

> Honor is flashed off exploit, so we say;
> And those strokes once that gashed flesh or galled shield
> Should tongue that time now, trumpet now that field,
> And, on the fighter, forge his glorious day.
> On Christ they do and on the martyr may;
> But be the war within, the brand we wield
> Unseen, the heroic breast not outward-steeled,
> Earth hears no hurtle then from fiercest fray.
> Yet God (that hews mountain and continent,
> Earth, all, out; who, with trickling increment,
> Veins violets and tall trees makes more and more)
> Could crowd career with conquest while there went
> Those years and years by of world without event
> That in Majorca Alfonso watched the door.[6]

We know of the great Scottish missionary David Livingstone, who took the word of God alone into the heart of Africa and was lost to the outside world for years. We can read the marks of battle on the crusader who has come home from the Holy Land. Robert Louis Stevenson could read those marks upon the leprous flesh of Father Damien, who left his native Belgium against the strong objections of his superiors to live among the lepers on the island of Molokai, sharing their filthy hovels far from Europe and just as far from the love of their

kinsmen dwelling on the islands nearby. He went to gather them out
of their debauchery and despair, to join him in the journey, and he died
every day he lived.

Nothing so geographically drastic happened to the saint whom
Gerard Manley Hopkins memorialized in the sonnet above. All he did,
to the eye of idle man, was serve as the porter at the Jesuit house in
Majorca. But his life, as his brothers knew and the world later learned,
was a long pilgrimage of self-sacrifice, temptations struggled through
and overcome, and spiritual vision. He fought as manfully as ever did
Godfrey of Bouillon at the walls of Jerusalem.

A modern-day Jesuit who does not wear a hair shirt as if it were a
clerical robe but a clerical robe as if it were a hair shirt, when he wears
it at all, may scoff at the "traditionalism" of his younger brothers who
look with nostalgia upon the old houses of discipline, keen learning,
childlike and soldierly devotion to the Church, and prayer. What does
the young man long for, with the ardor of the young? It is not to *be
dead*. The orders that have deviated from the road are dead. It is not
the vitalism of mere continuance. It is that life that can only be had by
dying. Jesus has given us the pattern,

> Who, being in the form of God, thought it not robbery to
>    be equal with God:
> But made himself of no reputation, and took upon him the
>    form of a servant, and was made in the likeness of men:
> And being found in fashion as a man, he humbled himself,
>    and became obedient unto death, even the death of the
>    cross.
> Wherefore God also hath highly exalted him, and given him
>    a name which is above every name.... (Philippians 2:6–9)

That is not a way among ways, like a choice of pastries at a bakery
or courses at a college. It gives to us the very heart of life. There can be

no life except through this dying, this self-opening, ever to be renewed, ever deeper, ever more radically dependent upon God:

> Verily, verily, I say unto you, Except a corn of wheat fall into the ground and die, it abideth alone: but if it die, it bringeth forth much fruit. (John 12:24)

Whatever is valid in all moral philosophy and in all religions of man turns toward this truth. So to be nostalgic in this sense is to say, "Bring me once more to that place where I may learn again to die. Bring me to Brideshead, to the school that bears humble witness to the boys and girls whose feet wore hollows in the stairs a hundred years ago, to the church whose sacraments have not changed, to the prayers my fathers said, so that I may the more readily and confidently learn to die and so live. I am weary of mere continuance. I am weary of concrete block upon concrete block. I am weary of the rut of change. I am weary of decay and debility. I am weary of the Self as god, the most wooden-headed and deadening idol ever to be mass-produced in that factory of idols, the imagination of man. I want life. Teach me to die."

And we cannot learn that, we will not learn that, unless we acquire again the daily habit of prayer. That is because every true prayer, at its heart, repeats the words of Christ and commends the spirit into the hands of God. But prayer has now become hard to learn. It is hard for me to learn, and harder to practice. We are out of the habit. What happens then? Two things, I will suggest.

The first is that we make up something to take its place. I notice that what are called the most "progressive" areas of the United States are the most irreligious. Yet in those places we see what I might call a *selective atavism*, the idolization of something supposedly ancient and therefore true and good, either dreamed up out of nothing or divorced from any cultural environment that would lend it meaning. The emperor Julian, surnamed the Apostate, turned away from the

Christian faith in which he had been raised and tried to revive the
paganism of old, but it was a fruitless venture, even though plenty of
devotees of the ancient Roman household gods and the great gods still
lived in the rural areas of the empire: Latin *paganus*, "hillbilly." What
we see now are the sad and risible and sometimes hideous attempts by
people who have no household gods to invent a mythos of earth-
mother and good witches and easy sex, a kind of diseased Shaker-ism
without the carpentry skills and the self-denial. It is selective atavism,
with neither a genuine past nor a future. The phenomenon is not limited to witchcraft, nor is it a feature only of our current times. Mus-
solini captured the hearts of young Italians by proposing to them a
return of the Roman Empire, not in its notable ethnic tolerance, its
great engineering projects, and the free movement it allowed its citizens
within its vast frontiers, but in military aggression and a fanatical
devotion to his person and to the state. He ended up hanging from a
meat-hook.

The second thing that happens without prayer is, if I may coin a
word, *thanatophilia*—an attraction to death, not because it is the door
to eternal life, but because it shuts the door on the misery or the ennui
of this life. In the Netherlands, it is now possible to summon the color-
ful suicide van to your door to deliver a shot of lethal poison, as in the
old days the bread man and the milk man would deliver the basic
nutrients of life. Nor do you have to be terminally ill to place the order.
In one recent case, the young woman was in fact quite healthy, but she
wanted to die because she was all alone and feeling blue; and in a dead
world of men who know no relation to God and therefore only aleatory
and superficial relations with their neighbors, that blue feeling deepens
into the bleakest despair. But poison is cheaper than friendship would
be. This thanatophilia applies also to clergymen who have traded
Christ for Moloch, blessing the hands that open the womb and cut the
unborn baby to pieces. It applies to all who see human life as a cancer
upon the earth; who abominate the large and happy family; who

approve of sexual machinations insofar as they are machinations and sterile—"safe" from life and the complete self-donation of love.

Daily prayer, especially prayer that follows the canonical hours of the day from matins to compline, is an *exercise* in the old sense of the word—a drill for an army—as are daily practices of self-denial and discipline. We greet the morning light, we pray for the strength to use the day well, we give ourselves over to the demands of the day, we give thanks for what has passed, and we deliver ourselves at nightfall into the hands of God. Most of us, including me, are not used to such exercise. What does it fit the soul and the body to do? We need not speculate. We need only consider what has been done already. We need not imagine a Brook Farm or a Blithedale. We need only open our eyes. Men who were trained in this exercise quite literally built Europe, which was not so much a geographically distinct land mass—it is not—but a world united by the roads from monastery to monastery and from village to village that grew up around the monastery. The monks cleared forests, drained swamps, harnessed the power of water to work grain mills, and built chapels, schools, and churches. We have seen what the friars did with the supposedly savage and ineducable Indians of southern California. That was only what they had done all over Europe, North Africa, and the Near and Middle East.

But those things, as important as they are, are secondary. The one thing most needful is that prayer prepare a home for God within the soul, or rather beg God himself to do the preparing. Herbert, thinking of the mysterious night of Christ's nativity, writes:

> O Thou whose glorious yet contracted light,
> Wrapped in night's mantle, stole into a manger,
> Since my dark soul and brutish is thy right,
> To man of all beasts be Thou not a stranger:
> Furnish and deck my soul, that Thou mayst have
> A better lodging, than a rack, or grave.[7]

## Pilgrim, Come Home

I return now to Odysseus. He has arrived in Ithaca, tested the intelligence and courage of his son and the loyalty of his wife, slaughtered the one hundred and eight suitors who had been devouring his estate, cleansed the great hall with fire, and gone finally to reveal himself to his wife, Penelope. She turns the tables on him. It is perhaps not the easiest thing in the world to recognize even your own husband after twenty years. She pretends to concede, then orders that their bed be moved out from their chamber.

At that, Odysseus bursts out with exasperation:

"Woman—your words, they cut me to the core!
Who could move my bed? Impossible task,
even for some skilled craftsman—unless a god
came down in person, quick to lend a hand,
lifted it out with ease and moved it elsewhere.
Not a man on earth, not even at peak strength,
would find it easy to prise it up and shift it, no,
a great sign, a hallmark lies in its construction.
I know, I built it myself—no one else ...
There was a branching olive-tree inside our court,
grown to its full prime, the bole like a column, thickset.
Around it I built my bedroom, finished off the walls
with good tight stonework, roofed it over soundly
and added doors, hung well and snugly wedged.
Then I lopped the leafy crown of the olive,
clean-cutting the stump bare from roots up,
planing it round with a bronze smoothing-adze—
I had the skill—I shaped it plumb to the line to make
my bedpost, bored the holes it needed with an auger.
Working from there I built my bed, start to finish,

> I gave it ivory inlays, gold and silver fittings,
> wove the straps across it, oxhide gleaming red.
> There's our secret sign, I tell you, our life story!"[8] (23.205–
> 227)

The bed cannot be moved without being destroyed. Odysseus himself built it to be that way. Thus seven or eight centuries before Christ declared that divorce was a violation of the intent of the Creator from the beginning, Homer contrived an astonishingly powerful symbol of the union of man and wife, *around which and depending upon which all other social goods are built.* That union, biological and personal, builds the room, builds the house and home, builds the estate, and builds the polis itself. Take away that union, and all the rest begins to fall apart. We have seen this dilapidation in our time.

The poem does not end with the bed, wherein Odysseus and Penelope enjoy the sad pleasure of telling one another what has happened in those twenty years and then enjoy the delights of love and the restoring sweetness of sleep. We see that things are not really settled until the family of Odysseus is reconciled with the families of the slain suitors. That comes about not through judicial trials, much less through repentance and forgiveness, but by a battle that threatens to erupt into full-scale civil war. There is, however, a distinctly nostalgic feature to the battle. Odysseus' aged father, Laertes, who has absented himself from the manor house ever since the suitors descended upon it, to live out his days with the herds, wearing tattered clothes and knowing little more than sorrow from dawn to dusk, has joined his son and his grandson to face down the angry mob. It is Laertes, not Odysseus, whose spear slays the father of the chief of the suitors. All then is in order, and at that point Athena interrupts and puts a forcible end to the fray. So the poem concludes. The *kosmos* of Ithaca is restored.

What will happen then, we do not know, nor does it matter. Odysseus, the man of many dodges, is home, and there is once again a real home for him and his family and their faithful servants to dwell in.

If we feel that there is something missing at the end of the *Odyssey*, it is because we are not ancient Greeks listening to the rhapsode as he sings the immemorial song. Our imaginations, whether we admit it or not, have been formed by the Scriptures and the Christian hope. It seems as if Odysseus has stopped short *and as if his home were less than the home for which we long.*

Part of that is because the home is a spiritual place, which we do not fit for our tastes; we must instead be made fit for it. King Lear begins to come home, then, when he is out on the heath in the middle of the storm and considers, in what really is a prayer of repentance, of *metanoia* or spiritual return, that he has not fulfilled his kingly duty to the poor:

> Poor naked wretches, wheresoe'er you are,
> That bide the pelting of this pitiless storm,
> How shall your houseless heads and unfed sides,
> Your looped and windowed raggedness, defend you
> From seasons such as these? O, I have ta'en
> Too little care of this! Take physic, pomp;
> Expose thyself to feel what wretches feel,
> That thou mayst shake the superflux to them,
> And show the heavens more just. (III.iv. 28–36)

The wizard Prospero abjures his magic art at the conclusion of *The Tempest*, preparing to leave the isle where he has been dwelling unknown to his would-have-been murderers for twelve years. He has reconciled himself to those men, forgiving them rather than yielding to vengeance. His daughter, Miranda, will marry the virtuous son of his one-time enemy King Alonso of Naples, and everyone will soon be well on his way:

And in the morn
I'll bring you to your ship, and so to Naples,
  Where I have hope to see the nuptial
  Of these our dear-beloved solemnized;
  And thence retire me to my Milan, where
  Every third thought shall be my grave. (V.i. 307–12)

Home, and home; Milan, and the grave, but the latter in hope:

Then shall be brought to pass the saying that is written,
Death is swallowed up in victory.
O death, where is thy sting? O grave, where is thy victory?
The sting of death is sin, and the strength of sin is the law.
But thanks be to God, which giveth us the victory through
  our Lord Jesus Christ. (1 Corinthians 15:54–57)

It is no mere theme for sentimental theater. The most profound theologian of my lifetime, the gentle-spoken and shy Pope Benedict XVI, retired five years ago from the papacy to a life of prayer and peace. On February 7, 2018, he sent this short letter to the Milanese newspaper, the *Corriere della Sera*:

I am deeply moved, that so many readers of your daily paper should wish to know how I am passing this final period of my life. I can only say about it that, in the slow dwindling away of my physical powers, I am nonetheless, within, on a pilgrimage to home. It is a great grace for me, in this last stretch of the road that is sometimes a little wearisome, that I am surrounded by such love and goodness that I could never have imagined. In this sense I consider the question your readers have asked as likewise an accompaniment along the way, for which I can do no other than give them my thanks, and my assurance in turn that all of you are in my prayers. With heartfelt greetings.

He is going somewhere, and as he nears the goal, he finds himself immersed more and more deeply in a love that he cannot describe or explain in human terms. He is, if I may be so bold as to say it, being transformed as he goes, changed within, moving from glory to glory. It is like a gradual shedding of everything superficial, everything that, like the "troublesome disguises" that arouse Milton's impatience, obstructs us in our love of God and neighbor and clouds our sight of beauty.

### The Trumpets Sound

It is more than that there is nothing to fear. Death, says Herbert in his poem by that name, was once

> an uncouth hideous thing,
> Nothing but bones,
> The sad effect of sadder groans:
> Thy mouth was open, but thou couldst not sing.

That was because we "looked on this side of thee, shooting short," not seeing beyond to the destination. But the death and resurrection of Christ has put blood into Death's face, so that he is now "fair" and sought for, not as an escape from the troubles of this life, but as a positive good. We have now a farther and more penetrating view of Death as we look forward to eternity:

> For now we do behold thee gay and glad,
> As at dooms-day;
> When souls shall wear their new array,
> And all thy bones with beauty shall be clad.
> Therefore we can go die as sleep, and trust

Half that we have
Unto an honest faithful grave;
Making our pillows either down, or dust.

Death is not continuance, as people imagine in their sentimental, half-pagan way when they say that dear departed Uncle John is now in heaven watching baseball or working at the perfect table-saw that never snags the wood. We shall wear a *new array*, and so the words of the penitent David come true in a full sense, never to fail: "Purge me with hyssop, and I shall be made clean: wash me, and I shall be whiter than snow" (Psalm 51:7). So Dante has his voyagers to the mountain of Purgatory, led by the angel pilot, singing that psalm of deliverance, *In exitu Israel de Aegypto*: "When from the land of Egypt Israel came" (Psalm 114). The blessed souls are not singing about deliverance from the body, to which they long to be reunited in the resurrection of the flesh, but from sin, the sludge and grime of it all, the obstructions, the occlusions.

Dante had the happy insight to place these souls in a boat together rather than having them whisked to the mountain one by one, and this is another crucial point. The political progressive wants to fashion a perfect society here upon earth. It cannot be done. An invention called the mirror shows us why. Look in it and behold the weak, self-ish, nearsighted, grumbling, heart-callused, foolish, frustrating, and indefeasible cause of the breakdown of every single imagined utopia upon earth. Strive for perfection upon earth, using human persons for your stones, human lusts for your mortar, and human foresight for your architectural plan, and do not be surprised when you end up with rubble and blood instead, and you reel back into the beast. If it is true that the two prime commandments are one, "Thou shalt love the Lord thy God with all thy heart, and with all thy soul, and with all thy mind," and "Thou shalt love thy neighbor as thyself" (Matthew 22:37–39), then we will love our neighbors with a perfect love only when we love God as Jesus has said. But if this is impossible for fallen man to do without the perfecting grace of God, then we can progress along the journey to the perfect society only by being transformed by that grace. We draw close to one another when we draw close to God.

So Dante's souls journey together to Purgatory. Always in the *Inferno* the presence of a fellow sinner is at best a sad reminder of your failure, at worst a torment, and sometimes what is in a way worse than a torment, an everlasting annoyance, as one of the ice-bound traitors complains about another, "with his head in my way to block my sight." On the journey up the mountain of Purgatory, Dante meets many a gregarious soul, for they pray for one another and encourage one another, as do the souls of the once standoffish and envious. They who once looked askance at the good that another person enjoyed must now quite literally *rely upon one another*, shoulder leaning upon shoulder, as they sit with eyes sewn shut, the brink of a precipice ten or twelve feet away. Yet as they pray they also call upon a community, that of Mary and Peter and all the blessed saints.

Away from the loneliness of our progressive time—a time of progressive childlessness, of progressive antagonism between men and women, of progressive cultural amnesia—there beckons the old hope that is ever new. Milton describes it thus in his elegy *Lycidas*, composed in honor of a Cambridge classmate drowned at sea:

> So Lycidas, sunk low, but mounted high,
> Through the dear might of him that walked the waves,
> Where other groves, and other streams along,
> With nectar pure his oozy locks he laves,
> And hears the unexpressive nuptial song,
> In the blest kingdoms meek of joy and love.
> There entertain him all the saints above,
> In solemn troops, and sweet societies
> That sing, and singing in their glory move,
> And wipe the tears forever from his eyes. (172–181)

The philosopher Jacques Maritain, denying both the reduction of man to mere stuff and the exaltation of "progress" at the expense of man and his divine beginning and end, writes:

> Genuine Christianity does not forget the original greatness of man. It abhors the pessimism of inertia. It is pessimistic in the sense that it knows that the creature comes from nothingness, and that everything that comes from nothingness tends of itself toward nothingness. But its optimism is incomparably more profound than its pessimism, because it knows that the creature comes from God, and that everything that comes from God tends toward God.[9]

I long on earth for a return to the way of life that is indeed a way. The trumpet sounds, and the sleepers wake. Not one good thing we have known in this world will be lost, but all flesh will be transformed, says Saint Paul, in the twinkling of an eye, the twinkle that is like a merry glint of love.

> And I saw a new heaven and a new earth; for the first heaven and the first earth were passed away; and there was no more sea.
>
> And I John saw the holy city, new Jerusalem, coming down from God out of heaven, prepared as a bride adorned for her husband.
>
> And I heard a great voice out of heaven saying, Behold, the tabernacle of God is with men, and he will dwell with them, and they shall be his people, and God himself shall be with them, and be their God.
>
> And God shall wipe away all tears from their eyes; and there shall be no more death, neither sorrow, nor crying, neither shall there be any more pain: for the former things are passed away.

And he that sat upon the throne said, Behold, I make all
things new. (Revelation 21:1–5)

Come, let us be done with the progress of death. Let us resume the
pilgrimage.

# NOTES

## Introduction

1. Dante, *Purgatory*, trans. Anthony Esolen (New York: Modern Library, 2004), 12.61–63.

2. C. S. Lewis, *The Screwtape Letters*, (New York: Macmillan Co., 1943), p. xv.

3. Edmund Spenser, "Two Cantos of Mutabilitie," in *The Faerie Queene* (London: Penguin, 1979), I.ix.40.8–9.

4. Homer, *The Odyssey*, trans. Robert Fagles (New York: Penguin, 1996), Book 14, lines 155–172.

5. Marcus Tullius Cicero, *A Dialogue on Old Age*, (Boston: Ginn & Co., 1891), 9.29.

6. *The Wisdom of Confucius*, ed. and trans. Lin Yutang (New York: Modern Library, 1938), p. 100.

7. Edmund Burke, *Reflections on the Revolution in France*, originally published 1790, repr. in *The Harvard Classics* (New York: Collier, 1909), vol. 24, p. 235.

8. Ibid.

## Chapter One: Man in Time

1. Gabriel Marcel, *Homo Viator: Introduction to the Metaphysic of Hope*, (South Bend, Ind.: St. Augustine's Press, 2010), "The creative vow as essence of fatherhood".

2.    T. S. Eliot, "Dante." In *Selected Essays*, (New York: Harcourt, Brace and Company, 1950).

3.    Charles Péguy, *Portal of the Mystery of Hope*, trans. David Louis Schindler Jr. (Grand Rapids, Mich.: Eerdmans, 1996), pp. 11–12.

4.    Josef Pieper, *In Search of the Sacred* (San Francisco: Ignatius Press, 1991), p. 43.

5.    Walker Percy, *Lost in the Cosmos: The Last Self-Help Book*, (New York: Farrar, Straus & Giroux, 1983).

6.    Anthony Esolen, *The Hundredfold* (unpublished manuscript), no. 17.

7.    Gabriel Marcel, *Homo Viator: Introduction to the Metaphysic of Hope*, (South Bend, Ind.: St. Augustine's Press, 2010), "The creative vow as essence of fatherhood".

## Chapter Two: Man in Place

1.    Ignazio Silone, *Fontamara,* trans. Harvey Fergusson (New York: Atheneum Publishers, 1960).

2.    Ibid.

3.    Ibid.

4.    Ibid.

5.    My translation.

6.    My translation.

7.    Flannery O'Connor, *The Complete Stories*, "A View of the Woods," (New York: Farrar, Straus and Giroux, 1971), p. 335.

8.    Ibid., pp. 341-42.

9.    Ibid., p. 345.

10.   Hilaire Belloc, *Hills and the Sea* (London: Methuen & Co., 1906), p. 203.

11.   Ibid., p. 208.

## Chapter Three: Lost among the Ruins

1.    Thomas Wolfe, *Look Homeward, Angel* (1929; repr., New York: Scribner, 2006), p. 165.

2.    Dante, *Purgatory*, trans. Anthony Esolen (New York: Modern Library, 2004), 6.67–75.

3.    Ibid., p. 506.

4.    Ibid., p. 421.

5.    Josef Pieper, *Leisure, the Basis of Culture*, trans. Alexander Dru (1952; repr., San Francisco: Ignatius Press, 2009), p. 66.

6.    Wolfe, p. 450.

7.    Ibid., p. 434.

8.    Evelyn Waugh, *Brideshead Revisited: The Sacred & Profane Memories of Captain Charles Ryder* (London: Penguin, 1981).

9.    Ibid.

10.   Ibid.

11.   Ibid.

12.   Ibid.

13.   Romano Guardini, *The End of the Modern World*, ed. Frederick D. Wilhelmsen, trans. Joseph Theman and Herbert Burke (Chicago: Henry Regnery Company, 1956).

14.   Anthony Esolen, "Leo XIII: 'Without Faith, Liberty Degenerates into License,'" *Crisis*, December 27, 2012, https://www.crisismagazine.com/2012/leo-xiii-without-faith-liberty-degenerates-into-license.

15.   Helen Hunt Jackson, "Father Junipero and His Work," *The Century Illustrated Monthly Magazine*, May 1883, p. 18.

16.   Ibid., June 1883, p. 200.

17.   Helen Hunt Jackson, "The Present Condition of the Mission Indians in Southern California," *The Century Illustrated Monthly Magazine*, August 1883, pp. 519, 529.

## Chapter Four: The Static Idol of Change

1.    Edmund Spenser, "Two Cantos of Mutabilitie," in *The Faerie Queene* (London: Penguin, 1979), vi.1.

2.    Ibid., vi.5.

3.    Ibid., viii.1.

4.    *Faerie Queene*, I.ix.43.

5.    Gabriel Marcel, *Homo Viator: Introduction to the Metaphysic of Hope*, (South Bend, Ind.: St. Augustine's Press, 2010), from the preface.

6. Dante, *Inferno*, trans. Anthony Esolen (New York: Modern Library, 2002), 26.119–120.

7. Jacques Maritain, *On the Philosophy of History* (Aeterna Press, 2015), p. 19.

8. Lucretius, *On the Nature of Things*, trans. Anthony Esolen (Baltimore: The Johns Hopkins University Press, 1995), 3.1065.

9. Ibid., 2.29–33.

10. Ibid., 3.968.

11. Ibid., 3.959–960.

12. Ibid., 4.1006–7.

13. Torquato Tasso, *Jerusalem Delivered*, trans. Anthony Esolen (Baltimore: The Johns Hopkins University Press, 2000), 7.12, 13.

14. *Faerie Queene*, II.vi.44.1–5.

15. Ibid., III.vii.50.1–3.

16. Ibid., III.viii.42.1–2.

17. Ibid., I.vii.7.2–3.

18. Ibid., I.vi.5.4.

## Chapter Five: Lost Innocence

1. Dante, *Purgatory*, trans. Anthony Esolen (New York: Modern Library, 2004), 28.144.

2. Francis Parkman, *The Conspiracy of Pontiac and the Indian War after the Conquest of Canada*, 10th ed., (Boston: Little, Brown, 1892), vol. 1, pp. 39–40.

3. Frederick Schwatka, "The Sun-Dance of the Sioux," *The Century Magazine*, vol. XXXIX, no. 5 (March 1890), p. 758.

4. Edward Eggleston, "The Aborigines and the Colonists," *The Century Magazine*, May 1883.

5. Henry David Thoreau, *Walden and Other Writings* (New York: Modern Library, 1992), pp. 86–87.

6. James Hilton, *Lost Horizon* (New York: Harper Perennial, 2012), p. 76.

7. Thoreau, p. 88.

8. Hilton, p. 205.

9. Ibid., p. 206.

10. Charles Péguy, *Portal of the Mystery of Hope*, trans. David Louis Schindler Jr. (Grand Rapids, Mich.: Eerdmans, 1996), pp. 5–6.

11. C. S. Lewis, *God in the Dock: Essays in Theology* (Grand Rapids, Mich.: Eerdmans, 2014), p. 324.

12. Letter to the Editor, *The Century Magazine*, vol. XXVI, no. 5 (September 1883), p. 789.

13. Ibid., p. 782.

14. Ibid., p. 789.

## Chapter Six: More Than Small Change

1. Edmund Spenser, "Two Cantos of Mutabilitie," in *The Faerie Queene* (London: Penguin, 1979), vii.41.

2. Ibid., vii.58–59.

3. John Henry Newman, "Genuine Developments Contrasted with Corruptions," Chapter 5 in *An Essay on the Development of Christian Doctrine*, 10th ed. (1845; repr. London: Longmans, Green & Co., 1897), pp. 169–206.

4. Horatio R. Storer, M.D., "Contributions to Obstetric Jurisprudence," *North-American Medico-Chirurgical Review*, vol. III, January 1859, pp. 64–72; available at horatiostorer.net.

5. Newman, p. 172.

6. Ibid.

7. Ibid., p. 185.

8. Ibid., p. 186.

9. Ibid., p. 200.

10. Ibid., pp. 203–206.

11. John Paul II, *Rise, Let Us Be on Our Way* (New York: Warner Books, 2004), pp. 51–52.

12. Ibid., pp. 52–53.

13. George Herbert, *The Complete English Works* (London: Everyman's Library, 1995), p. 78.

14. C. S. Lewis, Afterword to Third Edition, *The Pilgrim's Regress*, (Grand Rapids, Mich.: Eerdmans, 2014), p. 234.

15. Ibid., p. 237.

16. *Pilgrim's Regress*, p. 25.

17. M. G. van Rensselaer, "Lichfield Cathedral," *The Century Magazine*, vol. XXXVI, no. 3 (July 1888), p. 390.

18. Rensselaer, "Recent Architecture in America," *The Century Magazine*, vol. XXIX, no. 3 (January 1885), p. 337.

19. Ibid., p. 335.

20. Henry James, *The Bostonians* (New York: Penguin Classics, 2001), Chapter 28, p. 207.

21. John M. Ellis, *Literature Lost: Social Agendas and the Corruption of the Humanities* (New Haven: Yale University Press, 1997), pp. 74–75.

22. Ibid., p. 75.

## Chapter Seven: Back to the Family

1. Walker Percy, *Lost in the Cosmos: The Last Self-Help Book* (New York: St. Martin's, 1983), p. 13.

2. Dante, *Inferno*, trans. Anthony Esolen (New York: Modern Library, 2002), 5.40–45.

3. Dante, *Purgatory*, trans. Anthony Esolen (New York: Modern Library, 2004), 1.71.

4. *Lost in the Cosmos*, p. 44.

5. Daniel Carter Beard, *The American Boy's Handy Book: What to Do and How to Do It* (New York: Scribner, 1882), p. 83.

6. Ibid., p. 227.

7. Ibid., pp. 310–311.

8. Eliot McCormick, "A Boy's Appetite for Fiction," *The Century Magazine*, vol. XXX, no. 4 (August 1885), p. 651.

9. C. S. Lewis, *The Screwtape Letters* (1942; repr. New York: HarperOne, 2015), p. 64.

10. Ibid., p. 118.

11. Ibid., pp. 53–54.

12. Ibid., p. 120.

## Chapter Eight: O Grave, Where Is Thy Victory?

1.    Malcolm Muggeridge, *Confessions of a Twentieth-Century Pilgrim* (New York: HarperCollins, 1988); reprinted as *Conversion: The Spiritual Journey of a Twentieth-Century Pilgrim* (Eugene, Ore.: Wipf and Stock, 2005), p. 110, emphasis in original. Citations here are to the 2005 edition.

2.    Ibid., p. 112.

3.    Ibid., p. 107.

4.    Ibid., p. 110.

5.    Gerard Manley Hopkins, *Poems and Prose* (London: Penguin Classics, 1953), "The Windhover," p. 30.

6.    Hopkins, "In Honor of St. Alphonsus Rodriguez," pp. 66–67.

7.    George Herbert, *The Complete English Works*, "Christmas," (London: Everyman's Library, 1995).

8.    Homer, *The Odyssey*, trans. Robert Fagles (New York: Penguin, 1996), 23.205–227.

9.    Jacques Maritain, *On the Philosophy of History*, (Jacques Maritain Center, University of Notre Dame), https://maritain.nd.edu/jmc/etext/philhis2.htm#p50.

Ave Maria, 58
Avezzano, 32–34

**B**
Babylon, xxx, 53, 96
Bach, Johann Sebastian, xxx
Balder (Norse god), 143
Banfield, Edward, xiii
Beard, Daniel Carter, 186–190
Belgium, 143, 205
Belloc, Hillare, 40–43, 48, 54
Bennett, Josephine Waters, 162
Bentham, Jeremy, xxx
*Beowulf,* 2
Bethlehem, 133
*Blithedale Romance, The,* 100
Bohemia, 4, 53, 104
Book of Common Prayer, 24
Boston, 148, 151,
*Bostonians, The,* 160
Boy Scouts, 186
Bradbury, Ray, 116–17
Brasilia, 38
*Brave New World,* 125, 177
*Bread and Wine,* 31
*Brideshead Revisited,* 50
Browning, Elizabeth Barrett, 180–81
Browning, Robert, 164

Buddhism, 114
Burke, Edmund, xxvi–xxvii
Burnett, Frances Hodgson, 195
Burt, A. L., 153
Burt's Home Library, 153–54

**C**
Caedmon, 203
Calderón, 64
California, 64–67, 209
Calvary, 76
Calvino, Italo, 110–111
Calypso, xvii, xx
Camelot, xi–xii
Canaan, 35
Canada, 57
capitalism, 77, 105
capitalist, xvi, xxxi
Capra, Frank, 113
Cardinal Newman, 75, 135
Catholic Church, xxx, 92, 151
Catholic Counter-Reformation, 86
Cato, xxiii, 179
*Century Magazine, The,* 64, 127–28, 158, 182
Ceres, 21–22
Ch'ien, Szema, xxv
Chartres, xxx

# Stuff After Death

How to Identify, Value, and Dispose of Inherited Stuff

Mary Miley Theobald

# CONTENTS

# INTRODUCTION

*Anne sits quietly in the living room of her grandmother's tidy home, watching her relatives walk about on eggshells. Her grandmother was dead. Everyone was sad. The funeral was over. And now they would somehow divide up Grandma's things. At least Grandma had left a will, something the lawyer said only about a third of all Americans did. But it had been short and simple, with vague instructions about dividing everything equally between her five children. But what was equal? Was the Chinese-looking bowl equal to the old Santa cookie plate? Aunt Sandra said that she remembered Mother telling her that the painting above the sofa was valuable, but no one knew anything about it. Uncle Bob wondered how to tell the difference between real and fake pearls. Two aunts were discussing the silver service when Uncle Ray said he thought had been in the family for several generations and was worth a small fortune. What were they going to do now?*

*Across town, Ellen walks through her brother's townhouse, feeling like an intruder even though everything in it now belonged to her. As Jack's only living relative, she knows there will be no family feud over his belongings. Cold comfort, since it also means she will have to handle everything herself. And she doesn't have weeks to spend; she needs to fly home to her husband and children as soon as the funeral is over. How on earth did you sell old guns? You couldn't take them on the plane, could you? What was she going to do with all those tools in his workroom? The oriental rugs under her feet were surely valuable, if they were genuine. And what about Jack's prized collection of German air medals from World War I and II? Ellen intended to sell these things and use the money for her children's college educations, but she didn't*

ii

*have time to organize a yard sale and besides, it seemed disrespectful to Jack's memory to dispose of his things in such a cavalier manner. What was she going to do now?*

*Down the street, Dave and his wife begin sorting through a large house full of everything Dave's father had accumulated in 81 years. The Alzheimer's care facility where he now lives costs more than Dave can afford, and he needs the proceeds from the sale of Dad's house and household goods to pay for his care. What was he going to do now?*

Whether you are the sole heir or one of a hundred, dividing and disposing of a family member's personal possessions is a daunting job made harder by the fact that few of us are adept at evaluating objects. And before you can decide what to do with an item, you need to know what it is and roughly what it is worth. None of us wants to "sell stupid." Unless you are a professional appraiser or a museum curator, you probably know very little about the objects your grandparents own. Even your parents' belongings can be a mystery.

"Where there's a will, there's a war," wrote one lawyer. We've all heard appalling stories of siblings fighting for years over the parents' assets until lawyers' fees had depleted the estate, of people who smashed objects rather than see them go to someone else, and of family members who never speak again after falling out over their mother's jewelry. We've all assured ourselves that it could never happen in our own family. The purpose of this book is not to provide you with legal advice—for that you'll need to consult your attorney or any of several books * that treat the topic. **This book will help you assess what you have, so you can distribute things equitably among the heirs, sell them at their maximum value, or donate them where they will do the most good and take the appropriate tax deduction.**

The transfer of stuff from one generation to the next happens every day of the year, one family at a time. This book will make it easier.

* *For instance, The Family Fight: Planning to Avoid It, and What Your Lawyer May Not Tell You About Your Family's Will: A Guide to Preventing the Common Pitfalls That Can Lead to Family Fights.*

# CHAPTER ONE

## Don't Miss the Can Opener

The Greatest Generation is dying, by some estimates, at a rate of 3,500 a day. They suffered through the Depression, sacrificed through World War II, and when peace brought the boys home, they built one of the most prosperous economies the world has ever seen. Along the road from have-nots to haves, they acquired many children and more possessions than their parents had dreamed possible. This is the generation that never threw anything out, because hard experience taught them that they might find themselves hungry, shirtless, or unable to afford a new roll of aluminum foil. Their heirs are the Baby Boomers, the largest population bulge in American history, a group that moves through the decades like a meal through a boa constrictor. While they never experienced severe want, they are an acquisitive bunch nonetheless. Within the next decade, the Boomers themselves will start to pass away in significant numbers and pass along their possessions. It is an endless cycle of taking and giving that none of us avoid.

Our turn usually comes at the worst possible time, when grief has wrung us dry and left us vulnerable. Overwhelmed by funeral arrangements, financial issues, wills, notification of friends and family, social security forms, legal hassles, travel arrangements, medical insurance—all the while trying not to neglect our jobs, our children, and our surviving family members—we need another major undertaking like we need the flu.

The fortunate few will find that their loved ones wrote wills that leave clear instructions for property division: the crystal bowl to Cousin Sue, the ruby necklace to Jane, the coin collection to David, the remainder to Goodwill. The odds, however, are against this. The majority of Americans—in some estimates, two thirds—die without a will. Even those who have one usually neglect the specifics in favor of phrases that speak generally about dividing property equally or fairly between the survivors.

Whether we are selling items at a garage sale, auctioning them to the highest bidder, giving them to the Salvation Army, donating them to a museum, or dividing them up among the heirs, we need to know what we are dealing with. Out of respect for the deceased and an obligation to the heirs, none of us wants to do anything foolish, like selling that dusty painting of a dull country scene to a man at the yard sale for $20, only to learn it was a Constable that the man re-sold for $450,000. But the plain truth is, *most things are worth far less, in terms of monetary value, than we think. A few things are worth far more.*

Always remember that the value of an item is only as much as someone will pay for it at that moment in time. Value is a constantly changing concept. Things that were valuable some years ago are no longer worth much today (think Beanie Babies), and things that were commonplace years ago can be very valuable today (think Roy Rogers lunch box). But not all old things are valuable. *Contrary to popular belief, prices don't automatically go up over time.*

Eric, an experienced appraiser who has worked for several auction houses and estate liquidators, tells his favorite story about the most valuable object at one estate sale. "It was a can opener," he says. "And it was a nice estate with many valuable items," he says, "but this one can opener was very rare and sold for thousands of dollars, more than any other single item."

2

Beverly has worked for ten years at one of the city's finest antiques store, a business that also handles some estate sales. She remembers finding a metal Victorian birdcage in the coal bin—no one else even knew what it was. She cleaned it up and sold at the tag sale for $1,000. "Then I had to explain to the family why it was worth more than the silver chest full of sterling silver tableware," she says. "People are often shocked at how little some things are worth, and how much other things are worth."

When talking about an item's monetary value, two terms come up: wholesale and retail. Generally speaking, you are selling items *at wholesale* to a business that will sell to the customer *at retail*. Suppose Joe inherits an antique table appraised at $5,000. That means the table should bring about $5,000 *at retail*—at an auction the final bid should be around $5,000; at an antique shop, the table would have a sticker saying $5,000 on it. But people who run auctions and antique stores are not going to pay Joe $5,000 for a table they can turn around and sell for $5,000. The antiques dealer might offer Joe $2,000 for the table *at wholesale*, allowing himself a potential profit of $3,000, less whatever discount he gives his customer. The auctioneer might take a third of whatever the final bid comes to. But auctions are tricky things and there are no guarantees. Maybe the table comes up for sale during a night when most of the audience is there to bid on some fine quilts. Few bid on Joe's table, and it brings only $2,000, minus the auctioneer's third. Or maybe Joe is lucky and a bidding war breaks out between two people who just *have* to have that table, and the final price is $8,500. It all depends on the crowd. Alternatively, Joe could donate the table to a museum and take a tax deduction of $5,000 which, since he is in a 35% tax bracket, will save him about $1,750 off his tax bill. Joe could bypass the middleman and sell his table directly (at retail) to the customer at a garage sale, where he would not likely get anything close to its value, or through an ad in the newspaper or Trading Post, where he might get lucky and connect with someone who really wanted that particular size and style table, or on an Internet site like www.eBay.com or www.Craigslist.org, where the table would probably bring more because of the larger number of furniture lovers exposed to it—or it might bring less because of costly shipping additions. As you can see, the "value" of an item is a moving target.

Don't try to take *Antiques Roadshow* to the bank. This popular television show is fun to watch, but all most viewers hear is the inflated value these appraisers give. Remember that the estimates on television are high end to begin with, and they are *retail estimates*. The owner might get half that amount if he decided to sell, probably less. And estimates for insurance purposes, another dollar figure sometimes quoted on the show, are usually higher than retail.

*What are things worth? With rare exception, they are worth the wholesale value to the heirs.*

And how much is that? Is the framed picture over the fireplace worth twenty dollars or twenty thousand? Is it an inexpensive print or a limited edition original? Is the artist collectible or unknown? Is it an oil or a water color? What is that shiny punch bowl worth? Is it sterling silver, silverplate, or polished pewter? English or American? Two hundred years old or thirty? Are any of the books worth much? Are there any first editions? Are the pearls genuine? Is the bracelet real gold? It may take a bit of time and effort to get the answers, or it may be as simple as learning what to look for. Keep reading.

# CHAPTER TWO

## The Rush Job

Not everyone has the luxury of time to deal a house full of Stuff in the optimum manner. While it is preferable to take weeks, even months, to research and consider each item and decide what it is, whether it has any value, who should have it, or how it should be sold, recycled, or disposed of responsibly, reality often interferes. With families scattered across the country—or across the globe—the difficulties mount. Maybe the surviving children live in other states and have only a couple days to go through Dad's belongings and empty the house in preparation for its sale. Or Aunt Lena passed away in an assisted living apartment, and the management is gently urging you to clear out her things so the next person on the waiting list can move in. Like it or not, the pressure to act quickly may mean having to forego certain desirable steps in the process.

Keep in mind before you begin that most Stuff can be categorized as having either monetary value (that antique tall case clock in the hall) or sentimental value (the portrait of Grandmother as a young woman). Some have both (Mom's diamond engagement ring). Lawyers will tell you that it is usually the items with sentimental value that provoke the bitterest conflicts among heirs. Money can be divided fairly with a calculator, but Grandma had only one rocking chair where she sang her grandchildren to sleep, and they all want it.

The first task is to distribute the items mentioned in the will, assuming you can find one. If Mother wrote that her ruby dinner ring was to go to Judy and her antique sterling silver was to go to Jane, then it doesn't really matter that one is worth $4,000 and the other $950—and it is probably best if no one is aware of the discrepancy. Mother probably valued them equally herself and felt she was being fair.

After that distribution process is completed, the hard part begins: dividing the remaining personal possessions according to the proportions specified in the will, say, one third to Judy, one third to Jane, and one third split equally between Jennifer and Jed. Does anyone want the picture over the fireplace? Well, Jennifer might . . . but if it's worth $29,000, do the other heirs want to sell it and divide the proceeds, or let Jennifer have it? Jane wants the crystal goblets and Jed wants the stamp collection. Are those rough equivalents to the painting? And what should be done with the Stuff no one wants?

There are several options to consider when time is at a premium. Suppose your bachelor uncle has passed away. In his will, he leaves a few sentimental items to you and your brother, and the rest of his estate to your mother. Your mother's health is too poor to allow her to travel, your brother is stationed overseas, and you are unable to spend longer than a weekend on the other side of the country where Uncle died. What can you do?

**1. Use an estate appraiser and auction off the bulk of the estate.** Contact at least two estate appraisers (or estate liquidators or auctioneers) and have them come to Uncle's house to look over his estate and give you a quote on their services. These people can do a turnkey operation for you if you want it, although of course, you will pay for these services out of whatever proceeds result from the sale of the Stuff. They can pack, mail, or ship any items you want to keep, specifically those mentioned in the will. They can pick out the more valuable furnishings and take them away for sale at their next scheduled auction. Unless they have a special license, they may not be able to sell liquor and guns, but they will know who to contact for these. They can sort through the remainder, hauling the stacks of newspapers to the recycling center and the rolls of rusty chicken wire to the dump. They can sell boxes of kitchen tools and old books for a couple bucks or take them to Goodwill if you tell them that's what you prefer. Or they can offer you a flat price, say $15,000 for the entire contents of the house, and what they auction off or throw out is left up to them. (And if you decide to contract with a nonprofit like Goodwill to dispose of the contents, you can use that quote of $15,000 as the credible value of the contents when you declare the donation on your taxes.)

*This option is the least desirable in terms of money for the heirs, but it may be the most desirable for heirs who are too old, too ill, too far away, or too busy to handle any of the work themselves.*

There are two types of appraisers: real estate and personal property. You might want both if you have a house to sell as well a houseful of Stuff. Look in the Yellow Pages under "Estates" or search the Internet, but try to get personal recommendations, admittedly difficult if you are from out of town. The funeral director or an upscale antique store should have a good recommendation or two. Check with the Better Business Bureau to make sure the name isn't toxic. Personal property appraisers are not required to have any particular qualifications or education levels to conduct business, so you need to be careful about hiring "just anybody." Some are nothing but auctioneers who hold up an item without knowing or caring what it is, as long as it sells fast. Many reputable appraisers specialize in certain areas, say dolls or jewelry, and may be ill-equipped to recognize the pair of eighteenth-century Hogarth prints on the wall.

Because antiques dealers buy a good portion of their inventory from auctioneers and estate liquidators, they are good people to ask for recommendations. Bob sells antiques and collectibles at regional antiques shows and warns, "I go to auctions several times a week. There are eight auctions houses in my area, and I only do business with four of them. I think any antiques dealer could tell you who was honest."

One indication of knowledge and integrity is the appraiser's professional status. Ask if he or she is a member of the American Society of Appraisers or the Appraisers Association of America, or if he has the letters GPPA after his name (Graduate Personal Property Appraiser). Ask what their specialty is. Membership in these associations mean that the person has been in business several years, has taken a professional appraisals course, has learned how to write appraisals correctly, and has studied the ethics involved. You can use www.appraisers.org or www.appraisersassoc.org to find appraisers who are members of these two groups and search for those who specialize in either gems and jewelry or personal property. That said, there are exemplary appraisers who are not accredited, and I would not disqualify someone who was not accredited if they had solid recommendations. Contact a reputable auction house and ask for recommendations for the sort of appraisers you need. Before you talk to an appraiser, have as much of the following information as possible ready:

1. your reason for an appraisal: to sell the item, to insure the item, to donate the item (these are different types of appraisals and will usually produce different values);

2. any information about the item: description, measurements, artist, age, when and where purchased;

3. a photograph of the item and any identifying marks.

Why are estate appraisers better than auctioneers? They are usually more knowledgeable about the value of objects, especially antiques. Some appraisers are also auctioneers; other appraisers work with specific auctioneers.

*People who appraise your Stuff should not buy it. That's a clear conflict of interest.*

The estate appraiser/auctioneer holds regular public auctions or on-site estate sales and will sell your Stuff for the highest price possible. He'll take a commission, as little as 10% if you have several items that he knows he can flip quickly to a particular customer, or as much as 60% if you have consigned boxes of miscellaneous tools and junk that will take time and sell for only a dollar a piece. The percentage is negotiable and depends on things like how far a distance he has to haul your Stuff. The auctioneer also makes money on the other end, in the form of a "buyer's premium" that amounts to 10-15% of the bid. He gets that money from the buyer.

Some appraisers will hold an on-site sale or auction if your location is convenient to a large customer base. Stuff often sells better in a residential setting. This is called an estate sale or tag sale and usually lasts a couple days. Everything is pre-priced, and the prices usually fall the second day. They'll sell what they can to the public and haul the rest away. The tag sale will take several weeks to prepare: every item needs to be examined, priced, and carried into view, and the event needs to be advertised, but the heirs do not have to be present. In fact, it's best if they are not, unless they are genuine customers intending to buy.

Contact an estate appraiser before you've done any removals, and ask if they will meet you on site for a discussion of their fees and their recommendation. It will probably take an hour. They should not charge for this service, just like interviewing a lawyer about your case should not cost you. You are shopping for professional help and should interview at least two. After examining the house's contents, the appraiser can tell you which of several options they recommend:

1. An estate sale on the site. If the location is convenient to lots of people and the estate includes some high quality Stuff worth a total of at least $10,000, this will probably be the way to go. Nice antiques, art, rugs, and handcrafts tend to sell better in the home than in a store.

2. If there are just a few exceptional items, they could move those to an antique shop or art gallery and sell on consignment. This takes time—many things will not sell for months, maybe years, but if you're in no hurry for the money, it could work best. A typical cut for the store would be around 40-50%.

3. Buy the contents of the house outright and you're done with it. This means less money for you, but it's over.

4. An online estate auction where every item is tagged with a number and the house is open for a day or two for preview only. This is an inspection time where individuals and antiques dealers can breeze in, pen and paper in hand, and take note of any items they want to bid on. They go home, log onto the auctioneer's website where every item is listed beside its picture, and bid for the things they want. After a few days, the top bidders are notified to pick up their property.

No one knows everything, and a good estate appraiser will have contacts with experts in many fields that she can call on for help when the estate contains Stuff like oriental rugs or antique silver or hand-carved decoys. This ensures you get the most money for your Stuff. And since the appraiser is getting a percentage, it is to her advantage to get you the highest price.

Most auctions are "open" which means the items are going to be sold for whatever they bring. No "reserves." A reserve is the floor below which the item will not sell. (As in, "I want to sell this table but not for less than $200." Then $200 is the reserve.) In an estate sale, every single item is priced. Prices may be negotiable but not usually on the first day.

*Alexander is a knowledgeable antiques buff who occasionally attends estate auctions. Not long ago, at a local auction house, the auctioneer helpers held up a table described as a "nice tea table, good wood." Alexander thought it looked better than nice. Its features made him suspect it was very old, possibly made by Goddard and Townsend, cabinetmakers who dominated the furniture business in eighteenth-century Newport, Rhode Island. The bidding opened at $100. Only one man bid against Alexander, and he soon dropped out. Alexander paid less than $500 for a table that was later authenticated by Sotheby's and is worth six-figures. The moral of the story? The local auction company is not a good choice for heirs selling antiques.*

Another alternative is to use a professional organizer or move manager who will sort, sell, and dispose of your estate for a fee. Find such people through their website at www.nasmm.com for the National Association of Senior Move Managers, or at www.napo.net for the National Association of Professional Organizers. They are not typically knowledgeable about antiques, but if the estate you've inherited consists of Stuff less than 75 years old, that won't be an issue. These two types of professionals aren't the same—move managers don't always handle organizational jobs and professional organizers don't always handle moves—but they do overlap to some degree. You won't hire the wrong sort. They'll tell you if your job is out of their area of expertise and probably recommend someone more suitable.

**2. Donate to charity.** Everyone is familiar with service organizations such as Goodwill, Amvets, the Salvation Army, the Disabled American Veterans, or Vietnam Veterans of America that accept donations or even pick up Stuff for re-sale in their retail stores. Keep in mind that local chapters of these organizations have different rules. For example, some will pick up furniture, others will not, and large items like sofas can be difficult for you to drop off. Most will accept clothing, accessories, books, kitchenware, bedding, furniture, lamps, rugs, and decorative items. These groups generally do *not* want computers or electronics that don't work; pianos; mattresses; large kitchen appliances like refrigerators, stoves, washers, and dryers; guns; magazines; newspapers; chemical products like paint thinner, drain cleaner, and pesticides; or cans of gasoline.

Call the local chapters of these nonprofit organizations. Do not ask if they have home pickups. The answer will probably be no, but many of them really do have the ability to come to your home and help if the situation warrants. Tell them your circumstances ("I'm far from home and trying to dispose of my uncle's estate."), your timeline ("I have only a week."), and ask, "How can you help me?" Engaging in a conversation will reveal what, if anything, they are able to do, and it is often more than you'd expect. Depending upon the branch—and all are quasi-independent and have different capabilities—they will either send a team out to assess and pick up Stuff, advise you to take Stuff to their collection point, or suggest you go elsewhere.

Problems for most nonprofit organizations include pianos, pool tables, and large appliances like freezers (they don't have the manpower or equipment to move those large things), old tires, building materials like drywall, lumber, wall-to-wall carpet (costs more to leave at the landfill), and mattresses and box springs (sanitizing issues and bedding laws prevent them from handling these). The director of one of the country's largest Goodwill branches says, "The problems are usually in the basement, the attic, the garage, and the shed. We can handle just about everything in the living quarters of a house. It's when you get to those other spaces that we have difficulty. We don't have the expertise, the rigging, or the crew needed to move these items, some of which need to be broken up to get them out of the basement or attic. And we don't have the equipment to sanitize bedding, so we can't take mattresses." These organizations aren't in the business of hauling your belongings to the dump for you, so they will only accept the Stuff they can resell or recycle. If they are willing to handle the entire houseful of Stuff, that would include making some trips to the dump or recycling center.

Donate judiciously to selected charities. If you have a little time to sort and a vehicle to deliver, take canned goods and paper products to the local Food Bank, books to the local library, and toys to a shelter for families or a YMCA daycare facility. Some building materials and tools can go to Habitat for Humanity, but not much. They don't want old carpet, old appliances, rusty nails, or scrap lumber. Call first and ask.

You should estimate the value of the items you donate so the heirs can have a tax deduction. (More on that to come.) Who gets the tax deduction is something your lawyer will need to answer. It depends on the will, or lack thereof, any trusts created by the will, and the state law where your relative died. Often the belongings transfer to the heirs at the time of death, so a donation's value can be deducted by the heirs at the percent stated in the will. Two children who each inherit 50% of their parent's estate can each claim half of the value of the charitable deduction. But not always.

Old cars or boats can be donated to Goodwill or other nonprofit to sell at auction. They will send you a letter so you know what the car sold for and can declare the donation for a tax deduction. Occasionally, if the car is in reasonable shape, the organization will decide to keep it for their own use or give it to a family, and its value will be higher, giving you a higher tax deduction.

**3. Give away directly.** Put a neat pile of Stuff at the curb with a Help Yourself sign. Or stack in a communal place in the retirement center. You cannot claim a tax deduction for a direct giveaway, only for Stuff given to bona fide nonprofit organizations.

*After Amy's grandmother died, Amy gathered things she thought others in the retirement complex could use, such as canned goods, paper towels, soap, ammonia, and shampoo, and put them in the laundry room next to a Help Yourself sign. Within hours, everything had disappeared.*

**4. Throw away.** None of us wants to add to landfills unnecessarily. Sadly, throwing Stuff away is sometimes the only alternative. And not easy if you have large items that require trips to the dump. You may need to rent a U-Haul or pickup truck. At the dump, take anything that looks like it would be useful to someone else and set it aside. In many cases, these will disappear before the next day has dawned.

If you have more to throw out than you can or want to handle, call a professional "junk man." In the good old days, this person hauled all your Stuff away for free in exchange for whatever it was you were discarding. That custom has gone the way of the nickel candy bar. Now you have to pay for the service, but it may be well worth your while. There are several national junk services with franchises in most parts of the country. Got Junk, can be reached at 1-800-GOT-JUNK. Another is Junk King at 1-800-995-5865 or www.junk-king.com. College Hunks is another, and they really do hire a lot of college students. Check their website for details at www.collegehunkshaulingjunk.com. These services will send a truck and a few men, load your stuff, clean up after themselves, haul everything away, sort through it, and decide what they can donate, recycle, or take to the dump. Or call a private refuse service and pay them. Or call the local county and request a (paid) pickup.

**5. Don't throw out diamonds or cash!** No matter what, make time for a thorough sweep of the home to search for hidden cash, jewelry, checkbooks, safe deposit keys, gold coins, or other valuables. Check all purses and wallets for cash, credit cards, driver's licenses, and other IDs. Check the freezer, between the mattress and box springs, and the back of dresser drawers. Old people aren't the only ones who hide valuables, but this generation was particularly distrustful of banks and investments, having seen so many of them fail during the Depression. The director of a large Goodwill branch told about an employee who had recently found a diamond solitaire among a bunch of socks. They were able to figure out who had donated that lot and returned the ring to the heir. Not everyone is that honest.

# CHAPTER THREE

## The Thorough Effort—Doing It Yourself

Spending time on the disposition of the deceased's possessions will bring greater appreciation for the Stuff you end up keeping, greater compensation for the Stuff you end up selling or donating, and greater peace of mind regarding the whole process. It will also take a lot of time and labor and it can have related costs that you might not realize. One estate sales professional put it this way: "Some people have the time or inclination to do it themselves, but it is very time consuming. We've had people take a year or two to clear out a house because they want to save money and not use a professional. But they've lost the revenue of the house for the year to say nothing of their time and energy." Very true.

Ideally you will have help. This is the quintessential family project, and the more everyone is involved in the process, the less they tend to complain about being shortchanged. People are needed to carry things to the dumpster, drive larger loads to the dump, empty the refrigerator and pantry, collect boxes for packing, and sort through files, garage cupboards, basements, tool sheds, attics, closets, bathroom cupboards, kitchen drawers, and storage rooms. That said, experience shows that usually one or two people end up doing the bulk of the work, even though there are other heirs.

Sorting is the key job. Battlefield doctors call it triage: deciding who must be operated on immediately, who can wait, and who is beyond medical help. Work in teams—two heads are always better than one when it comes to remembering or identifying things. Naturally you should encourage relatives with specific knowledge to sort those items: send the handyman in the family to the tool shed where he can spot the keepers better than the young lad who doesn't know pliers from a wrench. Designate one room for donations and another for throw away, if that is your plan. Choose a downstairs room.

*Do not polish, paint, or touch up old Stuff. If something is filthy, wipe it with a damp cloth but resist the temptation to use any chemicals or cleaning solutions. The value of many an antique or collectible has dropped significantly when misguided owners tried to "improve" its looks.*

As you and the heirs work through the house, take time to check *everything* for hidden items. Elderly people—and not-so-elderly folks too—often hide valuables in secret places and forget to tell anyone about them. Be on the lookout for hidden cash, jewelry, checkbooks, safe deposit keys, savings bonds, and other valuables that have been squirreled away someplace "safe." Do not sell, throw out, or give away anything until it has been thoroughly checked.

1. Check every single zipper pocket in every single purse, and every fold of every wallet for cash, credit cards, drivers' licenses, and other IDs.
2. Check any containers in the freezer. A 2011 survey found that 27% of Americans who keep sizeable amounts of cash in their homes hide it in the freezer.
3. Lift the mattresses. The same survey found that 11% hid cash under the mattress.
4. Check the oven.
5. Empty every dresser drawer and examine for papers taped to

the back or bottom.

    6. Flatten all socks and gloves.

    7. Check all pockets, especially in pants and coats.

    8. Check the toes of all shoes and boots.

    9. Pull out all drawers and look under any shelf paper linings.

    10. Ruffle the pages of every book, a quick exercise that will also let you know if there are any hollow books that were used to stash small items.

    11. Look in all kitchen canisters and containers. Sift through the flour or sugar for small objects.

    12. Lift sofa and chair cushions.

    13. Check every pouch and side pocket of all luggage, gym bags, and brief cases.

    14. Check drapery hems for coins or small jewelry.

    15. Look inside the toilet tanks.

    16. Examine the backs of all framed pictures.

    17. Be alert for loose floorboards in the attic or items wedged in the rafters.

Heirs with the time and inclination to conduct a thorough evaluation of the estate have more options than those who are pressed for time. Consider hiring an independent, personal property appraiser to come to the house. Independent means they have no interest in buying the items so have no stake in the outcome—they are not trying to lowball you; they are not friends of one of the heirs; they have credentials and an ethical standard. An appraiser is paid by the hour, never a percentage of the appraisal. They can come for an hour or two and point out the valuable items you might not have realized were special, or they can come give you a detailed, written appraisal of certain pieces. It might help to know the value of things when it comes to the distribution of Stuff among the heirs. You may be comfortable having each heir choose items, one at a time, without regard for value, or you may prefer to have each choose items that in the end total the same approximate value. Some antique stores and auction companies know appraisers who will work this way, for an hourly fee.

Avoid hiring a "friend who knows something about antiques" and won't charge you as much as a professional. The amount you pay as a fee for such people will save you a couple bucks that day and cost you hundreds or thousands in the long run.

*Alicia asked Lora, a personal property appraiser, to look about the house her late in-laws had bequeathed the family. Alicia said, "I might want to keep an item, but if you tell me its worth $20,000, I'd rather sell it—I've got kids to send through college." So Lora examined various antiques and dishes and crystal and named a range of value to help Alicia make up her mind. In the course of the walk-through, Lora pointed to a large stoneware jug that she said would probably sell for $8,000-9,000. Astonished, Alicia admitted she had intended to throw it out. The moral? Don't begrudge the appraiser's fee. Even if they find nothing of great value, you can sleep at night without fretting over what might have gotten away.*

Taking the time and effort to investigate your inherited Stuff will lessen your chances of selling stupid, and you'll make more intelligent decisions about donating or keeping Stuff. Become your own appraiser. It's not impossible, but it does take some effort.

To research the value of an object, start with the computer to find information that is free. Using a couple words to describe the object, type any descriptive marks into google or your search engine. For example, here is a delicate, pink porcelain rose, about two inches in diameter. The bottom shows a mark and the word "Germany" and a word that looks like "Kandarbeit." Typing "Kandarbeit Germany porcelain rose" into google leads to an automatic correction—the hard-to-decipher word starts with an H, not a K, and there is a list of sites to check out. The word seems to mean "handmade." Nothing is found on www.eBay.com. A pair of yellow Handarbeit roses just like this pink one has been listed on www.etsy.com, chipped, $5, for over two months without any interest from buyers. Three pink Handarbeit roses, exactly the same as this one, were listed on www.liveauctioneers.com for $20-30 for the trio, but there were no takers there either. If further information is needed, the library will have books on German porcelain, but in this case, it would seem to be an unproductive use of time. Conclusion? Little interest in such items; no value. Price at $2 for the garage sale or consider donating.

Heirs have many options in dealing with inherited Stuff. Regardless of the choices made, it is usually desirable to have some idea—sometimes a precise idea—of the item's monetary value. This helps decide whether or not to keep it or how to count it in a fair distribution among the heirs. For items that are donated to a nonprofit organization, an estimated value is necessary for the donor's tax return.

Here are some of the ways you might handle your inherited Stuff:

**1. If the estate has much antique furniture, china, or silver, or oriental rugs, or art, you may want to call in a reputable antiques dealer or estate sales professional, preferably two or three for comparison purposes, rather than doing all the research and selling yourself.**

If there are antiques among your Stuff, you have several ways to sell them. An antiques dealer may be interested in buying some of the antique furniture or household goods. References are important: if you are from out-of-town, ask around for the name of "the best" antiques store. Make an appointment for someone from the store to come by and look over the household furnishings while everything is still in place. If there is a lot of one particular category of goods—if Grandma collected china plates, for example—mention that to the antiques dealer so they can send the person most knowledgeable in that field. Don't expect miracles: antiques dealers cannot tell you at a glance what everything in Grandma's house is worth, but they should be able to tell you on the spot which items they would buy from you and how much they would pay. Knowing what a dealer will pay for an item will help you make your decision about its ultimate disposition.

Antiques dealers are generally more knowledgeable about antiques than estate appraisers, although such a sweeping generalization is open to exceptions. You may have seen the specialized antiques appraisers on television shows like *Antiques Roadshow*. These are some of the best in the trade who know a lot about a particular subject, such as clocks or weapons, but they wouldn't know much as much about the value of a thirty-year-old upholstered chair as would an estate appraiser.

To sell all your Stuff at once, find an estate sale professional. Ask for referrals from your lawyer, realtor, antiques dealer, or funeral director. Interview them. Check references. Attend one of their sales, if time permits. Understand their contract.

Auction houses can also be a good place to sell Stuff, but antiques and high-end objects will bring more at a regional auction house where the clientele comes from several cities and can also bid online. Small, local auction houses are good for selling household goods, but generally not your upscale Stuff. These small operators will sell to the highest bidder, of course, but their bidders aren't really looking for fine antiques, so the items go for a low price. Consider selling the antique items to an antiques dealer and consign the rest of the household furnishings to a local auction house.

If you decide to hire an estate sale professional, he or she may decide to send some of your Stuff to specialized dealers in order to maximize the price you get. Stuff like books, coin and stamp collections, and guns may go elsewhere.

If there is serious disagreement among the heirs about the distribution of the estate, an antiques dealer or estate appraiser can serve as a solution. Send everything in contention to auction and let the heirs who want it bid alongside the general public. Whoever wants it most, bids highest and gets it, whether it is a stranger or a relative. The heirs share in the division of the proceeds whether they have successfully bid on anything or not. Of course, if one brother is wealthy and the other two are poor, the wealthy one will be in a position to bid higher on the things he wants. But factoring in the general public means he'll have to pay fair market value or greater if the bidding is lively. And the two poor brothers will each get 1/3 of this higher price.

After you have gathered the opinions of the antiques dealers or estate appraisers, you can start the serious sorting process—the triage—separating out the junk from the things people want. Pile everything intended for the dumpster in one room or one pile, and do not cart anything off until all present have had a look.

*When Barbara's mother died, Barbara began clearing out her apartment before her brother arrived, knowing he had less time than she did to spend sorting through all the Stuff. She threw away only items that were clearly junk, only to find too late that her definition of junk was not the same as his. To her brother, some of those things had significant sentimental value, but it was too late. Moral? Someone's trash is another's treasure.*

**2. Donate to a charitable nonprofit organization.** Donate what the heirs don't want to a service organization such as Disabled American Veterans, the Salvation Army, or Goodwill, checking to see what they will accept and whether they will pick up. Estimate the value of items before donating and keep a list for tax purposes. (See Chapter Four) They will not estimate value for you.

Donate selectively. Take canned goods, non-perishables, and paper products to the Food Bank, books to the public library, and toys to a shelter for families or a YMCA daycare facility. An old car can go to a church, the Kidney Foundation, Goodwill, or other charity that will sell it and tell you the amount so you can declare it as a tax deduction.

**3. Donate to museums, especially history museums, county historical societies, and historical houses.** You can be a museum benefactor even if your last name isn't Rockefeller! It may surprise you to know that far more objects are donated to museums by ordinary Americans than by those whose names you would recognize.

Don't make the mistake of thinking that museums are interested only in items with monetary value. Often the things they prize most have little worth in the marketplace but tremendous historical value. Staff at one Frank Lloyd Wright house museum was delighted to have a box of used toys from the 1940s. Curators at General George C. Marshall's house in Virginia furnished their kitchen with everyday spatulas, strainers, and knives from the

1940s and 50s, and in December they set up a scene in the living room with Christmas toys and decorations from the 1950s, much of which was donated. The DAR museum in Washington D.C. gratefully accepted a radio and a set of martini glasses dating from the 1930s to accurately depict their colonial revival room. Old Christmas ornaments are prized by historic houses from the late nineteenth or early twentieth century. Pre-1950s cook books, magazines, and sales catalogs such as Sears or Montgomery Wards are often in demand by historic house curators who use them for research and reference as well as for display in period rooms.

You don't have to be intimately acquainted with the historic houses in the region, just call the local historical society or search online for a list and short description. Call the ones that might match with your items and ask to speak to the curator who will probably be able to tell you over the phone what items the museum would be interested in having.

By the way, museum curators are prohibited from appraising things. They can identify items and tell you what you have, if they have the time (which many do not), but they cannot give you a value. They will not even recommend a particular appraiser, but they may give out several names of appraisers from which you can choose.

They hardly advertise this fact, but some museums do purchase items they want badly enough. Few have funds for such purchases, but they can sometimes find a donor or board member who will front the money. If money is your main goal and the museum is eager to have your item, ask if they would be interested in it for X amount. You'll need to come up with the price—they will not name one—and a professional appraiser is necessary here.

**4. Hold your own garage sale or yard sale.** If you are clearing out a house and have at least a week to prepare, garage sales can dispose of a lot of unwanted Stuff, especially Stuff that is too good to throw out but not good enough to interest an estate sale professional. Take out an ad in the newspaper and list online for a Saturday sale. If you have a lot and don't mind people tracking through the house, leave everything in place and have your own tag sale. Calling it an estate sale rather than a garage sale implies a higher quality of merchandise.

Garage sales are a lot of work. There are many books to help you with advice. Sometimes the local newspaper has a kit to give away. And there are online sites that give helpful tips for those who haven't done this lately. Just be sure you have reliable help for security purposes as well as labor, plenty of change, and a flexible attitude toward price. If neighbors want to join your garage sale, so much the better! A multi-family sale will attract a bigger crowd and you can split any advertising costs.

**5. Sell through the Internet.** Selling online is hard work! Selling at retail directly to the customer (on www.eBay.com, www.Craigslist.org, www.WeBidz.com, www.uBid.com, or a similar site) might make you more money, but it requires a willingness to fuss with photographing, packaging, boxing, and mailing, and the patience to sell one at a time. And remember that only about half the items listed online ever sell.

Using eBay or other similar sites allows you to sell merchandise at the retail level instead of wholesale, and to reach a far greater market than a garage sale. You are, in effect, holding your own estate auction but pocketing most of the proceeds—an especially good idea if you have a family member with the time and knowledge to handle this. You can provide the motivation by splitting the proceeds with him or her. She can do the advertising, monitoring, packing, and shipping; the heirs can get an effortless percent. Or you can hire the services of eBay's Trading Assistants who do the work for you for a percentage of the selling price, usually a third or a little more. Or you can get a book or work through a tutorial and learn how to do it yourself. Selling on most Internet auction sites is not free. You usually pay a small amount to the site, but only if your item sells.

Craigslist is free. While eBay is basically an auction site, Craigslist is more of an electronic classified section, like in the newspaper or *Trading Post*. It draws local people who can come inspect the goods before buying, and the purchases are nearly always made with cash. If your item is especially large, like a sofa, or if it is something that people will need to look over before they are comfortable purchasing, like a guitar, Craigslist may be the best route.

Some things sell better online than others. Toys, for instance, and vintage clothing are hot, but this isn't the best place to sell antique furniture. Damaged items seldom sell. If you have dozens of something, selling in bulk might be more sensible.

You will need good photos, close-ups and full front and back and bottom, plus any signatures or marks indicating maker, date, or provenance.

*Robert has been selling stamps, coins, dolls, and sports memorabilia on eBay since he retired eight years ago. He began by selling off his own collections that he no longer wanted, but now it has become almost a fulltime business as he buys and sells daily, often listing several thousand items at one time. "Old things, nostalgia, sell best," he says. "Published price guides for collectibles are not in line with eBay; they list prices that are about 50% higher than you'll get on eBay. To find out what a particular collectible is worth on eBay, check past sales of that item. That'll give you a range of past sales, and you'll be better informed when setting your own price."*

**6. Sell items yourself, advertising through traditional methods like the classifieds of the local newspaper or a Trading Post.** A good idea, particularly when you think the item you are selling will appeal largely to older people who may prefer traditional classifieds to the computer.

**7. Sell to antiques/collectibles dealers.** After having researched your objects so you have some idea of value, take pictures or samples with you to an antiques store, an antiques show, or an antiques mall and find the vendors who sell your sort of merchandise. It will be harder to find a vendor at an antiques mall—these are places where an individual rents a booth but is rarely present. Sales are handled at a central desk. Ask for the name and phone number of vendors who look like potential buyers and arrange to meet them later.

Or call an antiques dealer to come to your house and look over the Stuff. He can help identify and set the price he would offer you. This will not cost you. Or you can hire an appraiser (which will cost you) to come out and identify and value Stuff.

If you find a receipt for an antique, get in touch with the store that sold it. Chances are, they will buy it back. Not, obviously, for what your relative paid for it, but for what it is worth today, which is probably less but may be more.

**8. Sell Stuff yourself at an antiques mall.** Rent a stall at a decent antiques mall for a few months and sell old Stuff and collectibles yourself. You do not need to be present; the mall has a central desk where purchases are made. Visit all the antiques malls in your region and choose a good one—some are just junky flea markets. Most malls charge a percent of sales plus rent. Give yourself a time limit of three months and mark things way, way down after the second month. Visit your booth and rearrange things every week so it looks like you have new Stuff.

**9. Sell through a consignment shop.** Consignment shops are especially well suited to getting rid of clothing, furnishings, and decorative items. You usually end up with half of the selling price. You get nothing at the outset, of course, not until the item sells.

**10. Hire an auction house to sell your Stuff.** There is a big difference between a local auction house and a national (or international) one like Sotheby's, Bonham's, or Christie's. The local outfit can do a good job selling your everyday Stuff like household belongings, tableware, canoe, tools, lawn mower, and so forth. They sell to the general public and to antiques dealers, not usually through the Internet. The big guys will only be interested in high-end objects such as fine art, antiques, fine wines, and important jewelry. Many of their clients bid through the Internet. There is a middle ground too, regional auction houses that, while not located in your town, can reach those specialized buyers, many of whom are Internet bidders. These auctioneers conduct themed auctions to attract specific collectors and buyers. For example, some recent themes include American Indian Art, Fine Jewelry and Timepieces, American History, and Historic Firearms and Early Militaria. Their primary buyers are dealers and collectors, not the general public.

Take pictures of your better objects and contact these national and regional houses. If they are interested, they will quote an estimate of what they think the item will bring at auction. No guarantees—it could be significantly higher or lower. You will pay to pack and ship the item to them and will have the option of insuring it while it is in their care. It isn't expensive to insure for a few weeks or months, and it brings peace of mind. They will take a percentage of the selling price, usually around 15%. It will probably be months before you see any money. Read the contract carefully. There may be costs that have not been mentioned, such as a charge for advertising or photography for their catalog.

Everyone has heard of the two big international auction houses, Christie's www.christies.com and Sotheby's www.sothebys.com, but there are literally thousands of others of varying size and specialty. Any list of major houses would include (in no particular order):

Bonhams www.bonhams.com
Skinner's www.skinnerinc.com
Doyle's www.doylenewyork.com
Heritage www.ha.com
Cowan's www.cowansauctions.com
Susanin's www.susanins.com
DuMouchelle's www.dumouchelle.com
Bunte www.bunteauction.com
Stanton's www.stantons-auctions.com
Leslie Hindman's www.lesliehindman.com
Leland Little www.llauctions.com
Moran www.johnmoran.com
Google others.

Local auction houses hold auctions on a weekly or monthly basis, usually collecting Stuff in one location and selling a mix from multiple owners. They may hold an auction at a house or farm or bring items into their warehouse for the next auction. Their primary buyers are the general public and local antiques dealers.

**11. Sell furniture along with the house.** Realtors will tell you that houses show better with furniture in them. If you are responsible for selling a house, leave in place the furniture no one wants and offer to sell all or part of it with the house. This works best with pieces that fit particularly well into the house, such as bar stools, fireplace equipment, and custom-made draperies, and with large items like sofas and chairs. People moving into larger quarters might appreciate having furniture for extra bedrooms, washers and dryers, porch/patio furniture, and other quality items, if the price is right.

**12. Barter online.** Bartering your belongings through on line websites lets you exchange things you don't want for things you want. No money changes hands but you are usually responsible for paying the shipping for the item you send. Sites such as www.trashbank.com, www.swaptreasures.com, or www.barterbucks.us offer a forum to swap or sell, and there are others that specialize in music and videos, books, or a commercial business clientele.

List all the book titles on www.paperbackswap.com. Never mind the name of this site—they swap hardcovers and audiobooks as well as paperbacks.

**13. Give away.** Stuff piled neatly at the curb or stacked in a community room with a sign that says "Help Yourself," usually disappears quickly. No tax deduction for you, since the recipient is not a nonprofit organization but appreciation counts too! At least the Stuff isn't clogging the landfill.

Are there young adults in the family with new apartments who need glasses and sheets? One heir piled all the useful household objects—dishes, glasses, Tupperware, casseroles, bed sheets, pots and pans, can openers, coffeemakers, blenders, sheets, towels, etc.—in one room and invited his son's friends who had just graduated from college to help themselves. They did.

Since 2003, an online service called Freecycle has posted items that people want to give away. Their mission is to keep Stuff out of the landfill and, based on the theory that one man's trash is another man's treasure, they serve as a clearinghouse for giveaways. You list what you want to give away and someone in your area comes to get it. Learn more at www.freecycle.org.

**14. Recycle.** Many houses have stacks of newspapers, magazines, and paper bags that can be recycled. Kitchen cupboards and tool sheds are often full of miscellaneous glass jars. Obsolete textbooks, old encyclopedias, telephone books, and Reader's Digest Condensed books can be recycled instead of tossed.

**15. Throw away.** Trips to the dumpster or the dump are unavoidable. If the home still has refuse service, ask if you can pay them extra to haul away your castoffs. Things to toss include most things made of plastic: bags, containers, and Tupperware. Do not throw out paper like canceled checks, bank statements, or anything with a Social Security number on it. Shred these. Many homes have tax records back thirty or forty years. Shred them. If there is too much to shred, Goodwill branches often have a shredding service.

Use the chapters in this book to help you identify and value the Stuff you want to sell. Deliver remaining items to Goodwill or to the dump when the day is done, or call a junk service such as Got Junk at 1-800-GOT-JUNK or Junk King at www.junk-king.com, or College Hunks at www.collegehunkshaulingjunk.com for a paid pick up.

# CHAPTER FOUR

## What Is It? What Is It Worth? What Do I Do With It?

Ahh, here at last is the nitty-gritty of valuing your Stuff. This information will help you identify, value, and dispose of the Stuff you and the other heirs have inherited that no one wants.

What if you don't know what it is or if it's worth anything at all? Here's a large red vase. Is it a priceless antique or a dime store product? Time to turn detective. Search the item for markings or clues, then turn to the Internet. First type in a brief description of the item (vase) and its markings and see what comes up. Then look for similar items at auction sites such as www.eBay.com    or www.craigslist.org. Search www.liveauctioneers.com, typing in "vase" and looking through all the "Sold" items for a similar item and its selling price. Look at the bottom of the page for the category Auction Results Database. Another good site is www.Worthpoint.com with a Question & Answer service and a seven-day free trial, which works well if you have only a couple items to check. If you need to know more about an object, examine it closely for a name or manufacturer and country of origin, then look online or at your library for more information. Check price guides at your library. These usually have pictures and descriptions, although you can't rely on the their prices—they are usually too high. Figure 50% or less. Some good price guides include *Kovel's Antiques and Collectibles Price List, Warman's Antiques and Collectibles Price Guide, Miller's International Antiques Price Guide, Encyclopedia for British Pottery and Porcelain Marks, and Pictorial Guide to Pottery and Porcelain Marks.* Check with www.artfact.com where you can pay a few dollars for a month's access to recent sale prices of Stuff, maybe just like yours.

Keep a sharp eye out for old advertising (signs, posters), antiques, art (oil paintings, sculpture, watercolors, signed prints), baseball and other sports memorabilia, leather-bound books, Christmas decorations, clocks and pocket watches, coin and stamp collections, cookie jars, dolls (Barbie, Shirley Temple, Madame Alexander), fishing lures, folk art (decoys, carvings, primitives), fountain pens, board games, antique furniture, figurines, guns, jewelry (costume and real), fine linens, militaria, quilts, samplers, oriental rugs, sterling silver, teapots, tools, and toys. Items in their original boxes are also worthy of note. Anything that is chipped, cracked, broken, or missing parts should be tossed.

A country of origin mark, like "Made in Italy," dates the object to 1891 or later. That's when an American tariff went into effect that required all imports to be identified by country of origin. If you find a foreign object without those words, it is either earlier than 1891 or it was not intended for export to America. It could have been purchased in another country and brought home as a souvenir from a trip or by someone who was stationed overseas in the military or who lived overseas as a missionary or student.

# Advertising

Some people call advertising "poor man's art." Although advertising has existed since ancient days, the collectors most likely to buy your inherited advertising items are collecting things from the late 1800s to the 1950s.

For our purposes, the category includes signs (usually tin, wooden, or porcelain enamel); posters promoting movies, travel destinations, theater shows, vaudeville, circuses, liquor, and the like; product packaging (tins, boxes, bottles, medicine); and trays. There are many other types, such as matchbooks, calendars, or magazine ads, but they seldom have much value unless very old. The most popular topics that bring the most interest and, therefore, the most money, include beer, liquor, soft drinks (especially Coke), gas stations, military (like "Loose Lips Sink Ships" or recruiting posters), automobiles, trains, and tobacco.

Fakes and reproductions abound in the advertising category. (A reproduction is an honest copy of an original; a fake is a copy made with intent to defraud. Many reproductions become fakes when an unscrupulous person "ages" them.) For example, any Coke tray you have is most likely not original, and most advertising posters are reproductions.

As always, start by identifying your Stuff. Go to www.eBay.com and see if there is anything like your item offered for sale. Check the tab marked Sold Listings, and see what price those items brought. Remember, half the Stuff on eBay never sells, so you can't tell much by seller's asking price alone. Look in your library for one of the advertising collector's guides. General ones like *Warman's Advertising* and targeted ones like the *Encyclopedia of Porcelain Enamel Advertising* can be ordered from another library by your librarian; used copies are available cheap on www.amazon.com. These guides will help you identify and describe what you have. Check the guide's publication date. If it is only a couple years old, the buyer's price they assign may be roughly accurate after you halve it to get an approximate seller's price. If the book is older than a few years, no problem; just use it to help identify your object and then go online for more up-to-date valuations. If the dollar amount looks to be more than a hundred dollars, give or take, check some of the regional auction houses across the country to see if they might be interested in selling the item for you. Contact them online and send a picture of all sides of your Stuff, its measurements, and anything else you know about it.

# Art

Any estate will include art of some sort. Whether it involves original art and sculpture, dime-store posters and prints, or the grandkids' fourth-grade masterpieces, there are certain to be pictures hanging on the walls and probably some others stuck away in the attic. Are they originals or reproductions? Oils, watercolors, prints, or photographs? Old masters or Grandpa's paint-by-number hobby? It isn't always easy to tell. Most art in most homes is not valuable, but we all know the stories about the person who bought a pretty picture for $25 at a yard sale and discovered it was an original worth hundreds of thousands of dollars. How can you avoid that hapless seller's angst?

If your loved one bought fine art, you are probably aware of it already. You may even know if they preferred watercolor landscapes or glass sculptures. But even if you are unaware of any art collecting habits and think what's hanging on the walls is merely reproductions or prints purchased at some garage sale, there is still the chance that one or two items have monetary value—and that makes it worth the effort to ferret out the truth.

Start by examining and documenting what you have. A paper trail of receipts, appraisals, or information about the artist may accompany original works of art, so keep an eye out for records of that sort stashed in files or taped behind the picture. Measure the item. Take a picture of it. Genuine, original art objects will usually be signed. Examine the front, back, and bottom for an artist's signature and maybe a date. If legible, search the name on the Internet to learn who it is—a contemporary artist who is still living? A long-dead one? If the signature is illegible, play code breaker and try to decipher enough letters to figure out the name. Use the Internet or the index of art history books. Libraries at universities and art museums have dictionaries like *Fielding's Dictionary of American Painters, Sculptors, and Engravers* or *Who Was Who in American Art* that may help you. And they have librarians who often help the general public. You can get even more specific with resources like *Dictionary of Women Artists* or *Handbook of 17th-, 18th- and 19th-Century American Painting* or *Dictionary of Sculptors in*

*Bronze* or *Dictionary of British Flower Painters*, and while these are likely to be found only in university and art museum libraries, your public library can often borrow copies from them for you. Your public librarian is a terrific resource here. Take a quick look at online sources such as www.askart.com, www.artcyclopedia.com, and www.artnet.com.

Contemporary artists are harder to research in books but easier to find online. If they are still living, they will almost certainly have a website. Relevant books include the Dictionary of Contemporary American Artists and *Who's Who in American Art*.

*A scrawl on a bit of paper inside a miniature portrait case looked like the letters O-f-f-i-???? In the index of a book titled* Early American Portrait Painters in Miniature *was a listing for Officer, Thomas, an early nineteenth-century portrait painter.*

If you can find only initials or a partial name, like the example above, there are books that can help you flesh out the rest of the name. You are likely to find these only at university or art museum libraries, but if one of those is not located near you, see what your public librarian can do for you via interlibrary loan. *American Artists: Signatures and Monograms, European Artists: Signatures and Monograms, Dictionary of Signatures and Monograms,* and *The Visual Index of Artists' Signatures and Monograms*.

Once you have determined the artist, the next question to ask is, What is it? If the picture is on canvas, framed, but without glass, it is probably a painting done in oils or acrylics. If it is under glass, it is likely to be a print or watercolor. An impression bordering the picture indicates it is a print—the indentation is made when the metal plate was pressed into the paper as the print was being made. Is there a pencil signature at the bottom beside some numbers? That tells you the artist's name and the number of prints he or she created in that edition: 15/50 means you have the fifteenth of fifty prints that were made before the artist destroyed the plate. A print run of 50 means the item is rarer—and more valuable—than a print run of 10,000. Latin words like *fecit* or *sculpsit* indicate who made it (*fecit*) or engraved it (*sculpsit*) or who painted the original painting that the print is copying (*pinxit*). If the picture looks to be on canvas, it may be an original, but be aware that there are many contemporary artists, like the popular Thomas Kinkade, who mass-produce their work onto canvas. These can sometimes be sold on eBay for a modest amount, but there are so many out there that the re-sale value is low.

Research your original prints in books like *American Engravers upon Copper and Steel* or *American Printmaking 1880-1980*. To find dealers who sell prints by the same artist as your (and who, therefore, might be interested in buying yours), try www.ifpda.org for the International Fine Print Dealers Association website.

Make an appointment with a fine art appraiser to bring or email your pictures along with any information you have found (dimension, artist's name, date, receipts, and whatever you've learned from the Internet). To find one, call a local art gallery or auction house and ask for a recommendation. A curator from an art museum might take the time to help you identify a painting, but some museums have a policy against this practice. All curators are prohibited from valuing art or objects. The fine art appraiser can tell you what you have and what it's worth, and will usually give you some options for selling it.

*Ben has inherited a dark painting that looks like an oil painting, but it is framed under glass. It is a historic scene of a peasant woman working at a table. He remembers his mother saying it came from a grandparent, so it must be "old." The signature on the lower left says T. Van Vreeland. Googling that name leads to an F. Van Vreeland—yes, the T. could have been an F.—and one of those sites, www.askart.com, shows several paintings by a Francis William Van Vreeland that are unmistakably similar in style to Ben's. So now we have his proper name, dates, and a brief biography. He was known for watercolors, so the peasant-at-the-table is probably a watercolor, not an oil, and he lived from 1879-1954. Googling the proper name leads to a number of sites, most of which ask Ben to pay for access to the prices Van Vreeland's paintings have recently fetched. He tries the free sites first, like www.liveauctioneers.com. A kitchen scene sold recently for $300. A landscape went for $375. A scene with a woman is being offered by one auction house with an estimate of $200-300. An indoor family scene sold for $230. A large auction house recently sold two Van Vreeland landscapes, one estimated to go for between $600-800 actually went for $550 and the other, estimated at $400-600, went for $300—both times less than predicted. The artist seems to have been quite prolific, and there are many auction sites that will give Ben more information* *for a small fee—some will charge a couple dollars for one day's access, others for one month—but he may have enough to go on without doing that. The sites also tell him which auction houses have successfully sold Van Vreeland's work recently, and he can contact them about selling his.*

Other ways to research the dollar value of your art object online include www.artfact.com, www.artprice.com, www.artnet.com, www.askart.com, www.findartinfo.com. There are modest fees involved, but most of these sites have a one-day subscription price, so gather up all the art and artists you want to research and go at it all at once.

What about finding a famous artist's work among your inherited Stuff? There it is, hanging on the living room wall, a signed Picasso etching! Or a Dali. Or a Chagall, or a Miro. Eureka! A fortune! Well . . . don't count your money too quickly. These are the most common fakes in the art world. No one knows how many thousands are out there. A fine art appraiser will be able to sort the wheat from the chaff. Or you can google "fake" and the artist's name and research yourself how the fakes differ from the real McCoy.

Selling your art on what is called the secondary market is not easy. Few art galleries are interested in these items, although it never hurts to ask. They might take your painting on commission and keep 20-25% of the selling price. Auction houses are good possibilities, if you can find one that has sold items like yours in the past. Success is more likely at an estate sale, where pictures on the wall in an attractive setting can sell for a decent price. Interior designers often attend estate sales. If you have only a few paintings to sell rather than an entire estate, you should still contact an estate sales professional, who may be willing to add your art to another upcoming estate sale. An appealing subject will help—children, flowers, dogs, scenery, hunt scenes, and bright colors beat the heck out of dreary landscapes and still lifes with dead game.

If your painting or sculpture was done by a local artist, check online to see if he or she is still living and who represents him. Contact that gallery and ask if they are interested in buying it back—not for the price your relative paid, of course, and probably for a good deal less because it was purchased at retail and is being sold at wholesale. But if a gallery is interested in re-selling it, great! The art could have gone up in value since your relative purchased it, but it is more likely that it has depreciated. *Be aware that most art does not appreciate.* Art is—or should be—purchased because someone liked it, not for an investment.

*Wanda and her husband have owned an art gallery for several decades. One of their good clients, an elderly bachelor, had a nice art collection that he had assembled over many years. When he died, his nephew was eager to cash out the estate. He found Wanda's gallery through the receipts and papers his uncle had saved and asked them to buy the paintings back. He was surprised that they were not interested. They offered to sell them online on the secondary market, which would take a while, they told him. He refused. The paintings, some of which had been purchased in recent years for $4,000-5,000 each, would have brought about half that online. Instead, the nephew took them to a local auction house where they sold to a general public audience for about $500 each. If he had been more patient, he could have received a lot more, said Wanda, but perhaps he needed the money fast.*

A local artist sells best in his or her locality. So if you live in Texas and have a painting by an Illinois artist, contact a few Chicago galleries and see if they have a resale program. Regional auction houses—not small, local ones—can do a decent job of selling original art. Find them online. Western art sells faster and for more money in the western states where cowboys, rodeos, and Indians are part of the local culture. The same is true for paintings of landmarks and scenery. Paintings of New York City will sell better in New York than San Francisco. Beach scenes and shell prints will find a home faster in Florida than in Wisconsin.

*Jeff is an appraiser who, on a job at one house, found a painting in a closet with a blanket over it. The heirs were about to give it away because it was "ugly." He researched the piece and sent a picture to Christies and Sothebys. They estimated it would sell for $100,000. It actually sold for $275,000.*

You can sell your art online yourself through the usual eBay and Craigslist types, but art specific sites are better. Google "sell fine art" to find companies.

Often overlooked is the fact that picture frames, especially old, ornate ones, can have value. Sometimes more than the picture itself! Look on the back at the construction: Old picture frames will not have stapled corners or metal strips joining the corners. Again, a fine art appraiser will recognize this.

# Bicycles

Is there anything more forlorn than an old bike leaning against the wall of a shed, its once-gleaming chrome spotted with rust, its tires flattened by rot? A shiny new bicycle is a snap to sell on Craigslist. Unfortunately, that isn't what you are likely to find among the household belongings you've inherited.

Your local Goodwill branch may take old bikes, but if so, you will probably have to deliver it yourself. Call a bike shop in your area and ask if there is an organization in town that repairs and gives away used bicycles. Sometimes an informal group of bike-loving, mechanically minded, charitable people takes on this sort of project, especially with children's bikes, especially in the summer and fall in anticipation of Christmas.

If you are considering trying to sell, a bicycle shop can be the best place to start. Bring yours in for an examination and an estimate on fixing it up—new tires and a thorough cleaning may be all it needs to put it in salable condition, and you'll get a lot more for a clean bike with new tires than you will for a decrepit one. If refurbishing involves more than that, you may find it isn't worth it. When new adult bikes start at about $200, putting significant money into something that, when finished, may be worth $80 makes no sense.

One of the best places to sell your used bike is the online classified site, www.Craigslist.org, because its prospective buyers come from nearby. When selling an item that people want to try out before buying, like a bike, or an item that is large, heavy, and expensive to ship, like a bike, Craigslist should be your first stop. And it doesn't hurt that it's free.

## Boats

Found a fishing boat, kayak, sailfish, or canoe behind the shed? An ad in the local newspaper, Trading Post, or Craigslist would be a good bet. Small boats are not hard to sell, but the work is on you. The easiest route to take is to donate it to a nonprofit like Goodwill that will haul it away and give you a tax deduction.

## Books, Magazines, and Newspapers

Whether you are breaking up an entire private library full of antique, gold-embossed, leather-bound volumes or dealing with a few boxes of dusty old books that Uncle Fred stored in his attic, a financial windfall may be in store on the shelves of your relative's house. There are often several generations of books in one household, handed down over the years, and some may be rare or collectible. For some people, books are precious in their own right and throwing them away amounts to heresy. Fortunately, many of the books you have inherited can have a future if you can take a little time to deal with them.

A rule of thumb—paperback books seldom have any monetary value, but hard covers, especially if they are first editions or have local interest, are in decent condition, and have original dust jackets, can surprise you. Leather-bound books have value, even if it is only the cosmetic sort. Interior decorators often buy these for their clients.

If the estate includes a lot of hardcover books, call a local book dealer to come to the house to browse for valuable volumes while they are still on the shelves and easy to see. You'll find such people listed in the Yellow Pages under "Books" or online at www.abaa.org. Look for someone who advertises that he buys old books, not the national chains like Barnes & Noble. Your local book dealer is interested in hard cover books, old and new, and will make you an offer on the ones he can re-sell.

Throw out (or better yet, recycle for content) obsolete textbooks, old encyclopedias, phone books, and Reader's Digest Condensed Books. Box the rest, hard cover and paperback alike, and deliver to the local public library. Do not bring magazines. The librarians won't want many of your books for their own shelves, but most libraries have a support group called the Friends of the Library that sells donated books for a dollar or so and uses the proceeds to buy current titles. Libraries may accept some new hardcover books—say, less than five years old—for their own shelves. Small community libraries in rural areas are more likely to appreciate your donation than larger, better-funded institutions. Some libraries resell books to a group that comes by periodically to examine all donations for Internet sales potential. Even the books no one wants are usually recycled for their paper content rather than sent to the landfill.

Goodwill, the Salvation Army, or other local charitable service organizations will accept used books for resale (not the categories listed in the previous paragraph). Veteran's Administration hospitals appreciate current paperbacks and audiobooks for their mostly male patients. Large print and audiobooks of all sorts are eagerly received by nursing homes and retirement centers, especially the publicly funded ones that have little left in their budgets for amenities. Call these institutions first to make sure they are equipped to accept donations. If your loved one was living in a retirement community when he or she passed away, that facility may have a library for residents that would accept some of your books. A historic house museum might appreciate books that date from the same period as the house.

*Old books are not necessarily valuable.*

**Bibles:** *Family Bibles, unless owned by some important historical figure, have no monetary value.* Most of those who inherit the contents of a home will find a Bible or two on the bookshelves. Some people are reluctant to throw away a Bible, especially if it is old, but in most cases, it has no monetary value. If there is any genealogy information written inside it and someone in your family has an interest in charting the family tree, make sure to offer it to him or her; otherwise, call your state library or county historical society to see if they would like to have it for their genealogy collection. You can also look online for buyers who are interested in genealogy. EBay is one possibility; for another, google the word "genealogy" and the last names listed in your Bible to see if you can connect with some interested researchers.

If the Bible is in a language other than English, it is less likely to have monetary value and you will have a harder time selling it online.

Some very old Bibles may have monetary value. What is "very old?" Older than you think. Those dating from the 1900s or 1800s are very common and therefore not desirable to book collectors. If your Bible dates from the 1700s and earlier, it might have some value. Books of that era, however, may not have a publishing date on the front pages, so if you suspect your Bible is that old and don't see any indication of date, you need to take it to a rare books dealer for expert opinion. You should not have to pay for a quick-glance opinion, but you would expect to pay for an appraisal.

Consider donating an 18th-century-or-older Bible to a museum—you can take a deduction on your income taxes for its appraised amount, or, if you haven't had it appraised and don't want to spend the money for an official appraisal, do one yourself by finding similar Bibles for sale online and seeing what they sold for. Average a few sales and you have a reasonable value to declare.

No one wants old textbooks unless they are over a hundred years old. Very old books dating from the eighteenth and nineteenth centuries are welcomed by historic houses of roughly the same period, perhaps for display in their bookcases or for research purposes. They can also be sold to book collectors.

If you find a book you think might be valuable, check to see whether it is a first edition. This is a bit more complicated than it sounds, as the first edition means the first printing, and there might have been more than one printing in the first year. A little research helps: books such as *First Editions: A Field Guide for Collectors of*

*English and American Literature* can give you information to help you determine whether you have something valuable. But characteristics other than first edition status determine value. Does your book have its original dust jacket? Was it signed by the author? Is its binding broken? Are the pages stained, folded, torn, or marked up with pen or pencil? Is it a book club edition? *Bookman's Price Index, Huxford's Old Book Value,* and other price guides tell you what similar books have sold for recently. You might find those in a large public library, but more probably in a university library. Another way to look up current prices is to use www.bookfinder.com, www.alibris.com, www.abebooks.com, www.biblio.com, www.abaa.org, or www.addall.com to see what a similar copy of your book is selling for online.

Now that you know approximately what your book is worth, you can decide how to dispose of it. You can take the short cut and contact a local book dealer. He will come to your house if you have a lot to show him, or meet you at his store if there are only a few volumes. Expect to get about half of the book's retail value. Many people auction their old books on eBay, where they can keep more of the price for themselves, but there is no guarantee you will net more money there. If you chose that route, don't ignore the cost of advertising, packaging, and mailing, not to mention your time.

*Always ruffle the pages of a book before you sell or toss it. As crazy as it sounds, some people stash money, bonds, or important papers between the pages.*

**Comic Books:** In 2012, a Detective comic book from 1939 sold for over half a million dollars at Heritage auctions in Dallas. But—and there's a big "but"—it was rare, in perfect condition, well preserved, and professionally graded. It made the news precisely because it is so unusual.

But less-than-perfect comic books have value too. Collectors come in all stripes. Most towns and all cities have at least one store that sells comic books, old and new, and a trip to a couple of those should tell you what you need to know about the value of yours. They will probably make you an offer.

If you prefer to do it yourself, comic book price guides are available in some libraries or for sale in bookstores, comic book stores, or on amazon.com. Selling comic books on eBay is another way to dispose of these if you have the time and patience to sell them one by one, assuming you've accurately researched the value. Trouble is, the market price is very dependent on condition. A little tear on one page, a coffee cup ring, rusted staples, or folded pages can alter the price considerably.

A general rule of thumb is that comic books printed after 1980 have no significant value. There are just too many of them around. Most shops and collectors are looking to buy those that date earlier than 1969. And the first comic books came out in 1938, so none are older than that.

**Magazines:** If you are pressed for time, throw away or recycle magazines. If you have time, sort through them, looking for pre-1950 issues, and consider donating those to a museum or historic house dating from a similar period. If you find anything dating from the 1800s, check with a local rare books dealer or a specialty magazine dealer (you can find those on the Internet). Or do a little research yourself in one of several magazine price guides such as *Old Magazines: Identification and Value Guide*, available at your public library or the nearest university library, or look online at www.amazon.com.

Call the local elementary school and see if the art teacher or the kindergarten teachers would like magazines full of color pictures to cut up for art projects and collages. Recent issues of *National Geographic* or other periodicals that are not time sensitive (not news magazines or *People* that are out of date in a few days) might be donated to a nursing home, retirement center, or VA hospital—call first and ask. There is some market for very old issues of magazines like *Life*—you'll see them in boxes at booths in antique malls or at traveling antique shows—but these retail for only a few dollars and you would get very little in return for your trouble. So many people saved their *National Geographics* that these are worth almost nothing, but a *Saturday Evening Post* with a Norman Rockwell cover could have some value.

*When Robert's mother died, he found 300 neatly stacked issues of* Life *in her basement. Rejecting an offer to sell a few of them for $1.50 each, he turned instead to eBay where he cleverly offered them individually with the suggestion to "Buy your Birthday." Robert has sold 250 over the past few years for about $3,000, an average of $12 each.*

**Newspapers:** Recycle newspapers unless they are very old (say, pre-World War II) and might be of interest to a historic house museum or historical society.

Many people save newspapers with important headlines— *Titanic Sinks After Collision with Iceberg* or *Princess Dianna Killed in Crash*—thinking that they will be worth something someday. They are wrong. There are simply too many of these around for them to have any value. You might get a few dollars for them at an antiques show from a dealer who sells paper items like postcards, prints, posters, old newspapers, and advertising.

**Paperbacks:** Another option with paperbacks you don't want is to trade them for paperbacks you *do* want. Check out www.paperbackswap.com and www.titletrader.com where you can list the titles of your books, then mail them free to the first person who asks for them. That earns you credit you can use to ask for someone else's book. You pay postage when you send books, but the ones you order come to you free. These sites also allow hardcover books, CDs, and DVDs to be traded.

**College Yearbooks:** It would be no surprise to come across a collection of high school and college yearbooks when working through an inherited estate. Rather than throw them out, consider reuniting them with their school. Most colleges and universities are delighted to have old yearbooks donated. Graduates whose original copies have been lost or destroyed sometimes ask for replacements and are grateful when the school can comply. And it could be that the college was lacking that particular year, or had very few copies and wanted more. It doesn't take a moment to email the school's development office to find out.

Private high schools, prep schools, and boarding schools fall into this category too. Public high schools are seldom equipped to accept or store old yearbooks, but you could inquire.

## Cameras

Even in these days of digital cameras and cell phones with cameras, some old 35 mm cameras have modest appeal. Goodwill will take them off your hands if you can't sell them online or in a Trading Post.

Throw out any old 110 or 126 cameras. Millions were made in the 1960s and no one wants them today. Even if they did, no one is making the film. Check inside the cameras first for film—maybe there are some very old surprises waiting to be developed, although it will be hard to find a developer.

A camera shop might buy an old 35 mm camera for a very modest amount (and some few models could bring up to a couple hundred dollars), but your best bet is to find a high school where photography is taught. Donate your camera and its accessories to the teacher for a student to use. If you can connect with a student at the beginning of a semester before the course has started, you might be able to sell your camera. Camera clubs might have an interest. But all this effort is likely to get you nothing more than a few dollars, so the donation route may be preferable.

Very old camera equipment can be examined and evaluated at a camera store, where they will know if it has any appeal to a collector or a museum.

## Ceramic Stuff: Fine China and Everyday

Lovely sets of fine china meant the world to the generations that came before ours. They were especially fond of porcelain from France (particularly Limoges and Sevres) and Germany (particularly Meissen and Dresden) and bone china from England (particularly Chelsea, Bow, Bristol, Derby, Lowestoft, Minton, Worcester, Doulton, Spode, and Wedgwood). In the twentieth century, an American manufacturer, Lenox, became very popular, especially with the White House. It was not unusual for couples to own two or more sets of china with twelve place settings in each.

Sadly, there is little market for such sets today. Brides seldom choose old-fashioned patterns and young people seldom buy or want to inherit flowery antique dinnerware with a gold rim that must be hand washed and can't go in the microwave. They prefer modern place settings from Crate and Barrel that can go straight into the dishwasher. People just don't entertain with formal dinner parties any longer; they don't need twelve place settings of formal tableware. So don't count on the children or grandchildren to want Grandma's bone china.

China dishes are usually marked clearly on the back of the plates or the bottom of cups. The famous Meissen crossed swords or the Sevres crossed Ls (for King Louis) are among the best-known marks. A multitude of books at your library, like *Porcelain Marks of the World (Poche)* and *Kovels' New Dictionary of Marks (Kovel)*, will help you decipher your marks. For example, china made in Limoges was usually marked with the city, Limoges, the country, France, and the maker, Haviland. Online sites are helpful too, just google porcelain marks and the relevant country. If you can't determine what pattern you have, Replacements, Ltd., at www.replacements.com will identify it for free if you send them a photo.

The Tariff Act of 1890, intended to protect American industry, required foreign merchandise entering the U.S. to be marked with its country of origin. So china marked with its country in English (like Germany or Italy rather than Deutschland or Italia) dates from after 1890. Of course, this applied to imports, not to the merchandise American travelers bought while overseas, so if you had relatives who traveled, served in the military, worked as missionaries, or lived or studied abroad, they could have purchased unmarked items and brought them home.

An average-size public library carries three shelves full of books on ceramics, including general and specific price catalogs. Start by identifying your item in a general catalog, then go to a more specific one for more information and more pictorial examples.

You can sell your fine china tableware for a modest amount, depending on its brand, to Replacements, Ltd., at www.replacements.com where it will be sold piecemeal to people wanting to replace a broken piece of a pattern that is no longer made. It doesn't matter if you have a complete set or just a few pieces. You will have to pack up the china and send it, which will cost a good deal in packing and shipping such heavy, breakable things. They will not take anything cracked or chipped. No one will. Throw those out.

Japanese and Chinese ceramics were immensely popular in the twentieth century—and still are today, so you should be able to sell them. Sets of dinnerware from Japan, like Noritake, were imported throughout the twentieth century except for the World War II years, 1941-1945. If it is marked Nippon, it dates from 1890-1921. After 1921, U.S. law required Japanese imports to use the word Japan rather than the Japanese word, Nippon. Items not intended for export to America were not marked in English, yet some Americans acquired these items when they were stationed in Japan during the Occupation. Pieces made during the Occupation years of 1945-1952 will be marked "Made in Occupied Japan." These are collectible. One professional who specializes in helping seniors downsize says, "We have trouble selling things just because they are Occupied Japan. But items that sell for other reasons can be marked a little higher if they are marked Occupied Japan."

Chinese and Japanese ceramic marks intimidate Westerners unfamiliar with Asian characters. There were no hard-and-fast rules about how to mark ceramics, so identifying your vase or dish can be difficult. There are websites and books that can help, but if you get discouraged, www.gotheborg.com/index.htm may save the day.

There are many marks pictured on this site, and if those don't help you, they will try to read and identify your Chinese or Japanese marks for a small fee.

Blue and white china has its collectors, especially the oriental Blue Willow pattern that depicts a bridge and a pagoda and may or may not have been made in the Far East. These tend to be worth a bit more than other patterns.

*Generally speaking, the more information on the back of a piece of china, the younger it is.* If it says "Dishwasher safe," it isn't very old.

*How can you tell porcelain from pottery?* Porcelain is usually translucent. Hold a plate up to the light and you should be able to see the shadow of your fingers behind it. Porcelain is usually thinner than its thicker pottery cousin, although porcelain is stronger and will not break or chip as easily as earthenware or stoneware. A porcelain bowl or cup will probably resonate (ping!) when tapped with a pencil; a pottery bowl or cup will thud.

Everyday pottery dishes are best donated to Goodwill or the like. Here too, anything chipped, cracked, or missing its lid should be thrown away.

Decorative pottery, like bowls and vases and novelty items, run the gamut from junk to precious. Run any marks or descriptive information through google first to see what you can turn up. If you have a name of a manufacturer or potter, also check ceramic price guides. Names not included in ceramic price guides probably aren't collectible.

For example, suppose you have an old cookie jar with the word Metlox on the bottom. Google directs you to several sites about this California manufacturer, telling its history and linking you to books on the subject, to collectors who are actively looking for certain pieces, to descriptions of the different marks, and to recent sales on various auction sites. Checking www.liveauctioneers.com reveals an upcoming auction where a Metlox item is being sold, plus a whole page of examples that have been auctioned in the last few years at prices ranging from $5 to $600. Www.ebay.com has cookie jar pictures and prices too, ranging from $10 to $380. Surely one of these will match yours, and maybe the price is high enough to prompt you to contact the auction company that sold it and ask if they will sell yours too. Or do it yourself on eBay.

Ceramics made for children are eagerly sought by collectors, so if you come across an antique ABC plate or dish or something from Royal Doulton's Bunnykins or Wedgwood's Peter Rabbit line, you can sell them easily online, at garage sales, or as part of an estate sale.

Some Scandinavian-made pottery has value. And certain U.S. pottery manufacturers like Bennington Potters are likely to sell well.

If you find a Limoges plate with flowers or a scene painted on it and a signature or initial or monogram, you have probably found something a relative or friend made many years ago. Around the turn of the twentieth century, it was popular for nicely-brought-up young ladies to showcase their feminine talents by painting on china. Finishing schools often had classes in china painting, and thousands of Limoges blanks were imported into America from France for this purpose. These amateur items have sentimental value only, unless someone famous painted them.

Clunky stoneware crocks or storage vessels have monetary value, though they may not look attractive to you. Folk art ceramics are also highly collectible. Take them to an antiques dealer.

A precaution: hand wash your ceramic items unless they are clearly stated to be dishwasher safe. Gold rims, transfer designs, and other decorative finishes can fade or sustain other damage from harsh detergents and very hot water.

## Christmas Decorations

Just about every household will have Christmas paraphernalia stored in the attic or closet: boxes of tree ornaments, seasonal knick-knacks, a crèche scene, wreaths, outdoor lights, perhaps an artificial tree. Most of this is best sold at a garage sale or to vendors in an antiques mall who trade in used Christmas decorations. Old strings of lights should probably be thrown away over concerns about frayed or outdated electrical wiring.

Christmas decorations dating to the 1950s or earlier deserve better than a garage-sale fate. Historic houses of similar periods would probably be interested in having such things (even old lights) donated for their use in period Christmas decorating.

Tree ornaments are probably the most salable of Christmas decorations because they are so widely collected. Consider them in three broad categories: antiques (pre-1960s), modern collectibles (1970s to present), and ordinary modern. One way to recognize age is by size—old ornaments are generally smaller and lighter in weight than modern ones.

The Christmas tree didn't become common in America until after the Civil War. The honor of having the "first" Christmas tree in America is claimed by half a dozen states, but the custom didn't even begin to catch on until the 1850s. Even then, tree decorating was different: people made their own ornaments out of paper, nuts, cookies, candy, and small toys. These decorations were taken off the tree at a Christmas party and eaten or played with, not packed into corrugated boxes for use next year. German-made blown glass ornaments were first crafted about 1860 but didn't come to the U.S. in any quantity until F. W. Woolworth began importing them in the 1880s. Until World War II broke out in 1939, nearly all the blown glass ornaments in the U.S. were made in Germany, with a few coming from Czechoslovakia and Japan. Only after the original source was cut off in the 1940s did American companies, notably Shiny Bright, step into the market. In the 1970s and 1980s, old-fashioned German-style ornaments experienced a revival and are again being imported from Germany and eastern European countries. Much of the ornament market—indeed, most of the Christmas market in general—was captured by the Chinese in the 1980s and forward.

All this is by way of suggesting that the "old" Christmas tree ornaments in your grandmother's attic are probably no older than the time when she was a young married woman. How can you tell if the old-looking ones are genuine? Research. Become friends with your public librarian and borrow a copy of the *Pictorial Guide to Christmas Ornaments and Collectibles: Identification and Values* by George Johnson, or other similar guides. Librarians can usually get you a book from another library if they don't have it at your local branch, so ask. Remember that all such guides to antiques and collectibles are written for the buyer, not for you, the seller. Prices mentioned are what the buyer should expect to pay; the seller can hope for half that amount or less.

If your ornaments are genuinely old, you now have an idea what they are worth at retail. You can try to sell them yourself online or to appropriate antiques dealers. For serious collectors, the most desirable ornaments are those made between the two world wars (1918-1939). These can sell for hundred of dollars. Most others can be sold for a few dollars each.

*Nancy had inherited a dozen old Christmas tree ornaments that she wanted to sell. There were some unusual colored wax figures (Santas, snowmen, drum majors) that research said dated from the 1920s and 1930s. Thinking they would be valuable, Nancy checked into eBay and other online sales sites. Others like hers were selling for $1 or $2 each. The moral of this story? Old doesn't necessarily mean valuable.*

"Collectibles" are modern ornaments, issued in a series. The first major collectible ornaments were manufactured by Hallmark, starting in 1973. Others like the White House collection (since 1981), Christopher Radko designs (since 1986), Franklin Mint, Danbury Mint, Bradford Editions, et cetera . . . issue one or more "limited edition" ornaments each year and discontinue a design after one year or a few years in an effort to enhance collectability. There is a secondary market for some of these ornaments, as long as they are in excellent condition . . . better still if they are in their original boxes. You can reach that market directly if you sell online, at a garage sale, or flea market booth, or you can wholesale to antiques mall vendors or to vendors who specialize in the secondary market. One of the largest of these is Replacements Ltd., a Greensboro, North Carolina, outfit that buys and sells china, silver, and certain collectibles for resale. Call them at 800-737-5223 and speak to their Purchasing Department to see if they are interested in your ornament, or try online at www.replacements.com.

Find a village scene among all the Christmas stuff? Old ones can be valuable. Originally, Christmas trees were tabletop size, and they often had a miniature farm or village scene placed around the base, ringed with a wooden or metal fence. These little animals, people, and trees were hand painted and made of wood, lead, paper maché, or composition. German villages have farm animals and people known as *putz* figures; they are usually composition. French farm scenes, called *santons*, are similar but often include a crèche. *Santons* are made of molded clay. To learn what sort you have, type either phrase into your search engine and compare pictures to your figures. Japanese cardboard houses and buildings that make up a miniature village are collectible, retailing for about $10-40 dollars each. Find examples for sale online to compare with yours.

Collectors' Christmas plates, like most collectibles, saw their value plummet with the advent of the Internet. No longer was it difficult for collectors to find the piece they wanted; no longer would they need to pay a premium to fill in their collection because they never knew when they'd ever see another. You can certainly sell any Christmas plates you inherit, you just won't get more than a few dollars a piece unless they are very old, as in early twentieth century, or rare. This category is easy to research. You'll find examples online and can judge prices from that. You can also ask Replacements.com what they would pay for your pieces to get another price.

Traditional German nutcrackers have been handmade since the eighteenth century. Cheap knockoffs have been made in China since the 1980s. Nutcrackers first came to the attention of Americans after World War II when American soldiers stationed in Germany during the occupation (1945-1955) sent them home as souvenirs, so yours is unlikely to be older than the middle of the 20th century. Because American law since 1891 requires all merchandise imported into the U.S. be marked with its country of origin, telling Chinese copies from German originals is easy. Look on the base. The distinction is crucial to the item's value: collectors will pay a hundred dollars and up for good German examples. Cheap Chinese copies will fetch a couple dollars at a yard sale. Sell German nutcrackers to antiques dealers or online.

## Clocks and Watches

Clocks come in so many sizes, styles, and materials that generalizations are impossible. An antiques dealer would be the best person to sort the resalable from the junk. An old tall-case clock (grandfather clock) has value; a modern one has little. Mantle clocks that no longer run are a problem since there are so few people who can repair them, and the cost of doing so will likely exceed the value of the clock.

Certain watches (you know the names: Rolex, Cartier, Patek-Phillippe, and other luxury brands) have a resale market. Certain others that are rare and historical are coveted by collectors, as are some pocket watches. But the vast majority of watches have no monetary value at all.

You can reach collectors online. Auction houses can sell luxury watches for you, or you can do it yourself online, but here too, the market is weak. A discouraging note: The Wall Street Journal noted in 2011 that the average sale price of used wristwatches on eBay dropped 28% from 2008 to 2010.

Pocket watches that were wound with a key are usually older and more valuable than other pocket watches.

## Clothing & Accessories

Sort clothing into piles: new, old, and vintage (older than 1960). Clothing that is just a year or two old, especially designer labels, is likely to sell quickly at a consignment shop. Ditto accessories.

You already know that lots of organizations accept donated clothing and accessories. What you might not realize is that they even accept un-wearable clothing, like stained shirts, pants with holes, or impossibly worn and outdated items. Goodwill sorts all clothing donations, separating the items that are saleable from the ones that are not and then recycling the latter for fabric scraps that make rag rugs and other items.

**Vintage clothing.** If there is any clothing from the 1960s or earlier, contact a vintage clothing shop. Most specialize in clothing and accessories from the 1920s to the 1960s, but most will bend the guidelines for a particularly interesting item.

How can you tell the age of an item of clothing? Look at the zippers. Metal zippers mean the item is pre-1960. After that, plastic zippers took over. If there are buttons rather than zippers, like a button fly on a man's suit or buttons up the back of a dress, it probably dates from the Twenties or Thirties. The biggest giveaway is the washing care tags. If it has a tag with washing instructions, don't bring it into a vintage clothing shop—those weren't mandated until 1971.

Make an appointment with the vintage clothing shop owner to show what you have. Don't bring photos; bring the clothing. Condition counts. If it isn't wearable today, it has little value. That doesn't mean it has to be perfect, but large stains and torn lace will reduce the value hugely. The buyer will likely make you an offer on some of the pieces you bring, and she can advise you on the others. As always, two shops are better than one so you can take the best offer. Items from the Fifties and the Roaring Twenties are in special demand. Wedding gowns and military uniforms are often sold here. Before Halloween, vintage clothing shops become costume shops. Before Christmas, they sell a lot of jewelry. That means you are more likely to sell your Stuff (and get a better price for it) in September and November.

Vintage shops also buy accessories such as cuff links, stickpins, hatpins, tie clips, hats, gloves, scarves, coats, shoes, shawls, fans, evening bags, handkerchiefs, furs, and jewelry. You can estimate the date of your jewelry by the earrings—clip-on earrings are probably from the 1920s – 1960s, because both the earlier fashion during Victorian times and the later fashion from the 1970s forward favored piercing.

If the jewelry, cuff links, hatpins, and tie clips you want to get rid of are made of gold or silver, there will be marks like 18K, 14K or 10K on the gold and STER, Sterling, 925, or 900 on the silver, or PLAT or PT for platinum. If these items have stones, chances are good the stones are genuine. It wasn't common to put cheap "paste" stones in genuine silver or gold settings. Same with pearls. Pearls with 14K gold clasps or pins are probably genuine. These pieces should be taken to a reputable jeweler, preferably two or three, to see what they say. If the metal has no marks, it's likely the piece is costume jewelry and that is the sort you should take to a vintage clothing shop to sell.

Vintage clothing and accessories sell well on eBay, if you have the inclination. Tedious but profitable.

**Clothing for costumes.** Local theater groups and high school and college theater programs are happy to accept clothing that would translate into a costume for a play. Old ball gowns, shawls, fedoras, ladies' hats, men's suits, neckties, wedding gowns, and fur coats are probably the most appreciated.

**Furs.** There's an old fur coat in the closet. Or two. Or more. What to do with them?

The answer will depend largely upon your feelings about wearing animal fur.

People who are anti-fur will want to consider donating the coat to the Humane Society, which promotes cutting up old furs to use as surrogate mothers for orphaned mammals, making their nests warm and comforting. Search the Wildlife International database for a list of nearby rehabilitation centers. Or donate to PETA where they will pass an old fur coat on to a homeless person, who, according to PETA, "are the only people who have an excuse to wear fur."

Those with no moral objections to wearing fur need to learn what sort of fur they have. Is it chinchilla or weasel? Leopard or mink? Your local fur dealer will identify it for you for free and give you some ideas. They can appraise too, but that might have a small cost. Identifying the fur is the first step. After that, you can:

--donate to a theatrical program at a local little theater, high school, or university,

--have it remodeled and updated at a furrier's to wear again,

--donate or sell for arts and crafts, or make something yourself (a collar, muff, handbag, pillow, or vest),

--sell directly on eBay or other site, bearing in mind that traditional styles sell best,

--sell to online businesses such as Cash for Fur Coats or to one of the three main used fur dealers in the U.S. (Henry Cowit in NY, Ritz Furs in NY, or Chicago Fur Outlet—find information online) where they buy outright or sell on consignment,

--sell on consignment at a local secondhand clothing shop,

--trade in at your local furrier for credit toward another coat.

Furs are like cars, they depreciate dramatically the day you walk out of the shop and are generally worth less than you think. They also don't last as long as you think, so if you find an old fur, it may be worthless. Some minks, if well cared for, might last fifty years, but if the fur has been stored in the attic or basement, it has probably been ruined by heat, moisture, or pests.

**Hangers.** Gather up all the hangers and take them to the nearest dry cleaners for re-use.

# Collections

Selling a collection is different than selling one or two of an item that people collect. Your potential buyer is probably another collector, someone who already owns many or most of the items in the collection you've inherited and therefore does not want the entire group. While it is more work for you, it is often easier to sell the pieces individually to fill in the collections of others.

If your loved one was a collector, you will probably know that already. Heck, you probably gave him some of the items in his collection for Christmas or birthdays! Look for paperwork. A serious collector will have saved receipts, boxes, auction catalogs, price guides, and reference books, and made lists of their items. They may have joined a club—good news for you, since it connects you to others with similar interests who may want to purchase the collection or certain pieces. Do not put much stock in price guides—they are wildly optimistic about values and besides, they are giving retail prices for buyers, not wholesale prices for sellers.

People will collect anything, from Arrowheads to Zydeco music. Among the most common categories are autographs, dolls, stamps, guns, coins, figurines, postcards, silver spoons, rocks, seashells, insects, plates, miniatures, books, toys, baseball cards, comic books, and records. Typically, such collections are valuable only to other collectors, and collectors look for pristine examples. Objects that are chipped, dented, or missing a piece will not interest them. Collections can be valuable to you only if you invest the time and effort into connecting with others who share the same passion. The key is in reaching those people, a difficult task if you are not among their number.

*Collectibles are not as collectible as they used to be.* Blame the Internet. It used to be hard to find the particular item you needed to fill in your collection, and if you did stumble across it, you were so thrilled at your good luck that you paid whatever price was asked. Now that you can find lots of those items online, prices have plummeted. Supply and demand. And today, fewer people collect Stuff. The post-World War II climate of easy credit and consumption after two decades of scarcity (the Depression and the War) led the entire population into an acquisitive frenzy. Now all those people and their Boomer offspring are dying or downsizing, and the market is flooded with their Stuff. Not as many younger people aggressively collect. As one 2012 newspaper headline recently put it, "Collectibles: Sellers Outnumber Buyers." And you know what that means.

Generally speaking, if you find a collection of something and want to dispose of it profitably, the best place to start is online. Google the words "collectors, teapots"—or whatever the collection contains. This will lead you to any books on the subject, in this case, *Teapots: A Collectors Guide*, available used on amazon.com for a pittance (and probably available for free at your library). Then google "Collectors club teapots" to find any organized clubs that share the teapot passion, in this case, two informal clubs. Read and learn. If your search turns up nothing, you probably have a collection that isn't very interesting to others, but don't despair.

Next check eBay for teapots, or antique teapots, and click on the tab for Sold Listings. That way you'll see the price of any that sold and not get bogged down in ones for sale that may never sell. See if you can find something similar to your items here. Next try www.maloneysdirectory.com, where you will have to pay a small amount to get access to their database. This gives information about appraisers, collecting organizations, museums, auctions, and other experts, and will help steer you to disposing of your collection. Keep a sharp eye out for any related materials among the estate items, such as receipts, price guides, lists, club newsletters, or anything that will route you to a potential buyer and a reasonable asking price. Once you can identify your objects, look at the regional auction houses to see if any similar have been sold.

If it is a casual, inexpensive collection ("Grandmother collected owl figurines"), you can sell it yourself online or at a garage sale. A serious, pricey collection ("Grandmother was a lifelong collector of Japanese kakemono scroll paintings") needs to be evaluated by a museum curator or specialized appraiser who can recommend what to do with it, probably selling it through a national auction house.

Some things that were highly collectible decades ago, like coins, stamps, Hummels, collector's plates, and marbles, have fewer fans today. Religious memorabilia has only personal, sentimental value. "Limited edition" collectibles, be they ornaments, plates, figurines, or Franklin Mint collectibles, are worth far less than the original buyer paid. Hummels and Lladro figurines, once worth hundreds of dollars each, seldom bring more than $50 today. The cold reality? Expect to get very little from any collection you've inherited.

The larger regional and national auction houses are a good place to contact if you have a serious collection of advertising memorabilia, art deco, art nouveau, art pottery, coins, dolls, guns, posters, prints, railroad items, sports cards and other sports collectibles, stamps, and toys. Heritage Auctions of Dallas www.ha.com, a company that once specialized in coin collections, today claims to be the largest auctioneer for collections of all sorts, but they are not alone. Send photos and a description to several places and see where the interest lies. Don't be surprised if some turn you down. A "no thanks" just means they can't do the best job possible with your object. It may be lower in value than their usual consignments or they may not deal in that sort of Stuff. Take your Stuff elsewhere.

To locate auction houses near you, look at www.auctionzip.com. If you are interested in selling only a few items, it doesn't really matter if you have to ship them to Cincinnati versus San Francisco.

First comes the research. 1) What is the object? 2) How much has it sold for recently?

The easiest way to start is to see what, if anything, your items are fetching on www.ebay.com, www.worthpoint.com, www.liveauctioneers.com, and other such sites. You can search these three for free (or at least, free for a short time), but be prepared to pay a few dollars for access to some of the other auction websites like www.artfact.com. Published price guides are in many libraries, listing prices collectors can expect to pay, not prices sellers can expect to receive. If you can't find anything online or in price guides, you may have inherited a collection that has little or no monetary value.

But does it have donation value? Is there a place that would accept your collection as a donation? A school (butterfly collection? rocks and minerals?), a library (children's books?), a local historical society (Civil War bullets? arrowheads?), a daycare center (stuffed animals? Beanie Babies?), a nursing home (a plate collection to mount on the walls?), or a stamp collectors club might be the perfect place for your collection.

**Coins.** Many people collected coins, domestic and foreign, in coin folders. Others collected them for their silver content in bags. U.S. quarters, dimes, and half dollars dated 1964 and earlier contain 90% silver, so make sure to find those if you are sorting through sacks of coins. Do not clean or polish them! Take American coins to a reputable dealer for an appraisal. www.pngdealers.com gives Professional Numismatists Guild members nearest you.

**Foreign Coins.** Many people collected foreign coins out of an interest in a particular country or region. Others who traveled a lot threw all their leftover coins in a box to use later . . . and never did. Many of these are obsolete now. Some have value. Because most coin dealers in America have little experience or knowledge about foreign coins, you are better off searching online to identify and evaluate your coins. Start with www.worldcoingallery.com for a comprehensive and free website. Also, www.numismaster.com, but there are fees involved here. Another method, if you can't figure out the country of origin, is to type any words on the coin into a search engine and see what comes up.

Donate unwanted foreign coins to Change for Good, a UNICEF program begun in 1987 to collect unwanted coins and currency. Tape them to cardboard so they don't rattle around in the package and mail them to Change for Good, UNICEF, 125 Maiden Lane, New York, NY 10038.

**Dolls.** Adults often saved toys out of nostalgia for their youth. If that describes your loved one, you can estimate the date of the toy from their age. But if the toys were purchased by a collector, they may date from any era. The dolls you are most likely to find will date from the twentieth century. Some on the most popular are Shirley Temple dolls, Madame Alexander dolls, and Barbie dolls.

Shirley Temple dolls have been made by several companies starting with Ideal in 1934 (the name is stamped on the back of the head). The doll came in several sizes with clothes and accessories copied from the outfits Shirley wore in her movies. Little Shirley had more outfits than the Queen of England. Her success brought out a wave of copycats, not called Shirley Temple but given names like Curly Top that were meant to suggest the association. These knockoffs are worth far less than the real McCoy. When Shirley grew up, sagging sales caused Ideal to drop the line in 1940, but it was renewed in 1957 when her movies hit a whole new generation through TV. Now it was collectors more than children who wanted the dolls.

Madame Alexander dolls were among the most expensive dolls ever made. First sold in 1923, they were tremendously popular in the late 1940s through the 1960s, which is why you may find them in the homes of people who were children during those years. They are still being made today. These were sold in the finest department stores, beautifully clothed, with lifelike wigs and expressive faces. There are hundreds of models, some based on movie stars (Scarlett) or fictional characters (Little Women), others more generic.

Barbie is the relative newcomer who debuted in 1959. Ken came along in 1961 and Barbie's friends showed up thereafter. The most valuable are the Barbies made from 1959 to the early 1970s. They can fetch hundreds, if not thousands, of dollars.

Prices for Shirley Temple, Madame Alexander, and Barbie dolls depend upon the condition of the doll, of course, but also on whether it is accompanied by the original clothing, original box, original accessories, and original booklet or wrist tag. Before trying to sell yours, research it online at www.dollreference.com or www.collectdolls.about.com, or check your library for doll collecting books and price guides. Check prices for similar ones that recently sold on eBay.

**Teddy Bears.** Teddy bears didn't exist before 1903, when President Teddy Roosevelt made the news by refusing to shoot a baby bear during a hunting trip. Ideal Toy Corp., Gund, and Stieff are the most sought after, with millions sold in various sizes. As always, condition is very important.

**Postcards.** In the early 1900s, postcard collecting was quite the craze, popular with young people who traded, saved, and mounted them in albums. They can be dated by a postmark if they were actually mailed, by the subject in the picture (city skylines, cars, fashions), or by the style and information on the back. The stamps may be of interest to stamp collectors.

Get help identifying and valuing yours from dealers at antiques shows, as always, asking more than one dealer and comparing offers. To learn how to identify and value what you have, take a look at www.postcardy.com and www.vintagepostcards.org, websites full of information and links to more information. Once you know what you have, postcards can be sold online.

**Sports Memorabilia.** Serious collectors of sports memorabilia don't buy anything unless it's been authenticated—the market is flooded with fakes—so if you've inherited a baseball signed by Mickey Mantle (probably not!), you'll need to have it vetted by a credible service that does not buy or sell. Get recommendations through a reputable large auction house.

Sports cards, particularly baseball cards, are easily sold online because they can be dropped in an envelope and mailed for the price of a stamp.

**Stamps.** Find a stamp collection? Many, many people collected stamps in the twentieth century. It has been one of the most popular hobbies ever since the first postage stamp was created in 1840. It is still popular, although interest is waning.

Most collectors specialized. Some collected by country, states, historic events, famous people, or topics, especially transportation, mammals, and birds. Others preferred mint collections, commemoratives (a one-time printing not usually repeated), or first-day covers (envelopes postmarked with the first day of release). Figure out what you have.

The book, *Scott Standard Postage Stamp Catalogue*, is available at your library and gives recent retail prices. Expect to sell yours for significantly less. You can also check eBay for individual stamps. Limit your search to "sold listings" for a more accurate notion of value.

Find a local stamp club. Check www.linns.com where you can find the club nearest you as well as its meeting days and times. Check www.stampshows.com to find upcoming shows in your area. You can attend those with your collection and find out what you have what someone will pay you for it. Or you can consider donating to a stamp club to get a young collector started. Be warned: there are few young stamp collectors.

## Electronics

Computers, printers, monitors, televisions, mobile phones, and other consumer electronics may contain toxic materials like mercury, lead, and cadmium that should not (and cannot legally) be discarded in the local landfill, yet Americans toss about two million tons of electronics each year. If you inherit items of this nature—a highly likely scenario because, according to the EPA, the average American household has 24 electronic products—and you don't want them yourself, you will have to dispose of them correctly. For information on charities and recyclers in each state, see

www.epa.gov/ecycling. Or check with
www.electronicstakeback.com/how-to-recycle-electronics/ or
www.ecyclingcentral.com.

**Cell phones.** Most cell phone companies will recycle your old phone, whether or not it is their own brand, when you buy a new one. Goodwill will take them for recycling. Staples, Lowe's, Radio Shack, Best Buy, Sears, Home Depot, and other retailers participate in recycling programs.

**Computers.** If you can't sell it by yourself on eBay—and you probably can't unless it is almost new—many Goodwill outlets will take these, wipe the hard drives clean and re-use or recycle them in the United States (they will not send them to India or China). Most Goodwill branches participate with Dell in a national program to re-use and recycle safely. See www.goodwill.org. The National Cristina Foundation (in all fifty states) connects computer donors with those who can't afford them. See www.cristina.org. Manufacturers like H-P, Sony, Toshiba, Dell, and Best Buy have trade-in programs—they take any brand of computer and give credit on a new one of theirs. Check their websites for information on trade-ins.

**Televisions.** The real issue with electronics is televisions. These have high levels of contaminants, heavy metals that are dangerous and can't be easily discarded in a landfill. New flat-screen TVs are better, but you are not likely to come across those in Grandpa's house. Each state has its own regulatory provisions for the disposal of televisions. Some nonprofits aren't equipped to do what is legally required and so can't accept them. Some can. Call your local Goodwill or Salvation Army and ask. Even old televisions that no one wants may have scrap value to your local nonprofit.

# Eyeglasses

No matter how old they are or in what condition, drop off prescription eyeglasses at the local Lion's Club. Look in the phone book for their location, or call and ask where to take them; often it is a public library or other easily accessed public place. Or drop them off at the nearest LensCrafters, Pearle Vision, BJ's Optical, or the optical stores at Sears or Target. Someone in a developing country will appreciate your generosity.

# Furniture

Jim, a dealer in top-quality, used furniture who often buys from estate sales summed it up, "People need to understand the bad news. New furniture loses about 90% of its value when it leaves the store. Something you paid $1,000 for several years ago, even if its in great condition, is worth about $100 now. Exceptions are old Kittinger, Baker, or Suter pieces, reproductions made in the middle decades of the twentieth century. Those are worth more because they were virtually hand-made and nothing is being made like that any longer." Furniture made in the twentieth century by companies using traditional, handcrafted techniques will usually sell well in the region where their reputation lingers. Companies like Suter, Stickley, Henkel Harris, Hitchcock, Biggs, Kindel, Karges, and others made—or still make—high quality goods that are not easily found in today's market of cheap imports. A local name increases a piece's value in that area.

Auctioneers say that traditional, middle-class furniture has fallen in value since the economy turned south in 2008 and is now fetching half what it did before that date. The best-way, best-price place to sell used furniture is probably an estate sale rather than piece by piece on Craigslist, although funky pieces from the 1950s, '60s, and '70s can appeal to the younger crowd when sold that way.

The truth is that most furniture, aside from antiques, is outdated and may not worth trying to sell yourself. If it came from the '70s, '80s, or '90s, give it away. Goodwill might be able to get $20 for that upholstered chair, and they're welcome to it. If you decide to sell, consider www.craigslist.com where the buyer will probably be local and be able to pick up the piece.

Furniture has its fads too. One dealer said that Shaker chairs he sold a couple decades ago for $8,000 might bring $800 today. Wing chairs, all the rage for colonial revival decorating schemes, are slow to sell today. Victorian furniture, with its fussy and ornate styling, appeals to few people and almost no young people, who are the ones most likely to buy furniture. Still, it may be worth your trouble to photograph it and inquire at some reputable regional auction houses. Shipping costs may eat up any profit you make, so local buyers who can pick up at your house are preferable.

Old wooden furniture that has been refinished or painted is worth far less than it would have been if left alone. But what's done is done, and sometimes a fresh coat of paint can help sell a wooden chair or table that came to you with a battered or ugly colored coat of paint already on it.

## Glass and Crystal

What's the difference between crystal and glass? Have you heard your grandmother say that if you flick a glass with your finger or tap it with a pencil and it pings like a musical note, that means it's crystal? Well, it's not foolproof. Sometimes plain, cheap wineglasses make that nice ringing sound too.

Glass has been around since the ancient Egyptians. Leaded glass (also called crystal) was invented around the end of the 1600. In leaded glass, the calcium is replaced with lead, which results in a more brilliant, sparkling product with fewer air bubbles or imperfections. It makes the piece heavier than plain glass. English and Irish crystal has been popular in America, alongside American producers like Lenox.

Brides are as interested in fine crystal as they are in porcelain dishes and sterling silver tea services . . . which is to say, not much. There is more of this Stuff on the market than there are people who want to buy it, but yours may sell if it is particularly appealing. Check with www.replacements.com to see what they will pay you for your stemware and bowls, then look at the Usual Suspects (www.eBay.com, www.worthpoint.com, www.liveauctioneers.com) on the chance that something similar to yours has sold recently.

The lead oxide also makes the glass easier to work at lower temperatures, which allows artists to cut fancy decorations into the glass. This is called cut glass. A cut-glass bowl has sharp edges and is worth more than a similar pressed-glass piece made in a mold. You can probably tell the difference with your fingers. A very sharp edge means cut glass; a smoother edge is pressed. Cut-glass items include punch bowls and cups, compotes, small dishes, bowls, chandeliers, and even lamps. Pressed glass, a cheaper imitation of cut glass, has minimal value. As with ceramics, any damage eliminates almost all its value, although antiques with minor damage may still have some sales appeal. Some cut glass items sell on eBay; others languish. A good website is www.cutglass.org.

## Guns

Have you come across a gun or a closet full of guns? Before handling them, ask someone with some experience to check them all to make sure none are loaded.

**Guns.** Goodwill will not resell guns or ammunition, but they often work with their local police to find a safe way to dispose of them, so they might take yours as part of a whole lot of Stuff.

**Old guns.** Called antiques if they are very old and relics if they date from the first half of the twentieth century, old guns are often sold by specialized dealers to collectors. If you aren't knowledgeable about firearms, avoid gun dealers, many of whom will take advantage of rookies. An auction is more likely to result in the best price because many of these auction houses draw from a worldwide group of collectors.

Consider contacting an auction house: www.jamesdjulia.com or www.rockislandauction.com. Take a picture of each gun and send it along with your e-mail. If they aren't interested in your weapon, they can usually steer you to another auction house that is more appropriate. Get several responses before deciding which house to do business with.

If you are dealing with an inherited estate in a state other than your own, you may have difficulty transporting guns home. Carried in the trunk of your car, they should pose no problems.

## Handbags

If you find designer handbags of recent vintage, great! You can sell them online and actually get a good price for them on eBay, Craigslist, or other sites. Evening bags, old or new, often hold their value. Old ones can be sold to vintage clothing stores. Apart from those, used handbags have virtually no value. Your best bet is to donate to Goodwill or the equivalent.

## Hats

Hardly anyone wears hats today, so any you find will probably be quite old. Their value is modest. Consider donating them to a theater program at your local college, high school, or community theater where they would rejoice to receive a few fedoras or pillbox hats.

If you prefer to sell and your hats are particularly fetching, take them to a vintage clothing store and ask what they are and what they would pay you for them. If that doesn't please you, research at the library (*Vintage Hats and Bonnets 1770-1970* by Langley is a good reference) or search online for "vintage hats." Once you know what they are and how old they are, sell them yourself online. An interesting old hat can sell for a few dollars, but the competition is steep. Many, many vintage hats are listed on eBay and less than a third actually find a buyer.

A hat in its original hatbox will fetch a higher price.

## Jewelry

In every household, there is sure to be jewelry, men's and women's. Some of it may be listed in the will as a bequest to a certain family member. Some heirs will want to keep certain pieces; others will want the cash. One way to forestall arguments is to have the lot appraised so everyone knows what the pieces are worth. But appraisals cost money, so you'll have to decide whether the cost is worth it to you. Inquire at a local, reputable jewelry store about appraisal costs.

First set aside anything that is obviously costume jewelry. Take the rest to a local, reputable jeweler (I can't stress that enough) and ask him or her to cull out the costume jewelry—the fake pearls, the faux diamond earrings, and so forth. These you can give to children for dress-up, to a theatrical for costumes, or to Goodwill or the Salvation Army for resale.

The real Stuff should then be appraised by an experienced CGA or Certified Gemologist Appraiser. These people have the training to judge your jewelry and, equally important, they have no interest in buying it, so they have no incentive to lowball their estimates. Most will separate costume jewelry from real jewelry for you at no cost, and they may even point out the pieces that are genuine but of minimal value, like a topaz ring, so you won't waste your money appraising those. The good Stuff needs an estate appraisal. An appraisal for estate purposes is different from, and lower than, an appraisal for insurance purposes, which gives the replacement value, or what it would cost to buy another just like it. The estate appraisal is also good for the IRS if your estate is above the benchmarks for estate taxes established by federal and state law. The CGA will charge you for each item appraised. This will be invaluable when it comes to distributing the jewelry among the heirs    or    when    selling    it    online    yourself.

You may have heard that a real diamond will scratch glass and an imitation one won't. If only it were that easy! Most imitation diamonds are harder than glass, so even the fakes will scratch glass.

Selling used jewelry is harder than you might think. There is not a strong market for it. First of all, jewelry is a fashion item and old pieces are not necessarily desirable today. Most items that are sold are broken up for their gold, silver, platinum, or gems. Colored stones have a strong resale market. You will get paid more for diamonds (not the tiny diamond chips that weigh just a point or two, but the larger ones) because they can be pulled out of their setting, polished, and are "new" again. Retail jewelry stores sometimes have estate departments that will take certain items. Pawnshops are a possibility, as are vintage clothing stores. If the item is appraised at a high enough figure, auction houses might be a good alternative: international houses like Sotheby's or Christie's and smaller houses like Cowan's in Cincinnati or Bonhams in San Francisco handle fine jewelry.

Genuine old silver-and-turquoise Native American jewelry is one category that has increased in value over the decades, especially Navajo. Some jewelers in Santa Fe and Albuquerque specialize in this area. Search the Internet for several that have been in business for a long while and send them pictures of your items. Be sure to look closely for makers' marks and send close-ups of those too.

**Selling costume jewelry.** Vintage costume jewelry can bring in good money when it is sold online, especially if it is sparkly or signed by a desirable company like Trifari, Coro, Weiss, Sarah Coventry, Lisner, Money, Napier, and Ann Klein. And it has the advantage of being easy and inexpensive to mail.

**Selling gold jewelry.** Gold is an area where you are likely to find a lot of cheats, so go into it with your eyes wide open. Before you take gold jewelry anywhere, bone up on the current price for gold—check on the Internet or in the newspaper. This shows the buyer that you aren't totally clueless, and you'll be less likely to get cheated. Gold is priced per troy ounce, a measurement different from regular ounces. Make your own ballpark estimate before trying to sell. Here's how.

--Examine the karat mark and divide into piles. Most will be 10k, 12k, 14k, or 18k. If it isn't marked, it is probably gold plated or gold wash and worth next to nothing.

--Weigh each group separately on a postal scale to determine number of ounces.

--Convert ounces into troy ounces using an online converter or by multiplying regular ounces by .912. (Gold prices are quoted in troy ounces.)

--Deduct a percent for the part that isn't gold. 10 karat is 41% gold, so you'd deduct 59%. 12 karat is 50% gold. 14 karat is 58% gold. 18 karat is 75% gold, and the highest you are likely to see in America. 22 karat is 91% gold. 24 karat is pure gold. So 20 troy ounces of 12 karat gold equals 10 troy ounces of pure gold. Why don't you see much 22 or 24 k gold in America? Because it's too soft to make good jewelry. A neckchain of 24 k gold would pull apart with minimal effort.

--Multiply by the current troy ounce price.

That is what your gold is worth at retail, but of course you will not get that much for it. Many dealers will offer you half that. Shop around to get a better price. Reputable gold buyers should pay 80% to 90% of the retail value. Knowing approximately what that is will protect you.

*Fatima took her unwanted gold jewelry to a gold buyer who weighed it and quoted a price based on 14k. "But isn't this worth more?" she asked, indicating the mark on one piece that said 22k, an alloy common in India where she is from. The buyer, who "hadn't noticed," recalculated and offered her a higher figure. (She should have walked out the minute she realized he was dishonest.) Moral? Examine each piece and estimate it's worth before you see a buyer.*

Yes, there are pawnshops, online buyers, mail order schemes, and fly-by-night buyers who breeze into town and set up shop in a hotel room, but your best bet by far is a reputable, local jewelry store or coin dealer that buys gold and silver and sticks around for his reputation to matter. Let the buyer know up front that you are going to get two or three offers before selling and hold to that plan.

Gold-looking jewelry made in the twentieth century is sometimes marked GF for gold-filled, a deceptive term that means a very thin layer of gold over base metal. Watch out for 14k GF, which sounds better but is still just a thin, thin, thin coat of gold. It is worthless as gold, but it may have value as costume jewelry or vintage jewelry.

**Platinum.** Often mistaken for silver, platinum is worth far more than silver and is usually worth *more* than gold. Recently, gold prices have surpassed platinum, but that is not typical. It will have PLAT or PT marked on it.

**Pearls.** Is that string of pearls real or fake? There are a couple ways you can tell by yourself. If you have a strand of fake pearls that you know are made of plastic or glass, you can compare the mystery strand to those. Run the fake pearls across the biting edge of your upper teeth first, noting the very smooth feel. Then run the mystery pearls across your teeth in the same way. If they seem rough, gritty, or sandy *by comparison*, they are genuine. Another way to judge is by examining the clasp. A good string of genuine pearls will have a gold or platinum clasp; others will have steel, silver, or gold plate. Real pearls will have a knot between each pearl to

71

prevent them from touching (and scratching) each other. Fake pearls will not. Of course, it's best to consult a jeweler and know for certain.

Cultured pearls vary in value according to size, color, quality, and thickness of the nacre, or coating. You can't see this with your naked eye, but a gemologist can tell. The more nacre, the more lustrous and durable the pearl.

Natural pearls were discovered by accident as people opened shellfish. Not until 1893 did a Japanese oyster farmer named Mikimoto discover how to implant a particle into the shell and wait for the animal to coat it with hundreds of layers of nacre. (It's much trickier than it sounds!) The first cultured pearls were sold in Tokyo in 1899. This discovery, inevitably copied by others, made pearls available to millions of people around the world. Cheap cultured pearls are left in the oyster just long enough to acquire a thin coating of nacre. Expensive pearls take three years to produce; cheap ones, six months. Virtually all pearls today are cultured pearls. None will be more than a century old.

In recent years, the Chinese have perfected making round, freshwater pearls that look like cultured pearls (which look like natural pearls), making pearls even less expensive than before. The value of a "genuine" pearl can range from very low to shockingly high.

**Masonic jewelry, other fraternal jewelry.** What should you do with the fraternal jewelry you come across in the estate you've inherited? By "fraternal jewelry," I mean Masonic rings, sorority and fraternity pins, military academy rings, lapel pins, and other logo items that have special meaning to a particular organization. Fraternal groups ask that all such jewelry be returned to the organization, since these items shouldn't be worn by anyone except their members. Drop the piece in a padded envelope and mail to the local chapter or national headquarters. You'll get nothing for it (except thanks and a good feeling), so if there is a precious stone in the ring, for heaven's sake, have it removed by a jeweler. If the item is gold or silver, you may prefer to sell it for meltdown.

Fraternal organizations are also grateful when you return other logo items such as caps, fez, books, and papers. This can be a good way to honor the deceased, who no doubt valued these items very much.

**Gold coins.** Don't sell your gold coins for meltdown! Take them to a reputable coin dealer—they may be worth more than the gold content. Krugerrands, the most common gold coin for collectors, contain one troy ounce of gold, so their gold value can easily be calculated by multiplying by the current market price of gold.

**Silver coins.** The same is true for silver coins—the old dimes, quarters, half dollars, and silver dollars that many people saved when the country stopped using silver in coins. The last date to include silver is 1964. Those have 90% silver. The Kennedy half dollar of 1965-69 contains 40% silver. Since then, only a few special issue collectors coins have had any silver.

*Do not polish or clean your silver coins. Shiny is not better.*

---

### How to Clean Silver Jewelry

To clean tarnished silver jewelry, fill a dish with warm water and a few drops of dishwashing liquid. Gently scrub with a soft toothbrush. Dry with a soft cloth so the item doesn't spot. If that doesn't work, use a commercial cleaner or polishing cloth, available at a jewelry store, but not the harsh silver dips that will damage your piece.

---

# Kitchenware

**Small appliances, pots and pans, utensils, gadgets.** Send old toasters, blenders, mixers, and the like to Goodwill. In the unlikely event that you have a really old appliance, one that has been around since before World War II and is still in good condition (not corroded or missing handles), a historic house museum might be interested in it, or it could be worth a modest amount to a collector. Get a copy of the *Price Guide to Collectible Kitchen Appliances, from Aerators to Waffle Irons, 1900-1950* from your librarian or a used copy from amazon.com.

Believe it or not, there are collectors' societies for toasters, www.toastercollectors.org. There is good information on that site and also at www.toastermuseum.com where you can find pictures and prices of toasters, some of which sold for thousands of dollars on eBay or other auction houses! You should be able to identify your old can opener with the pictures shown at www.the-canopener.com.

**Plastic.** Throw away old Tupperware, Styrofoam, and any plastic containers. Newer Tupperware in good condition may sell for a few bucks at an estate sale.

**Copper pots and pans.** Copper pans, kettles, and boilers have monetary value since the price of copper has skyrocketed in recent years. These will sell on eBay or at a garage sale, auction, or estate sale.

## Linens for Bed, Bath, and Table

There is a decent market for fine old linens and cotton items, especially those with embroidery, cutwork, or lace. Handkerchiefs, doilies, dainty hand towels used for guests, lace curtains, christening gowns, smocking, and other fine children's clothing are collected, loved, and used by those who appreciate workmanship that is largely a thing of the past. Even old dishtowels and aprons from the Fifties are popular with some collectors.

Unless you know what to expect for such items, however, it will be hard to describe and sell them yourself online. An alternative might be the dealers at the better antique shows that come through town periodically. Some dealers have retail stores that can be located in the Yellow Pages or online. If one is near you, make an appointment to bring in your linen and cotton items and see what they offer. They will prefer—and pay more for—complete sets. For instance, a tablecloth with eight or twelve napkins will be desirable whereas the tablecloth alone may be refused.

**Sheets:** Many linen closets are stuffed with fine old sheets that, sadly, have no place on today's beds. Modern mattresses are far deeper than those of the past, which means that older, flat sheets cannot tuck under today's mattresses. While nothing is completely useless (such sheets could serve as drop cloths, makeshift curtains, or even rags), yesteryear's plain bed linens come close.

If the sheets are old and decorated with embroidery or lace, they may have value. Some people will buy an antique top sheet and use it with a new, fitted bottom sheet. Or they will use them to make curtains or trim pillowcases.

Goodwill will accept all linens (really, all textiles), even those that are stained, yellowed, or torn. What they can't sell, they recycle into rags and other items. Fancy 100% linen or 100% cotton pillowcases with embroidery, lace, or cutwork, have value to a specialty store that buys and sells antique linens or to a linen dealer who participates in a good antique show. These are readily auctioned on eBay because linens are easy to photograph, describe, pack, and ship.

**Blankets and Bedspreads:** Old blankets have little value, unless they are 100% wool and in good condition. Just price new 100% wool blankets and you'll appreciate what you have! Hudson Bay blankets are desirable today, as are Pendleton labels. Both brands have been popular since the days of the Indian trade. Take any 100% wool blankets home if you can. Use them to pack fragile things for the trip back. Dry clean. Sell in a yard sale or donate to a local charitable service organization.

Bedspreads have almost no value. At an estate sale, nicer ones might well for $5 to $20. An exception might be chenille bedspreads (chenille is French for caterpillar, which should give you the clue you need to identify this fabric by its rows of fluffy raised tracks), and a vintage linen dealer might take a good Bates spread. Otherwise, consider donating to Goodwill, the Salvation Army, Disabled American Veterans, or other charitable service organization.

Veterinarians, animal shelters, and the SPCA often appreciate donated blankets and bedspreads.

**Quilts:** Old American-made quilts can be very valuable. Even those in poor condition can sell for several hundred dollars, and quality antiques go for thousands. Even a quilt that is dreadfully worn, torn, or frayed can be cut down to make a crib quilt or a wall hanging or cut up for decorative pillow covers.

First, determine whether your patchwork quilt is machine or hand sewn. Gently pull at the seam of the patchwork pieces— irregular stitching indicates the top was pieced by hand (although a fine seamstress of the period could turn out stitches so perfect they might fool you into thinking they are machine sewn.) In all likelihood, the quilt is hand pieced. Even today, many quilters prefer to piece by hand, so that alone does not mean it pre-dates the sewing machine. Next, look closely at the running stitch that quilts the patchwork piece, the batting, and the backing together. A very old quilt that pre-dates the sewing machine will of necessity be both hand pieced and hand quilted. The foot-powered treadle sewing machine, while it existed before the Civil War, was rare until after that conflict (1861-65). Electric sewing machines became popular in the early 1900s.

It is more likely for old quilts to be quilted by hand—not until the 1980s did machine quilting become acceptable in quilt shows. Of course, not all quilts were made with the intention of entering them in the county fair. The utilitarian ones are apt to have been sewn as economically as possible, by machine.

The "big three" historic quilt patterns are the Double Wedding Ring, Dresden Plate, and Grandmother's Flower Garden. These were very popular in the 1930s. You can find books in your public library on quilts that will help you identify the pattern and the date, information that will help you place a value on the quilt before you try to sell it.

In recent years, a flood of cheap, American-looking quilts made in China has been sold in department stores. These can be very attractive, but they have little resale value. If you think your quilt is old, American-made, and handmade, take it home with you to resell. It's worth the trouble of dropping it in a box and mailing it home to yourself to deal with later.

Make an appointment with a textile curator at a museum that has quilts in its collection, likely the local historical society or a historic house museum. Tell the curator anything you know about the quilt: who owned it, where it came from, who made it, its age. If you know nothing about it, you can still help by saying where you got it. If it has a good "provenance" or object history, the museum might be interested in having it. It is unlikely they will offer to buy it from you, since museums rarely have money to spend on acquisitions, but you can have it appraised. The curator or museum can give you names of reputable appraisers in your area, or you can go to the website of the American Quilter's Society, www.americanquilter.com, for their list of certified appraisers—be aware of their hourly fee. Take the appropriate tax deduction the year you donate it. Museum curators never appraise objects. It's against their ethical code.

---

## Washing Old Linens

"Clorox in hot water is lethal to linens," says Erica, a woman who has dealt in antique linens and cottons for two decades. "When I was younger and didn't know any better, I destroyed a lovely piece by putting some Clorox in very hot water as I was washing it. It turned the piece yellow. Permanently. Dealers prefer that you not wash the linens you plan to sell, even if they are stained or dirty. You might set the stain. We'd rather wash it ourselves."

For those who plan to keep their linens and need to wash them, she recommends putting equal parts of 1) Tide with bleach in the soap powder form, 2) Biz (a non chlorine whitener), and 3) 20 Mule Team Borax in hot water and soaking stained items for one to four days. Rinse two or three times. Air dry flat, in the sun, if possible.

---

If you prefer to sell, take it to a high-end antiques shop in your area and speak to the owner. The Internet is another option. Many quilts are sold on eBay. If you have a good picture and your quilt is appealing, it may bring a higher price there.

If your quilt is very dirty, or came out of a barn or garage, consider washing it carefully before selling it.

**Handkerchiefs:** Decorative old handkerchiefs are collectible. Even monogrammed ones. People buy them for brides ("something old") or bridesmaids or to make lavender sachets or handkerchief dolls. Others press them between two pieces of Plexiglas and hang them in a window. Easy to sell on eBay or to vendors at antique shows who specialize in textiles.

**Table Linens:** Few young people want the bother of caring for old tablecloths, napkins, and placemats, but there are serious collectors out there who cherish fine table linens. Occasionally you'll find a retailer who specializes in such things, but most are sold through vendors at better antique shows. Dealers are not usually interested in modern fabric blends, only in 100% cotton or linen. It is hard to tell linen fabric from cotton or blends, even for experts, so if you don't know what your fabric is made of, just bring everything to a dealer for an opinion. Check with more than one and take your best offer.

**Bath Towels:** Unless they are virtually new, bath towels will have no re-sale potential. Goodwill or similar will accept them for use as rags. Or donate old towels to an animal shelter or the SPCA and donate them there.

# Washing Old Quilts

Suzanne was only about 21 when she inherited a dirty old quilt from the bottom of a trunk in Grandma's attic. She took it home, stuffed it into the washing machine, poured in plenty of detergent and bleach, turned on the hot cycle, and ended up with something resembling wet toilet tissue.

How should she have washed the old quilt? It's a question no one wants to answer. Textile curators and dealers in antique quilts invariably say, "Don't!" A dry cleaner will probably refuse, and that's a good thing because the fluids used would likely do serious damage. Not washing quilts may be excellent advice for museums and people who own rare and valuable specimens, but in the everyday world, quilts can come out of attics, garages, basements, car trunks, and sick beds. They can bear mysterious stains, foul odors, and suspicious animal hairs. They need more than a good shake before they can be brought home and spread over the guest room bed.

Here's what you can do with dirty quilts that are not "museum quality." Be forewarned that wet washing may cause the colors to fade or bleed.

1.    First check both sides of the quilt for tears or holes; repair those with a needle and cotton thread.

2.    Remove any rings and watches you may be wearing which could snag the fabric.

3.    Place the quilt in a top-loading washing machine and set the dial to large load and warm water. Add a small

amount of mild detergent like Ivory Soap Flakes, Ivory Snow liquid, or Dreft, perhaps half of what you would normally use for a load that size. Do not add bleach!

4.   Fill the washing machine with water and stop it before it begins to agitate. With your hands, gently squish the quilt up and down in the water for several minutes. Let it soak for a few minutes and squish again.

5.   Turn the dial to the spin cycle and spin. Let the machine fill up with clean water for the rinse cycle. Again, do not allow the machine to agitate. Stop the machine and squish the quilt around in the clean water by hand.

6.   If the quilt was extremely dirty, you may wish to repeat the wash and rinse cycle, letting the quilt soak a while before rinsing.

7.   Run the rinse cycle a final time.

8.   Spread a clean sheet that is larger than the quilt on the ground outside in a shady spot away from direct sun. Handle the wet quilt carefully because the weight of the water makes the fabric very fragile . . . two people are better than one. Lay it on the sheet, pattern side down, and spread it gently to dry. Don't even think of hanging it on a clothesline, draping it over a fence, or putting it in the dryer!

9.   Check every hour or so. Bring inside when thoroughly dry. Spread it over a bed for a day or two before folding to make certain it is completely dry. Do not fold on existing crease lines.

# Luggage

Luggage is found in virtually every home or attic, and probably old luggage at that. "Vintage luggage" (or, really old luggage) is quite collectible. You may have seen examples (and fakes) being used as props in displays at retail stores and in themed restaurants, or pictured in decorating magazines where they are usually stacked and used as end tables. The better luggage is sturdy, heavy even when empty, made of thick leather (usually cowhide) with brass cap corners over wood or cardboard, with brass locks. Crocodile or alligator leather is the most desirable, but it's rare. Don't overlook brief cases and attaché cases.

Original initials, monograms, or even full names and addresses stamped or painted onto the case adds to a suitcase's value. So do railway tickets, shipping labels, or steamship cruise line labels affixed to the piece. The most valuable to collectors are those made by Louis Vuitton, a French company that still makes expensive luggage after more than a hundred and fifty years. (It is said, however, that only 1% of all goods marked Louis Vuitton are genuine; the rest are Chinese fakes. But if yours were purchased by Grandma sixty years ago, they are *not* Chinese fakes.) Other luxury makers include Hermès (France), Moritz Madler (German), and Globe-Trotter (English), and the American companies Hartmann and Samsonite (particularly 1950s-era examples). Most of these should have maker's marks to help you identify them. These marks are generally found on the edge of the suitcase, inside the edge, or applied on the inside to the fabric.

Check the locks too. Some, like Louis Vuitton, have their name and serial number on each lock. High quality locks are made of good metal, the highest quality would probably be silver; below that, brass, iron, and tin. Many were electroplated nickel over base metal, which, when it wears away, shows a brassy looking metal underneath. If the metal is rusty or pitted, the lock is a lower quality and so, no doubt, is the luggage.

There are also cheaper luggage pieces made with simulated leather. If they look nice, they may have some value as props. Sell these to an antiques dealer at one of the area's better antiques stores, at an antiques mall, or to an interior decorator.

Used suitcases made of plastic or fabric are best donated to a service organization, but only if their condition warrants re-use. Otherwise let them take their last trip to the dump.

Wooden trunks can be sold to an antiques dealer. Those with rounded tops are useful at the foot of a bed for storage, but you'll probably get a better price for the flat top styles, because they can double as end tables or coffee tables.

It should go without saying: *thoroughly* search all bags, trunks, hatboxes, satchels, briefcases, or other luggage before disposing of them.

## Medicine

Odds are there will be many bottles of pills and medicines among the household belongings you've inherited. Even if the bottles have never been opened, medicine cannot be recycled to other patients, so they must be discarded. Every state—not to mention the FDA and the EPA and other federal agencies—has strict laws about the disposal of medicines that require hospitals, pharmacies, and manufacturers to incinerate their outdated or unused medicines. There are no specific regulations for drug disposal by individual consumers, but there are sensible precautions everyone should take.

The worst possible thing you can do with leftover medicine is flush it down the toilet or pour it down the drain. Environmentalists and scientists are starting to alert the public to the dangers of this practice, as rising levels of chemicals, hormones, steroids, and other drugs enter the water system and are not filtered out at wastewater treatment plants. Federal and state governments are in the early stages of data gathering, but the danger to marine life has been proven significant and pharmaceuticals have been detected in the drinking water supplies of dozens of metropolitan areas. Human beings who drink the water and eat the fish risk ingesting toxic substances. "There are thousands of compounds that could create havoc," says the Chief of Compliance at one Virginia water treatment plant, "and we can't and don't know what to filter out."

Some pharmacies will accept the return of unused medicines and dispose of them properly for you. Gather up your medicines and take them to the pharmacy that issued them and ask if they will accommodate you on a one-time basis. Some states do not allow pharmacies to do this; others do. Some pharmacies will help you; others will refuse. Your best chances are probably with the larger chains that have regular disposal programs of their own rather than with small pharmacies that have to pay for this out of pocket.

If no pharmacy will accept your unused medicines, the least bad place for them is in a sanitary landfill where they will not leech into the ground water supply.

The director of a free clinic in a rural part of the country recommends pouring unused pills or liquid medicines in a plastic milk bottle, adding water, and shaking until they are partially dissolved. Then add kitty litter or plaster Paris, let harden, and throw out in the trash. "This prevents children, pets, wildlife, or drug abusers from getting hold of pills," she says, "and it does the least amount of damage to the environment." The World Health Organization guidelines are similar. That organization suggests mixing the pills with water and cement. One assisted living center makes it a practice to fill pill bottles with glue before throwing them out.

The American Pharmacists Association recommends removing prescription labels from the bottles and destroying them separately to protect personal information.

## Memoirs, Letters, and Documents

Personal memoirs, diaries, old letters, and other historical documents are priceless, yet they seldom have any monetary value unless they are very old or the author is, or was, famous. These documents, or at least photocopies of them, should be donated to an appropriate historical society, university library, public library, or museum where they will be appreciated by future researchers. Generally speaking, older diaries and memoirs will interest these institutions most, but don't dismiss the value of 20th-century material. Your grandfather might have saved his diaries from seventy years ago or written his memoirs last year before he died, and the local historical society could find his recollections about shopping on Main Street a great help in restoring the town center.

The proper destination for such a donation depends upon the contents and the nature of the documents, which means someone will have to read them. This is often more difficult than it sounds, considering penmanship styles, faded ink, and yellowed, tattered pages. An uncle's account of his experiences as a Marine in the Pacific during World War II might go to the U.S. Marine Corps museum in Quantico. An immigrant's memoirs and papers might go to the Ellis Island museum in New York. An Iowa farmer's diary from 1890 might go to the State Historical Society of Iowa in Des Moines. The Holocaust Museum in Washington, D.C., actively solicits documents and memoirs from Jews and from American soldiers who liberated the death camps.

Think your relative's memoirs or diaries couldn't possibly interest anyone? Think again.

*Libbey's specialty is Christmas decorating customs, and she is elated to discover a document from any period of American history where the writer mentions how the family decorated for Christmas. "Just average people, telling the stories of their lives," she says. "Those are treasures for me." The hardest things for historians to learn are the common events of life, details that don't make the newspapers.*

Just about everyone who was part of the "Greatest Generation," as Tom Brokaw so famously nicknamed them, participated in World War II. Some parachuted into the Rhineland or stormed the Pacific beaches, while others served as nurses or worked in factories making ammunition or building airplanes and tanks. Everyone sacrificed. If your deceased relative was part of this generation, he or she may well have personal documents—letters from a soldier, diaries, memoirs—that would be welcomed, used, displayed, and cared for in one of hundreds of historical societies and military museums across the U.S. Stories about life on the home front during both World Wars are of great interest to historians, so your grandmother's experiences as a child collecting scrap metal for the war effort or details about your great-uncle's Victory Garden can illuminate American history in a very personal way, making it come alive for future generations. Most counties and all states have historical societies, and there are hundreds of military museums in this country. Honor your relatives by taking the time to contact a few of these institutions to describe what you have and ask if they would like a donation.

If your female relative served our country in the WACS or WAVES or in any branch of the U.S. military as a nurse, pilot, or clerk, the Army Women's Museum at Fort Lee, Virginia, will open a file on her with any pictures, letters, memoirs, or papers that pertain to her service. They have thousands of files and are growing.

Destinations to consider include local (county, city, or town) historical societies, state historical societies, state archives or state libraries, history museums, the public library, the university library where the deceased attended school, the Library of Congress, Civil War museums, and military museums (see list in Military Stuff section).

Finding the right destination is an exercise in matchmaking. If your offer is declined at one institution, don't assume that's a "no thanks" for all of them. A rejection could mean that whatever you're offering is no use to them, but it could just as well mean that the institution has dozens already and doesn't need any more, thank you very much, or that the nature of your donation is beyond the scope of their mission. If your family is breaking up your grandmother's house in Florida and her personal effects include her mother's diaries that chronicle growing up in Pennsylvania in the 1890s, odds are that the Florida Historical Society will politely refuse the donation. The Historical Society of Pennsylvania, on the other hand, will probably accept with delight. In case of rejection, ask the librarian or curator if he could recommend another institution that might be a better match.

*Among Jack's parents' papers were about fifty letters written by his great-great grandfather, an Army officer before the Civil War. The pages were difficult to read, not because the handwriting was poor—it was not—but because writer used both sides of the paper and the ink bled through to the other side. Planning to donate them to the museum at the U. S. Military Academy at West Point where his ancestor had graduated in 1823, Jack hired an independent appraiser to evaluate them for tax purposes. The appraiser read the letters, valued them at several hundred dollars, and summarized the contents. Jack then decided to donate the lot to the Library of Congress instead, because the contents were not overtly military, but personal.*

P.S. Postage stamps on old letters might be of interest to the stamp collector in the family, or they might be purchased by a stamp dealer (see Collections).

## Military Stuff

The generation that fought and won the two-front war against totalitarianism is passing away in greater numbers every year: a recent estimate suggested roughly 3,500 a day, but no one really knows. What is certain is that a larger percentage of this "Greatest Generation" served in a military capacity than the country has seen since the Civil War. More than 16 million men and women served during World War II, an astonishing 12% of the U.S. population at the time. When you add to those the veterans of Korea, Vietnam, the Gulf wars, and other conflicts, the number rises to around 26 million veterans alive today. As these people pass away, their relatives are finding photos, medals, military papers, letters, maps, diaries, uniforms, hats, caps, helmets, belt buckles, and other items among their personal effects. Items that the heirs do not want can take two main routes: to the collectors or to the military museums.

Collectors do buy and sell online, but the larger percent buy direct, where they can examine the items closely. Vendors buy and sell at gun shows and military shows: finding the upcoming show nearest you is easy on the Internet. Type in the words *militaria* and *show* to your search engine, or go to www.wwmeinc.com for a list. "Militaria" is the word used to indicate military-related merchandise, including guns, knives, swords, flags, medals, patches, insignia, uniforms, and helmets. Also check out gun shows—most have vendors selling all sorts of military items from all eras and nationalities who may be interested in what you have for sale. Take your Stuff to the show and find vendors who deal in similar things. As always, get several offers for comparison purposes. To learn more about any medals you come across, check your library or bookstore for books like the *Complete Guide to All U.S. Military Medals: 1939 to Present*, by Foster and Borts, or try to find your medals online at www.usamilitarymedals.com.

The major auction houses like Sotheby's and Christie's will not accept Nazi memorabilia for auction because they are concerned about the bad publicity that might erupt. Nor will eBay. Many other auction houses like Cowan's in Cincinnati do deal in this Stuff, and they find that their buyers are collectors with no ties to neo-Nazis. So if your relative picked up a German helmet during his tour of duty in Germany, you can sell it at Cowan's or other regional auction houses.

Vintage clothing stores are often interested in uniforms. Every Halloween, people buy them for costume. Sometimes theater groups need them. Cadet uniforms from military schools are desirable as well.

Honor your relative's service and help the future learn from the past by donating to a museum. Military museums abound in this country, and there are even a few American military museums overseas that commemorate American actions, usually in World War I or II. Some museums are operated by the U.S. government, others by private non-profit foundations. These institutions continually collect objects relevant to their mission, although they seldom purchase anything. Museums in general have small or nonexistent budgets for collecting and rely on donations to increase their holdings. Museums are more apt to accept your deceased relatives letters, diaries, and papers than they are medals or uniforms, unless, of course, these belonged to someone famous. Contact several institutions that sound like a good match, ask for the curator or public relations person, describe what you would like to donate, and see what they say. Be prepared to e-mail photos. If the answer is a polite no, ask if the person knows of another institution that might want your items.

*The Marine Corps Museum in Quantico is typical of military museums in its collecting policies. "We are always interested in letters, diaries, and photographs, because they tell the complete story," says the museum's collections manager. "We also want newspapers, especially shipboard newsletters and unit newsletters. We always want purple hearts, bronze or silver stars, and Navy Crosses, especially if they have the original certificates. Depending upon who the individual was, we might want other medals. And we really need anything aviation related," he adds. "It's best if people call or write with a description and/or pictures and we can discuss specifics with them."*

### Partial List of U.S. Military Museums

Most of the museums listed below are operated by the U.S. military. There are hundreds of others that are privately funded or state funded—it is impossible to list them all here. In truth, no one knows how many military museums there are in this country. Many are very specific, portraying only the history of a particular unit or battle. Museums commemorating battles from the Civil War, the Indian wars, the Mexican War, the American Revolutionary War, and the French and Indian War are numberless and exist in every state. State museums and state historical societies also deal with these topics. All of these nonprofit institutions accept donations of objects that relate to their subject.

You will want your donation to go to an institution that will take good care of it. To be sure a museum is professionally managed and its collection properly cared for, look at their website or ask if they are accredited by the AAM, the American Association of Museums.

## Army

The U.S. Army Museum System includes a diversified list of museums, including:

1st Armored Division Old Ironsides Museum, Baumholder, Germany

1st Cavalry Division Museum, Fort Hood, TX

2d Infantry Division Museum, Korea

3d Armored Cavalry Regiment Museum, Fort Carson, CO

4th Infantry Division Museum, Fort Hood, TX

82nd Airborne Division War Memorial Museum, Fort Bragg, NC

Adjutant General Corps Museum, Fort Jackson, SC

Air Defense Artillery & Fort Bliss Museum, Fort Bliss, TX

Airborne and Special Operations Museum, Fayetteville, NC

The Casemate Museum, Fort Monroe, VA

U.S. Cavalry Museum, Fort Riley, KS

U.S. Army Chaplain Museum, Fort Jackson, SC

U.S. Army Chemical Corps Museum, Fort Leonard Wood, MO

U.S. Army Engineer Museum, Fort Leonard Wood, MO

U.S. Army Field Artillery and Fort Sill Museum, Fort Sill, OK

Finance Corps Museum, Fort Jackson, SC

Frontier Army Museum, Fort Leavenworth, KS

Harbor Defense Museum of New York City, NY

Fort Huachuca Historical Museum, Fort Huachuca, AZ

U.S. Army Military Intelligence Historical Holding, Fort Huachuca, AZ

Fort Jackson Museum, Fort Jackson, SC

JFK Special Warfare Museum, Fort Bragg, NC

Fort Lewis Military Museum, Fort Lewis, WA

Fort George G. Meade Museum, Fort George G. Meade, MD

U.S. Army Medical Department Museum, Fort Sam Houston, TX

U.S. Army Military Police Museum, Fort Leonard Wood, MO

National Infantry Museum, Fort Benning, GA

National Training Center & 11th Armored Cavalry Regiment, Fort Irwin, CA

U.S. Army Museum of the Noncommissioned Officers, Fort Bliss, TX

The Old Guard Museum, Fort Myer, VA

U.S. Army Ordnance Museum, Aberdeen Proving Grounds, MD

Patton Museum of Cavalry and Armor, Fort Knox, KY

Don F. Pratt Memorial Museum, Fort Campbell, KY

U.S. Army Quartermaster Museum, Fort Lee, VA

Fort Riley Regimental Museum, Fort Riley, KS

Rock Island Arsenal Museum, Rock Island, IL

Fort Sam Houston Museum, Fort Sam Houston, TX

U.S. Army Signal Corps Museum, Fort Gordon, GA

Texas Military Forces Museum, Camp Mabry, TX

U.S. Army Transportation Museum, Fort Eustis, VA

Tropic Lightning Museum, Schofield Barracks, HI

Watervliet Arsenal Museum, Watervliet, NY

West Point Museum, West Point, NY

White Sands Missile Range Museum, White Sands, NM

U.S. Army Women's Museum, Fort Lee, VA


**Navy**

The Naval Historical Center in Washington, D.C., manages the Navy Department Library, and a dozen Navy museums, including:

Great Lakes Naval Museum, Naval Station Great Lakes, Illinois

Hampton Roads Naval Museum, Norfolk, Virginia

National Museum of Naval Aviation, Pensacola, Florida

Naval Museum of Armament and Technology, China Lake, California

Naval Undersea Museum, Keyport, Washington

Naval War College Museum, Newport, Rhode Island

Navy Art Collection, Washington, D.C.

Patuxent River Naval Air Museum, Patuxent River, Maryland

Seabee Museum, Port Hueneme, California

Submarine Force Museum & Historic Ship Nautilus, Groton, Connecticut

U.S. Naval Academy Museum, Annapolis, Maryland

U.S. Navy Museum, Washington, D.C.

U.S. Navy Supply Corps Museum, Athens, Georgia

USS Constitution "Old Ironsides," Boston, Massachusetts

## Air Force

As the newest branch of the military, the Air Force has fewer museums than the Army or Navy, including:

National Museum of the U.S. Air Force, Wright-Patterson Air Force Base, OH

Museum of Aviation, Warner Robins, GA

Air Force Armament Museum, Eglin Air Force Base, FL

USAF Museum of Aerospace Medicine, Brooks AFB, San Antonio, TX

Air Force Historical Research Agency, Maxwell AFB, AL

Air Mobility Command Museum, Dover AFB, DE

U.S. Air Force Academy Museum, Colorado Springs, CO

## Marines

The National Museum of the Marine Corps, Quantico, VA

Flying Leatherneck Aviation Museum, San Diego, CA

Marine Corps Recruit Depot Museum, San Diego, CA

Marine Corps Museum of the Carolinas, Jacksonville, NC

## Coast Guard

U.S. Coast Guard Museum, New London, CT

Coast Guard Museum Northwest, Seattle, WA

## Merchant Marine

American Merchant Marine Museum, Kings Point, NY

# Movies and Slides

Reel-to-reel movie film, slides, VHS tapes, and other outdated film should be thrown away, unless, of course, it contains the family's home movies. Get those converted to DVDs and preserved, if you care. Your local camera shop can help; so can sites like www.imemories.com or www.southtree.com.

Obsolete slide projectors in working condition can be sold on line to people who insist on doing things the old way. They are increasingly valuable as their numbers diminish.

# Music and Musical Instruments

**CDs, DVDs, and videocassettes.** Check out www.titletrader.com and www.paperbackswap.com. These sites host a free exchange for books and music. No money changes hands. You list the CDs and DVDs you don't want, mail them at your expense to the first person who requests them, and earn credits with each sale to order something you want. Not difficult.

DVDs of movies and documentaries might be donated to your local library, VA hospital, retirement center, or nursing home. VHS tapes find few takers, but they do sell for a pittance on places like eBay if you want to take the time. Probably not worth your trouble.

**Sheet Music.** Printed songs with the name of a city or state in the title (California Dreaming, Alabama Rain) will be welcomed at that state's museum or state library if you care to donate. Songbooks and books of piano music that were published before 1900 will have some monetary value; if before 1800, a good deal more. More recent songbooks or piano music has no value, but could be donated to a local piano teacher.

**Pianos.** Because pianos are such a huge problem to move (they weigh from 300 to 1,000 pounds), the options for disposing of them are limited and depend upon the type of piano.

First, figure out what you have. Grand pianos are classified by length. Baby Grands are roughly 4'8" to 5'6", Parlor Grands are 5'7" to 7', and Concert Grands are over 7'. Upright pianos, far more common, are classified by height. Studio pianos are 44" to 52", consoles are 40" to 43", and a spinet is only 36" to 39", a little higher than its keyboard. Antique models may be taller or shorter than these.

The hundred-year-old shoulder-height upright piano with hand-carved cabinet may be lovely to look at, but it probably hasn't been tuned in decades and can't be brought back to usable condition now. A local piano store or moving company will remove it for a price and take it to the dump. If the sentimental value is overwhelming, such pianos can be entirely restored. This is seldom done, though, because it costs as much as three or four new pianos.

Most of your average uprights have suffered years of neglect—they have not been played, tuned regularly, or repaired. If restoring them costs more than a few hundred dollars, they are probably not worth it, because a decent new instrument can be had for as little as $2,000.

Certain grand pianos are worth restoring. Steinways, Bechsteins, Bosendorfers, and some older Baldwins have potential because the new ones command such a high price that it makes sense to pay to restore an old one. "A new Steinway grand can cost $80,000," says one piano restorer, "so it's worth putting $25,000 into an old one."

If in doubt, have your piano inspected by a piano technician (ask for references at any piano store) who can tell you what, if any, value it has and whether or not it can be restored to use. If you want to know it's age and approximate value without paying $100-200 for a technician, you can try an online service for a small fee. Look at www.concertpitchpiano.com for directions on how to find the serial number and other relevant information that will let them look up those details.

**Guitars.** Finding an old guitar, hopefully in its case, presents several opportunities. It could be worth anywhere from a few dollars to many thousands, depending on manufacturer, age, and condition.

Is it electric or acoustic? If it is one of the major top brands— Gibson or Fender for electric and Martin or Taylor for acoustic— yours is not a thrift-shop guitar. It is potentially valuable. If you don't recognize the name, you might have a guitar that was cheap when it was new and is worth even less now that it's old, maybe $15-20. Donate to Goodwill or similar so they can resell it to a beginner. Or you may have an ultra-high-end guitar made by a "boutique" craftsman that is worth thousands. Check the name out online. Take it to a local guitar store, preferably two, to cross check information and let them identify it. You shouldn't have to pay for this service. You will have to pay if you want a written appraisal, but that won't be necessary unless it is a valuable instrument. The store might offer to sell it for you and if they did, would keep about 40% of the price.

If the guitar has been stored in the hot attic or damp basement, even in its case, it may need significant repair. A crack on a decent guitar may be worth spending a few hundred dollars to repair if you can then sell it for several thousand. Again, this is something you can learn at a good guitar store. You could market it as needing repair, but in that case you will probably have to discount it a good deal because buyers can't know what they're getting into.

If you decide to sell it yourself, you could auction it on www.eBay.com, where many guitars are sold to buyers all over the country—really, all over the world. But with musical instruments, it might be better to list it on www.Craigslist.com. That site draws local buyers who can come inspect it first. And Craigslist is free, another plus.

**Violins.** Probably no other instrument has been so widely faked than the violin. Do you have a valuable instrument? Maybe . . . if your grandfather played with a major symphony orchestra. It is more likely that you have a student violin, something that can be had for as little as $100. In any case, you need a qualified appraiser to value your instrument. Start by looking at www.fritz-reuter.com, a reputable Chicago violinmaker who can appraise, and who also offers links to other information.

Take your instrument (violin, cello, or viola) to a violin shop for evaluation. These are located in larger cities where there is a major symphony orchestra. Or call your nearest symphony orchestra's office to ask for recommendations. Or get a program, look up the names of the musicians who play stringed instruments, and call them. These musicians usually teach and will know where to go to buy and sell instruments. If all else fails, google "violin dealers" and take your pick.

Many people are surprised to learn that a bow, which is made of hair and wood, can be worth nearly as much as a violin. The bow is where the tone comes from. There are dealers who specialize in bows. Again, ask for recommendations from the experts in your area.

**Band Instruments.** Maybe there's an old horn or flute tucked in the corner of the attic. It's probably decades old, but it may still have a good life ahead of it. Find a local store that sells musical instruments (if you have trouble, ask a music teacher at any middle school or high school for a recommendation) and take it in for an evaluation. "If it's in decent shape, any band teacher would be glad to have it," said one high school music teacher. "But if it needs repair or professional cleaning, we don't have any money for that sort of thing." Many public schools loan instruments to aspiring band and orchestra musicians who can't afford their own.

If you prefer to sell your instrument on the secondhand market, the music store should be able to help you get it in good shape, and they might sell it for you. Otherwise, there is always advertising in the newspaper, Trading Post, or Craigslist. It's best to sell locally, because buyers usually want to try out an instrument before committing.

**Records and Record Players.** Collectors are interested in 78s and 45s. Original sleeves are an important component to the value. These are easy to sell and ship online for a modest amount, if you want the bother. If not, Goodwill and so forth will take them. Collectors are most interested in recordings from early country musicians, early rock and roll, and early jazz. Classical music recordings hold little appeal.

Some very old record players have monetary value—old Victrolas can fetch several hundred dollars, depending on condition.

# Paint

It's the rare tool shed that has no rusting cans of paint stacked in a corner. It is environmentally unsound to throw paint in a landfill, and it may also be illegal in your state, but throwing out dried paint is perfectly all right. Some states (California, Washington, and Minnesota) have special disposal requirements—to find out, whether they apply to you, call your local paint store.

If the paint in your cans has dried up, you can take it to the dump or dumpster. It's a good idea to pry the lid off when you throw it away to show the paint has solidified.

If the paint is still liquid, pour it into a cardboard box or double paper bag and let it air dry. Shredded newspaper will speed this up. Or pour kitty litter into the can and let it harden.

If the paint is newer, latex, and in good condition, call your local high school theater teacher and ask if you could make a donation. If there is enough to paint an entire room, offer it to Habitat for Humanity. See www.habitat.org for the one nearest you.

## Pewter

Most American and English pewter was made before the 19th century, when pewter plates and mugs were replaced by mass-produced ceramic plates and glass vessels. Pewter is an alloy, made mostly of tin. The minority metal can be copper, antimony, brass, zinc, bismuth, or lead. Take anything you suspect is old pewter to an antiques store for confirmation and possible sale.

Fake pewter, like Armetale, has little resale value. It is an aluminum alloy first made in the 1960s, but many of the pieces are made to look older. Real pewter is fairly heavy. If your object is light in weight, it is Armetale or a similar faux pewter. You might sell that online for a few dollars.

## Photos & Albums

Stuck up on the top shelf in a closet is a stack of scrapbooks full of photos, newspaper clippings, restaurant menus, and other memorabilia. You don't know who those people in the pictures are, and you have no interest in the yellowing articles about events long ago. You hate to throw away something that was once so precious, but what else can you do?

You can ask for an appointment with a curator or librarian at the county/city historical society, local-history museum, or state library and see if they have any interest in them from a cultural standpoint. While a scrapbook about a trip to France fifty years ago won't be of interest, pictures of the town from seventy-five years ago or newspaper clippings from a long-ago war can mean a lot to these organizations. Especially if the person who compiled the scrapbooks was a member of a prominent local family, founded a local business, served in the military or in politics, or taught school for decades, these scrapbooks can have considerable historical or cultural value. Think how proud the person who compiled them would be to know his or her work will contribute to a better understanding of the history of that region!

You can also hire a service to scan and organize your photo albums before throwing them out or giving them away. It isn't cheap, but if the albums mean something to you and are disintegrating, this will preserve the pictures on a CD. These services have a professional association, The Association of Professional Photo Organizers. Find a member near you at their website, www.appo.org.

## Rugs

The only rugs likely to have serious monetary value are handmade oriental rugs from the Middle East, India, Pakistan, and China, and hand-woven Navajo rugs made in the American Southwest. A good quality machine-made rug, like a Karastan, may find a buyer at an estate sale, or it can be donated to Goodwill or the Salvation Army type stores. Bound carpet in good condition might be accepted as a donation.

How can you tell a handmade oriental from a machine-made? It can be harder than people think. Check the underside corners for a tag that may tell you where it was purchased, the size, the original price, and maybe the pattern name (Sarouk, Hamadan, etc.). Look in files for a receipt and any other paperwork that relates to the rug. A tag that identifies it as a Brazilian Oriental or as having been made in Belgium or another Western European country means machine made; one made in Romania, Bulgaria, or another central European country could be either. Look at the back—if the detail and colors are as strong as the front, it is probably handmade; if the pattern and colors are not as clear as the front, it is probably machine made. Failing that, you can carry the rug to an oriental rug dealer or American Indian art specialist and ask. Taking a picture won't work very well in this case—there is too much that can't be discerned from a photograph.

If the estate has several oriental rugs, ask a local rug dealer to come give a verbal or written appraisal. He or she will almost certainly charge for this service. A verbal appraisal will cost less than a written. They can discuss your options at that time as well. In short, your options are to keep it, in which case you probably want to have it cleaned before taking it home; to sell it to the dealer (never a good idea to sell an object to the person who is appraising it), place it on consignment with a rug dealer, trade it for another rug you like better, donate it to Goodwill and take a tax deduction (an appraisal will come in handy here to prove its value), or sell it on eBay (not the best idea since people buying rugs really need to see them first and often expect to take them home to try them out).

An old, very worn oriental rug still has value—it can be cut up and the better parts made into decorative pillows that sell for a fair amount at interior design shops and rug shops, so inquire there.

The value of oriental rugs has a lot to do with decorating trends. At present, new rugs that look old are popular in most parts of the country, and they are cheaper than old rugs that are genuinely old. Subtle, soft, mellow colors are more desirable than the strong reds, oranges, and blues. Room sizes, typically 8 x 10 and 9 x 12, are most desirable. The oriental rug market varies from region to region, with certain patterns and colors preferred in certain areas. A dealer might recommend you sell your rug in another region to get a higher price.

The demand for oriental rugs has softened considerably in American and Europe due to the slow economy. Demand is driven by home ownership. "Renters don't buy oriental rugs," said one dealer who has been in business for 35 years. "They wait until they own a house." The housing market is depressed and likely to remain so for several years. That's why, unfortunately, this is the worst possible time to try to sell your genuine oriental rugs. If possible, hold onto them and wait a few years. Says a Cincinnati auctioneer, "A Persian rug I would have sold for $5,000 just a few years ago will now go for $800 – 1,500."

Today, in countries where oriental rugs have been made for centuries, labor is leaving the old craft. Some rug dealers think they are witnessing the death of an industry as workers move to better jobs and the cost of production rises. "The costs we pay have risen sixty to seventy percent in the last couple years," says one East Coast dealer, "and we don't see the quality we used to." What this means to you is that Grandma's old oriental rugs, purchased seventy-five years ago, are probably a better quality than anything being made today or likely to be made in the future. And that means their value should increase. On the other hand, the bad news is that there is a trend away from oriental rugs, much like the trend away from fine china, sterling silver, and lead crystal. It seems the younger generation is not as interested as their parents and grandparents were in these things. And that means there are fewer buyers out there.

Folk art rugs—rag rugs, hooked rugs, braided rugs—are quite desirable if handmade. Modern rugs have an even pile, no irregularities, and are as brightly colored on the front as on the back. Handmade ones will have irregularities.

Indian rugs, especially Navajo, are valuable, new or old. If you live in an area outside the Southwest, type "free evaluation Navajo rug" into google or your search engine and choose a couple services to compare.

## Sewing Machines

So Grandma had a sewing machine stashed in the attic? Odds are it's a Singer—by far the most common brand—and odds are no one wants it. It's rather attractive, though, isn't it? Depending upon cabinet height, it might make a nice side table or bedside table. Is it electric or the older treadle style? Does it work? Is there any resale value to it?

Like so many object categories, sewing machines have a collectors group, the International Sewing Machine Collectors' Society, or ISMACS. Their excellent website, www.ismacs.net, will help you identify your machine. To find out it's date, check the manufacturer's name and serial number, then look at the list on the ISMACS webpage titled "When was my Sewing Machine Made?" Or, if you have a Singer, you can go directly to the Singer website at www.singerco.com/support/machine-serial-numbers and examine their list of serial numbers, which goes back as far as 1870. (Older models—and the first year of production was 1851—are not listed because the original log books did not survive.) If you want to talk to a consumer affairs rep, call Singer at 800-474-6437.

The ISMACS online article on valuing your sewing machine, "How much is my Machine Worth?" contains sound information on how to estimate that elusive dollar amount, as well as the warning that few are worth the time and effort it takes to sell them. Millions of sewing machines were manufactured during the twentieth century and few were thrown out. A survey of "sold listings" on eBay shows that most antique machines sell for less than $100, while those with attractive cabinets usually pull in several hundred. In fact, many people buy the old sewing machine for the cabinet and dispose of the machinery part. They want an attractive table or the decorative drawers or the metal treadle base and don't care a rap about the machine. Remember that shipping costs are significant due to the weight, so try to sell to a local buyer.

The usual options for selling apply here: taking it to an antiques dealer or antiques mall, posting on eBay or Craigslist, or posting it on the ISMACS for sale whole or for parts. Donating to Goodwill is always an option. Take a deduction.

# Silver

It's silvery . . . must be silver, right? Not necessarily.

The first task is to figure out whether you have silverplate (base metal with a thin layer of silver electroplated to the surface), sterling silver (92.5% silver content), or another silvery-looking metal such as highly polished pewter or German silver (a silvery-looking alloy that is copper, nickel, and zinc without any silver at all). Look at the back of the piece. Generally speaking, American-made sterling silver will be marked STERLING or at least STER if the space is small. The vast majority of the silver found in American households today is—drum roll, please—American-made and dates to the twentieth century. If it is sterling (and therefore has value because of the silver content, if nothing else), it will be marked that way. It may also have other marks that indicate the maker or manufacturer. Old sterling is worth more than not-so-old, and if you are so inclined, you can research the marks yourself at websites like www.925-1000.com/americansilver__Menu.html. Or you can take it to someone who deals in sterling and they will happily tell you what you have and whether or not they want to buy it.

The second-most-common silver in America is English. English sterling will be marked with a set of hallmarks, little symbols or letters stamped into the silver. Look for the figure of a lion running toward the left with his paw raised—that means English sterling, or 92.5% silver content. English sterling pieces are usually marked with a set of four or five hallmarks: the lion plus other marks that identify the city, the maker, and the date the piece was made. (The occasional fifth mark shows the head of a king or queen and indicates that a tax was paid. That mark was used only from 1784 through 1890, but Victorians loved their silver, so there was a whole lot of it made during the 1800s.) If your piece is English sterling, it will be valuable beyond the silver content or meltdown value. Look up the marks to learn the date and other particulars. If you like solving puzzles, this will be fun! If you prefer, your library will have books listing American and international hallmarks. Or check a website that shows pictures of the various marks, like www.925-1000.com.

Does your family tree have roots in other countries? Perhaps the silver your family owned comes from Germany, France, or China. Each country developed its own standards and marks. Look up the marks online or in library books that de-code silver hallmarks. Sometimes the silver content is indicated by a number, like 900, meaning 900 parts per thousand or 90% silver.

Have you found some spoons that are very thin and marked COIN? Contrary to rumor, the word COIN does not mean the piece was made from melted down coins. It refers to the silver content—the piece has the same percentage of silver as silver coins once did. Just as the word Sterling means 92.5% silver, the word Coin means 90%. Many people think coin silver is worthless when in fact, it is worth almost the same as sterling! For heaven's sake, don't throw away any coin silver. It is probably nineteenth-century and collectible. An antiques dealer will buy these.

Just to make life difficult, lots of cheap silverplate and other shiny metal comes stamped with marks because they look nice. These are meaningless marks, perhaps a letter or a flower or a number. Manufacturers aren't allowed to use official marks like the lion. Genuine marks will be listed in the guides. The letters EPNS stand for Electro-Plated-Nickel-Silver and signify a microscopically thin layer of silver on top of a silvery-looking base metal. The terms "nickel silver" and "German silver" are misleading. They contain *no silver* whatsoever, just copper, nickel, and zinc.

If you are in a big hurry, take the items marked sterling and coin (even the dented, tarnished, or damaged pieces) to a place that buys gold and silver and sell them for the meltdown price. Toss or donate the silverplate and other metals; they have no meltdown value at all. Some auction houses won't accept silverplate, it's so worthless; others get rid of it by the box.

How do you estimate the meltdown value? Easy. Weigh the sterling silver on an accurate scale like a postal scale. (Don't weigh knives or candlesticks—knife blades are stainless steel so they don't weigh true and candlesticks are full of cement.) Then convert the number of ounces to troy ounces. Recently the price has hovered around $29/troy oz. There are converters on line, or just multiply the ounces by .9116 to get troy ounces. Multiply that by the current price of silver, which is listed per troy ounce in newspapers and online. Then, because sterling is 92.5% silver, not 100%, multiply the result by 92.5%, and you have the approximate meltdown value of your sterling. (For coin silver, multiply by 90%.) Will you get that much for it at a silver and gold buyer? No way. They have to make a profit too. 70-80% is reasonable, according to silver buyers. Let them know you are getting more than one offer.

Got a set of sterling flatware that no one wants? Twelve place settings of sterling flatware used to be the goal of every bride. Today, few brides opt for sterling. Who has the time to polish it or the servants to do the work? Some people are looking to fill out their set or replace missing pieces, so there can be some market for the flatware, but with the price of silver as high as it is these days, the meltdown value may be greater. Contact replacement houses like www.replacements.com or 800-737-5223, or bring to an antiques show or store where they deal in silver.

Candlesticks marked sterling have far less silver in them than you are led to believe by their weight. They are actually filled with cement covered with a thin sheet of sterling. Damaged candlesticks can be broken apart and the silver outer layer sold for meltdown.

Tea and coffee services, consisting of a large tray plus teapot, coffeepot, sugar bowl, creamer, and often other pieces such as waste bowls, were once a status symbol. Those who couldn't afford sterling bought silverplate sets—after all, it's hard to tell the difference without examining the bottom of a piece. So . . . the bad news is, there is little demand for silverplate tea services (a recent check of silverplate sets sold on eBay found them ranging from $10 for an entire set to $549). Sterling tea sets, however, are worth at least meltdown, possibly more because of their antique status. A hasty examination of recent eBay transactions shows sterling tea services selling for as little as $2,000 and as much as $10,000 or $15,000 or more, depending on style, age, and condition.

## Sports and Fitness Equipment

Gently used sports equipment, if it's not too old, has monetary value. Sell such items direct through the usual outlets—*Trading Post*, online sites, classifieds, and yard sales.

A nation-wide franchise called Play It Again Sports pays for used sports and fitness equipment. Locate one of their 500 shops at www.playitagainsports.com. These shops carry used and new merchandise relating to golf, tennis, baseball, hockey, snow sports, water sports (only stores near the coast), lacrosse, soccer, football, and wheeled sports. Roughly speaking, they will give you a quarter of the original retail price in cash or take the item on consignment or let you trade it in for something else. Shoes with cleats can bring a couple dollars. Top name brands are preferred.

A few caveats: Exercise equipment like treadmills, exercise bikes, and elliptical machines more than eight years old are probably obsolete. So are golf clubs more than ten years old; so are straight skis.

You will get more for your item if you bring it in during the season—the store's buyer may not be interested in buying skis in the spring because he'll have to hold onto them for six months, before customers are thinking about skiing. Go in the fall.

Donate sports equipment to a high school coach or YMCA. Find a local chapter at www.ymca.net/find-your-y/. Got golf clubs? Check www.thefirsttee.org for a list of chapters nearest you—this group works with young people ages 8 to 18, teaching golf and character development. They appreciate donated clubs, bags, and balls and will put them to good use.

# Tools

It's a rare house that has no tools. Even apartments and retirement residences usually have a toolbox with the basic hammer and screwdrivers for the handyman or woman. Hand tools and power tools can bring a respectable amount of money if sold online or at an estate sale or estate auction. Evaluate their worth by finding comparable items on eBay (research sold listings only) and take a tax deduction when you donate them to Goodwill or Habitat for Humanity. Other sites to search for comparables for old tools include www.vintagetools.net, www.oldtools.com, www.jimbodetools.com, and www.mjdtools.com.

Antique tools can be worth a good deal, so take the time to research anything that looks to be old. Like anything else, condition and rarity determines the value of hand tools. You can sand off surface rust, but deep rust ruins the value.

If they are in good condition, used power tools can be sold through Craigslist, eBay, the Trading Post, garage sales, or with the rest of your inherited Stuff at an estate sale or auction.

Fireplace tools and fenders, grates, andirons, and cast iron firebacks can fetch reasonable prices, but beware their weight when contemplating shipping. Better to sell those locally, through ads in the newspaper, Trading Post, or Craigslist.org. But as people switch to gas log fireplaces, there is less demand for this sort of equipment, so don't expect high prices.

An antique tool collection, on the other hand, should be handled according to the steps suggested in the section on Collections.

# Toys

People save or collect toys largely out of nostalgia for their youth. The toys you find among the belongings you've inherited probably date from the decade that the deceased was a child. Or perhaps they are the toys that belonged to his or her children, meaning they are a good deal newer and you will recognize them instantly. This sort of toy—Barbie dolls, GI Joes, action figures, and such—can be quite collectible. Check the latest copy of *Toys and Prices (Moen)*, available at your library or from amazon.com to give you an idea of how to price them should you want to sell them on eBay. Toys usually sell well on Internet auction sites. The first action figure (really a boy's doll, but no toy manufacturer would dare use that term in those days) was GI Joe who came on the scene in 1964, so it isn't age that makes these valuable; it is scarcity.

Antique toy soldiers are highly collectible. Not the plastic ones, these are usually lead or wood composition and meticulously handpainted. One website to check is www.treefrogtreasures.com. There you can see prices of, perhaps, similar miniatures and even ask questions about the identity or value of your own pieces.

Besides dolls and bears, other toys to watch for are tin toys. Few have been produced since 1980, but before World War II, Japan dominated the manufacture of these popular toys. After that war, German manufacturers took over. All imports should be marked with their country of origin.

# CHAPTER FIVE

## Avoiding the Family Feud

Although many people are loath to discuss the distribution of their belongings before they die, it is better for everyone if they do. Writing specifics into a will is the optimum plan because those wishes are legally enforceable, but if there is no will and no will to write one, a written and signed list of who-gets-what can forestall arguments later on. Writing names on labels and sticking them on the back of items can work, as long as the heirs respect the labels (and your sister doesn't sneak in and switch them).

In the event that the deceased made no will or left a general will that lacked specifics about the distribution of Stuff, here are some ideas that have worked for others.

1. Flip for first choice, then take turns choosing and marking your choice with colored stickers or post-it notes.

2. This is a variation of the cake-cutting trick—remember that? One person cuts the cake, the other chooses first. Make two lists, let the other person choose. With more than a few heirs, this

doesn't work as well—even King Solomon couldn't unravel problems with multiple heirs with different views of values and different, or the same, desires.

3. Conduct an auction. Distribute equal amounts of Monopoly money to each person and auction off all objects.

4. After splitting the Stuff, offer to purchase at fair market value whatever you wanted that you didn't get.

5. Consider sharing. Rotate Mom's sapphire necklace among all four sisters, handing it off at the end of each year.

6. Flip a coin for the item in contention, and let the loser choose the next two items as compensation.

7. If the objects are more important than their monetary value, take turns choosing an item until everything that anyone wants is chosen. If the monetary value is more important, that is, if it is important to the heirs that they inherit equal dollar amount of Stuff, have items appraised and marked with the appraised value, take turns choosing, but when one person is "ahead" of the others, allow the others to choose until their total catches up. Or assign values yourself if you don't want to hire an appraiser. Assign points rather than dollars, using a ten-point scale, with the nicer items worth ten points and the lesser items one point.

8. If the estate needs money for whatever reason, hold a tag sale and invite the relatives to come and purchase what they want. In this case, an even distribution is not relevant. Maximizing dollars is.

9. If the family feud is heating up, consider sending everything to the estate liquidator to auction off and invite the heirs to bid on the pieces they want. Yes, they'll be paying with their own money, but they will share in the profits from the sale. This process finds the fair market value for every item and ensures that those who want a particular item will pay a fair price for it.

10. Call in an appraiser to set a dollar value on each contested item. Allot each heir an equal dollar amount. If John really wants that portrait that is valued at $12,000, then he doesn't get anything

else until the others have objects that amount to $12,000. This practice tends to change people's minds.

*The rules aren't important. Agreement is. Agree on the rules. Follow the rules.*

**Warning.** The confusion and emotional strain of losing a loved one and breaking up an estate make this a perfect time for theft. A veritable parade of people are likely trouping in and out of the house, including caregivers, a maid or cleaning crew, neighbors bringing casseroles, relatives who have traveled a long distance for the funeral, and in-laws you've never met. Stuff evaporates. Strangers and siblings alike steal Stuff. What happened to the pearl necklace that your grandfather gave your grandmother? Disappeared. Where did those antique quilts go? Walked out.

The only way to prevent this is to give away, sell, or donate Stuff before the owner becomes ill or frail. Disposing of your own valuables before you die ensures that they go to the person you choose, forestalls arguments, and prevents family feuds. Sadly, this seldom happens.

Take precautions when your loved one is no longer mentally alert by removing the obvious valuables—particularly the jewelry, sterling, guns, and any valuable collections—from the home. Write down what you've taken and let the other heirs know so *you* won't be accused of stealing. If you can't account for all the house keys, change the locks.

During the days surrounding the funeral, leave someone at the house at all times. Thieves often target homes during funerals.

# ACKNOWLEDGMENTS

I interviewed dozens of people at dozens of business locations before writing this book, and want to thank several in particular who took time to educate me about their professions, including Eric Vaituzis, Beverly Binns, Wayne Burgess, Sara Garza, Bill Hirsch, Charles Layman, Jack Kreuter, Susan Campbell, and Tina Stoneburner.

The person I miss most is Emyl Jenkins, an expert appraiser who loved antiques. We had planned to write this book together, but cancer took her with no warning. This is for you, Emyl. I hope it comes up to your standards!

41868623R00070

Made in the USA
Lexington, KY
30 May 2015